Sexing the Teacher

Sexuality Studies Series

This series focuses on original, provocative, scholarly research examining from a range of perspectives the complexity of human sexual practice, identity, community, and desire. Books in the series explore how sexuality interacts with other aspects of society, such as law, education, feminism, racial diversity, the family, policing, sport, government, religion, mass media, medicine, and employment. The series provides a broad public venue for nurturing debate, cultivating talent, and expanding knowledge of human sexual expression, past and present.

Other volumes in the series are:
Masculinities without Men? Female Masculinity in Twentieth-Century Fictions, by Jean Bobby Noble
Every Inch a Woman: Phallic Possession, Femininity, and the Text, by Carellin Brooks
Queer Youth in the Province of the "Severely Normal," by Gloria Filax
The Manly Modern: Masculinity in Postwar Canada, by Christopher Dummitt

Sheila L. Cavanagh

Sexing the Teacher
School Sex Scandals and Queer Pedagogies

UBC Press • Vancouver • Toronto

15 14 13 12 11 10 09 08 07 5 4 3 2 1

Printed in Canada on ancient-forest-free paper (100% post-consumer recycled) that is processed chlorine- and acid-free, with vegetable-based inks.

Library and Archives Canada Cataloguing in Publication

Cavanagh, Sheila L. (Sheila Lynn), 1969-
Sexing the teacher / Sheila L. Cavanagh.

Includes bibliographical references and index.
ISBN 978-0-7748-1374-7 (bound); 978-0-7748-1375-4 (pbk.)

1. Women teachers – Sexual behavior. 2. Child sexual abuse by teachers. 3. Sexually abused boys. 4. Teacher-student relationships. I. Title.

LB2844.1.C54C39 2007 371.7'8 C2007-900556-X

Canadä

UBC Press gratefully acknowledges the financial support for our publishing program of the Government of Canada through the Book Publishing Industry Development Program (BPIDP), and of the Canada Council for the Arts, and the British Columbia Arts Council.

This book has been published with the help of a grant from the Canadian Federation for the Humanities and Social Sciences, through the Aid to Scholarly Publications Programme, using funds provided by the Social Sciences and Humanities Research Council of Canada.

UBC Press
The University of British Columbia
2029 West Mall
Vancouver, BC V6T 1Z2
604-822-5959 / Fax: 604-822-6083
www.ubcpress.ca

Contents

Acknowledgments

This book is informed by conversations, inspirations, and support given by many people. I would first like to thank Jean Wilson at UBC Press for her support, care, and attention to the book. I would also like to thank Robert Lewis for a careful and hard-working copy edit. Ann Macklem was the production editor and offered her expertise throughout the publication process. Although the UBC Press reviewers remain anonymous, each gave insightful and supportive criticism in the spirit of the book, and I wish to give them my special thanks. Their reviews of the manuscript were inspiring and affirming. I also wish to acknowledge the Aid to Scholarly Publications Programme for a grant in aid of publication and the generous support of the Social Sciences and Humanities and Research Council of Canada, which made the writing of this book possible through Standard Research Grant No. 410-2000-0357.

I also extend my thanks to friends and colleagues who listened to conference presentations (of the various chapters) and to those who, in various ways, shaped my analysis of the female teacher school sex panics: Bernadette Baker, Deborah Britzman, Kari Dehli, Emma Donoghue, Angela Failer, Helen Fielding, Dina Georgis, Helen Harper, Beth Jackson, Jan Jagodzinski, Michael Kehler, R.M. Kennedy, Frances Latchford, Leanne McCormack, James Miller, Andie Noack, Chantal Phillips, Mary Lou Rasmussen, Eric Rofes, Sharon Rosenberg, Chris Roulston, Katarzyna Rukszto, Trish Salah, Rinaldo Walcott, Harry Smaller, Lochlan Story, Mariana Valverde, Arja Vanio-Matilla, Leah Vosko, Jane Walsh, and Lorna Weir. While some of you offered casual thoughts during informal conversations and others offered close readings and scholarly criticism, you have all in different, yet important, ways made the book possible. I would also like to thank my research assistants, who exhaustively followed the news coverage of the female teacher sex scandals and in numerous other ways made the book possible: Erin Bentley, Diana Gibaldi, Vicki Hallett, Habiba Nosheen, and Marc Sinclair. Marc Sinclair, in particular, devoted countless hours to the bibliographic portion of the project and went well beyond the call of duty to enable me to make the publication date.

Finally, and most importantly, I wish to thank my partner Heather Sykes, who offered support, affirmation, and encouragement throughout the writing of this book. She is more loving, generous, and inspiring than words can say. I dedicate my first book to you.

Sexing the Teacher

1
Introduction: Queer Pedagogy and Sex Scandals in Education

> We are drawn to scandal by our desire to trip up the cultural censors, by a dream of escaping culture or transforming it ... Let me assume, then, that what draws us to scandal is the energy and promise of scandal itself ... It's the offense that matters, that holds out promise, gives us hope. (Kincaid 1998, 26)

> Transgression becomes a kind of reverse or counter-sublimation, undoing the discursive hierarchies and stratifications of bodies and cultures which bourgeois society has produced as the mechanism of its symbolic dominance. (Stallybrass and White 1986, 200-1)

In 1997, Mary Kay Letourneau shocked Middle America by having sex with a twelve-year-old boy-student. The press coverage was, by all accounts, titillating and sensational. Readers could not get enough of the story. People wanted to know why the all-American teacher – beautiful, blond, daughter of a wealthy and politically influential father – would jeopardize her relationship with a husband and children to have sex with a twelve-year-old Samoan American boy. Not only did she have an illegal affair with the preteen, but she mothered two of his children and, upon her release from prison seven years later, married her former student and left her more socially legitimate family in the lurch. The affair upset the public as it basked in the horrific image of the white female teacher seducing (or being seduced by) a boy of the Samoan Islands who seemed to be wise and experienced beyond his years.

The reverberations of the panic were keenly felt in Canada and throughout the Western world. In the wake of the Mary Kay Letourneau sex panic, a number of other high-profile cases hit the mainstream press. Since 1997, concerned readers have learned about sex scandals involving Mariama Buchanan (2005), Elizabeth Ann Carter (2002), Heidi Franziska Coleman (2001), Amy Gehring (2002), Victoria Harris (1995), Heather Ingram (2000), Jocelyn Jaster (2001), Debra Lafave (2005), Annie Markson (2001), Paola Queen (2007), Laura Sclater (2000), Katherine Tew (2005), Pamela Joan Turner (2005), and Allenna Williams (2007). A host of other white female teachers have also found themselves subject to sensational press coverage for sexual improprieties with boy-students. From 1997 to the present, more female teachers have faced criminal charges, professional censure, and public scorn in the United States, Canada, and England than in all earlier generations put together.

From public schooling's founding in the mid-1800s in Canada until the late 1990s, no more than a handful of female teachers had been accused of sexual improprieties involving male or female students. The number of female teachers now accused of indecent assault involving minors has increased exponentially. This is not to say that female teachers are now more likely to commit sexual infractions or that they are as likely to sexually assault students as are male teachers. According to reports issued by the Ontario College of Teachers and the British Columbia College of Teachers, the vast majority of discipline cases involving sexual harassment and sexual assault against students are perpetrated by male teachers. All studies and reports on the gender of sexual perpetrators in schools reviewed for this book show that male teachers are far more likely than female teachers to sexually harm students in Canada, the United States, and England (Freel 2003; Gallagher 2000; Hendrie and Drummond 1998; Jennings and Tharp 2003; Shakeshaft and Cohen 1994), but the moral panic doesn't recognize this statistic.[1]

There is little evidence to suggest that female teachers are now, in the late twentieth and early twenty-first centuries, committing sexual infractions at a higher rate than before the late 1990s. People are, however, more likely to file complaints against female teachers now than in earlier years, and these reports are more likely to lead to professional reprimands along with criminal investigations. The media now reports on the sexual improprieties of female teachers with a sensational flare and exuberance never before seen in the coverage of male teachers. One needs only to read the newspaper, to listen to daytime talk shows, to watch the evening news, or to purchase a national tabloid to witness the anxious concern and excited commentary about the lascivious and predatory sexualities of white female teachers. Everyone has something to say about the infamous Mary Kay Letourneau, about the sexual charisma of Debra Lafave – an American teacher who posed in a bikini for a motorcycle manufacturer and had oral sex with a teenaged boy-student[2] – and about the indiscretions of other Canadian-born female teachers caught up in flirtations or sexual relations with underage male or female students. The numerous media reports are written with both a foreboding tone and a sensational flare usually reserved for pop stars or serial killers.

Female students have been sexually assaulted and harassed by male teachers throughout the twentieth century and into the twenty-first, but this reality does not seem to warrant the same degree of media commentary. The lascivious white *female* teacher is another story. She makes headline news. The media sensation must not, however, be taken as evidence that female teachers are committing more sexual violations than in the past. There has been a change in our definition and understanding of sexual abuse in the educational milieu (Gallop 1997), a change that provides an important context for this book's examination of sex scandals involving female teachers. For example, it was not uncommon for male teachers to marry their female students following graduation in the early to mid-twentieth century. Male-teacher seductions leading to matrimony were seen as "natural" and "wholesome." Romance between male teachers and older female students was not only part of school life but well represented in mainstream film and popular fiction in North America and Britain. Flirtations between male teachers and older female students were not unusual, nor did they generate public and professional uproar. Today, we are scandalized when teachers act on or feel desire for their students – particularly when they are female. We wonder about what led up to the pedagogical romance and about how the classrooms of today have become settings for licentious behaviour. As I argue in Chapter 3, an erotic gesture or flirtation once seen as innocent or benign is now deemed unprofessional and subject to criminal investigations. The crushes between female teachers and older boy-students depicted in educational folklore, fiction, and movie classics are not only professionally inappropriate, but also border on the criminal by present-day standards.

Sexual assault and harassment of female students by male teachers in school cultures has also been commonplace in Canada, the United States, and England. In each of these countries, there has been sensational media coverage and professional uproar about the sexual transgressions of today's female teachers, and in subsequent chapters, I will focus on these three national contexts. In none of these countries has there been an outcry about the sexual improprieties of male teachers (unless they involve boy-students) comparable to what we now see in response to the sexual improprieties of female teachers. Until the 1980s, the education profession in Canada, for example, had not been politically galvanized by sexual assaults by male teachers against female students. Teachers' professional organizations, school administrators, and others involved in school life did not react with horror, nor was there a scandal of comparable proportions to what we now see shadowing female teachers today. If a male teacher was caught abusing a female student and parents complained, he was quietly moved to another school, where, in many instances, he repeated the offence with another student. Few cases of teachers' sexual misconduct came to court, and the public did not clamour for justice. Since the 1980s, there have been more public-education campaigns and policies developed for the identification and prevention of childhood sexual abuse, which accounts, in part, for the change that we see today. This does not, however, explain why female teachers, who commit significantly fewer sexual misdemeanours than male teachers, are the topic of heightened public debate, curiosity, professional discipline, and media sensationalism.

There is something queer or, at the very least, curious going on. How can we account for the school sex panics occasioned by lascivious female teachers in the past decade? We first need to consider the professional and media-driven uproar within the context of educational historiography. White female teachers in North American and British schools enjoyed a unique cultural representation in education until the 1990s – one that is strikingly distinct from representations of white male teachers (and female teachers of colour). For the first half of the twentieth century and well into the 1950s, the white female teacher was forbidden to marry, to have children and a family of her own (Cavanagh 2006a, 2006b; Danylewycz 1987; Oram 1983; Reynolds 1983; Vicinus 1985). Sex out of wedlock would cause a scandal, and so female teachers were expected to remain celibate. While most educational historians view the marriage bans as sexist and legislating against dual-income families, the bans were also about sexual and moral regulation. School board administrators, parents, ratepayers, and professional teachers' groups that developed over the course of the twentieth century were concerned about the gender identities and sexualities of white female teachers. This worry was framed as a concern about child welfare; people thought that "normal" adolescent student gender identity development would be compromised in schools taught by married (and/or sexually independent/masculine) women. Female teachers had to curtail their independent and undomesticated sexualities for fear of igniting controversy and, ultimately, dismissal. Virtues based on an ascetic ideal modelled on orthodox Christian teaching and doctrine were professionally mandated in most school districts.[3] Self-denial, deprivation, and personal discipline were ethical imperatives for most North American and British white women in education until the 1960s.

Extreme professional prohibitions did, however, have some queer and unintended effects. For example, celibacy and the strict moral codes applied to female pedagogues enabled women to live in all-female households and to pursue professional ambitions often denied other women. Lillian Faderman (1991) argues that the emergence of all-female occupations, like in education, led to the emergence of lesbian communities. The moral restrictions applied to love, marriage, and (hetero)sexuality enabled women to enter into what we now call lesbian relationships and to be financially independent of men, thereby opting out of heterosexual family units. Professional success also enabled women to be self-assured and independent in ways leading to a gender identification based on what we might now call female masculinity as conceived by Judith Halberstam (1998) and as I have written about it in the context of education administration (2006b). There is also a growing body of literature about how the early-twentieth-century school teacher opted out of heteronormative family structures and conventional sex/gender systems by choice or necessity and was read, in various ways, as "queer" or generically odd by school communities in Canada, the United States, and Britain (Blount 2000; Cavanagh 2005a, 2006b; Oram 1989; Vicinus 1985).

Not until the postwar period did psychoanalysts, sexologists, mental hygienists, pro-natalists, psychologists, and champions of heterosexuality, marriage, and motherhood begin to write extensively about the genders and sexualities of spinster-teachers. As the spinster designation came to signify "sexual abnormality" (lesbianism as opposed to mere abstinence), people began to wonder about the influence of *un*married women on school-aged children. Shortly thereafter, the career teacher was called upon to be attractive to men and open to marriage and motherhood, and a teacher's pregnancy was no longer something to hide. The white female teacher shifted from virginal to marriageable in less than a decade (Cavanagh 2004) – from innocent to heterosexual in the name of wholesome (i.e., white) family values. As I argue elsewhere (2004, 2006a and b), the white female teacher was subject to public and professional anxieties for most of the twentieth century. Marriage bans, prohibitions against pregnancy, and outlandish moral codes of conduct regulating dress, smoking, dating, and fornication – to cite a few examples – all speak volumes about heterosexual worries governing female teachers' genders and sexualities in the North American and British contexts.

Because the same prohibitions were not placed on male teachers, questions must be asked about how the public and the profession are particularly anxious about *female* teacher genders and sexualities. Although "marriage bans" have long since been dropped, there is an intensification of public debate about child sexual abuse involving female teachers that cannot be legitimated through recourse to statistics. I suggest that the earlier panic about female teacher gender and sexuality has transformed itself into a present-day panic about female teacher pedophilia. In essence, postwar worries about non-marital female teacher sexualities have transmogrified into current panics about female pedophilia in North American and British schools. Contemporary sex panics about "predatory" female teacher sexualities are modern manifestations of older, more deeply entrenched anxieties about unmarried and, hence, undomesticated female sexualities. The present-day fear is that the sexuality of the white female teacher has attached itself to the student. But the fear is not *really* about child welfare so much as it is about the threat posed by the female teacher to the institution of heterosexuality and normative sex/gender systems. This is, of course, not to say that children are not (or cannot be) sexually harmed by female teachers but that the legitimate worry about child welfare is being used in the service of sexual and moral regulation.

This book is driven by my curiosity about how the modern-day sex panic about lascivious and predatory female teacher sexualities is driven by what Gayle Rubin (1984) calls an "excess of signification" (279). Inspired by

French philosopher Michel Foucault's (1978) writing on the history of sexuality, Rubin wonders if sexual acts mean more than they should, and if this excess of signification is about the regulation of queer or, in other ways, non-normative sexualities in the service of heteronormativity. Foucault and Rubin are both, in different ways, concerned about how pedophilic panics (and the associated idea of childhood sexual innocence) function to legitimize the place of the courts in the domain of human sexuality. As Linda Martin Alcoff (1996) contends in her critical evaluation of Foucault's position on the policing of the pedophilic subject, by making sexuality the "business of the law," Foucault is concerned that we are, also, consenting to new and potentially more harmful systems of power, subjectification, and regulation than pre-modern institutions afforded. There is, in other words, a way in which a "widespread and officially sanctioned heterosexism and homophobia" (Alcoff 1996, 102-3) gets solidified through the coupling of homosexuality *with* pedophilia. Both occupy the conceptual terrain of deviant, dangerous, and threatening to normative heterosexuality. To arrest a pedophile is not just to "save a child" but to win a battle in the fight to salvage heterosexuality from a dangerous cloud of deviance hovering over the white nuclear family. But it is not just the slippage between homosexuality and pedophilia that is problematic and of concern to queer and radical sex theorists in the present-day. It is the use and management of the child in the name of protection that is, also, dangerously misleading.

Before I continue, I wish to underscore that the school is, unfortunately, a place where children – male and female – have been harmed by teachers, administrators, older students, and by those who have taken sexual liberties that we might correctly identify to be abusive. People are justified in claiming that boy-students, like girl-students, can be sexually assaulted and that the abuser is not always male. Female teachers *can* sexually assault and harm boys and girls, and we may decide (in opposition to Foucault) that we do need the law to intervene in gross instances of sexual abuse. The arguments made in this book should not be taken to suggest that female teachers cannot sexually harm their students (although I do wish to point out that this is, in the current moment, exceedingly rare). Female teachers – like all adult women – are capable of sexually assaulting and harassing male and female students alike, and the gendering of such abuse is in need of critical feminist and gay-positive scholarly and professional inquiry.

My intention in this book is not to trouble what are often legitimate and important child protectionist policies and interventions but to question the duplicitous use of the child in the service of something more than protectionism. There is, as I argue in the chapters that follow, a problem with a double-edged appeal to protect *and* silence underage youth. Too often the very people who want to save and protect those designated underage from adult predators are, also, unwilling to listen to youth, particularly when they offer narrative testimony that runs counter to the master narrative of child sexual abuse. This is where things get tricky. The paternalism driving the impulse to protect children (or underage teens) is often associated with a refusal to validate youthful claims to sexual self-determination. If an underage teen says he or she wanted (or even sought out) a sexual encounter with an adult, the testimony is not given legitimacy. Frequently, youth who make such claims are ignored, told they have been brainwashed by a manipulative adult sexual predator, or sent for psychological counselling. As Alcoff explains in her discussion about a panel in which Foucault took issue with the governmentality of the so-called "pedophile":

> A key aspect of this paternalism involves the refusal to accept the possibility that a child may authentically consent to sex with adults. The panelists point to the fact that children may not have the ability to articulate what they are feeling or wanting, and when they are unable to formulate their own desires the courts unfailingly presume to speak for them. Foucault characterizes this as the imposition of hegemonic discourses on the subjugated discourse of the child. Demanding that the child be able to articulate her or his consent involves bringing sex "into discourse," which will entail bringing it into the dominant discourse and subjecting it to the dominant discourse's codes of normality. (1996, 103)

Not only do the courts "presume to speak for the child" but, as I will discuss in more detail in subsequent chapters, even when the so-called "child" can speak eloquently about his (or her) desires, wants, and experiences of sexuality, the courts are unwilling to accept this testimony as credible evidence. The presumption that it is impossible for those under the legal age to consent to sex negates youthful claims to sexual citizenship. Foucault advocates listening to youth without presuming to know a core or essential truth about that child or teen in matters pertaining to sexuality (Alcoff 1996, 103). The female teacher sex scandals discussed in this book reveal outlandish instances where student testimonies were not only seen to be irrelevant but symptomatic of abuse. In other words, anything said by the student contra to the master narrative of childhood sexual abuse became itself an indicator of abuse. Within the master narrative of child sexual abuse, no healthy, normal teen could ever consent to adult sexual touching or flirtation.

Of course, I am not suggesting that we should take the words children and teenagers use to describe a given sexual encounter at face value. Social consent is not always transparent and intelligible, particularly when it concerns those designated underage. There is always a gap between what youth may want (or not want) and the words available to ask for (or to refuse) an overture in the domain of sexual relations. This is also true of adults. Following Freud and Lacan (see Miller 1998), I agree that desire and jouissance does not lend itself to figurative representation, let alone clear and transparent meaning in the domain of language. I am not suggesting that narrative testimony (and consent) is unimportant but that we must understand that there is more going on in the modern-day sex panics than meets the eye. It is always difficult to articulate a sexual desire or wish that is non-normative or rendered illegitimate in the public eye. We lack words to express much of what we want (and do) in the domain of the sexual, and the law steps in to fill the discursive gap. In an effort to understand the paternal and colonizing manoeuvres of legal and child protectionist discourse, I argue that female teacher sex panics are not just about child protectionism; they are about normalizing regimes and unacknowledged worries about the status of heteronormativity in the profession and the public at large.

I am, again, concerned about the "excess of signification" in the modern-day female teacher sex panics. The teacher sex scandals are driven by something more than child welfare because the public and the profession is disproportionately worried about the sexual proclivities of female teachers (who rarely commit the sexual misdemeanors of concern) as opposed to male teachers (who are most often found to have transgressed actual sexual boundaries instated to protect the underaged). There is something more at stake than the manifest complaint about harm to minors suggests. This book is about that something else. To begin, I first ask the question: What has so galvanized and upset the public and the profession about *female* teacher sexual transgressions?

By focusing in Chapters 2 through 5 on four sex scandals involving the conduct of female teachers with boy-students, I show that, according to all available reports, the boys initiated or were equally enthusiastic participants in what later came to be called a sexual infraction. In the sex scandal involving a lesbian teacher that I discuss in Chapter 6, I show that at the time of the affair, the teenaged female student thought that she was in love and chose to move in with her teacher. The case studies do not show that the underage male and female students were harmed by their sexual liaisons with their female teachers. All insisted that they weren't victimized or in any way harmed by their relationships with the accused teachers at the time of the affairs. In one instance, a teenager who had participated in a lesbian affair with her teacher saw herself as abused twenty years after the fact, and in another instance, a group of boys – under parental duress – told the courts (amid giggles) that they were harmed. Curiously, none of these students tried to take distance from the accused teacher at the time of the affair or exhibited what are now recognized as telltale signs of abuse (e.g., depression, anxiety, socially withdrawn behaviour, falling grades, and suicidal or delinquent behaviour). In some instances, the relationships lasted for several years, and while others were short, they were not marked by one sexual episode but by a longer, mutually sought-out flirtation. However, the students did become disturbed and upset by the media coverage, the parental and administrative intervention, and the insistence of child protectionists that they were – despite teen appeals to the contrary – victims.

Queer Times in School: Queer Pedagogies and Reproductive Futurity

In this book I use feminist film theory and queer, postcolonial, and psychoanalytic theories to understand the social and psychic dimensions of the sex panics occasioned by the conduct of female teachers. I argue that the panic about white female teachers' sexualities is not about child protectionism but about efforts to protect both an investment in heteronormativity and the bifurcations of masculinity and femininity that this normativity engenders.

In the chapters that follow, I draw on a range of cultural narratives to contextualize the stories about female teachers' sexual improprieties. I use film noir and the character of the legendary femme fatale to better understand the portrayal of white female teachers as sexual aggressors who are dangerous and threatening to so-called good white family folk. The cultural mythology of *Lolita* (a movie and book based on the seduction of a schoolgirl by an adult male) is used as a template through which to understand school-based pedophilic panics and how, in the cases to be explored, these panics attach themselves to white female teachers. I also use Freud's (1997) analytic of love and hate as a phenomenon that manifests itself in childhood beating fantasies to understand the function of Eros in educational pedagogy. As educational theorist Jan Jagodzinski (2002) explains through his Lacanian framework, a love-hate dynamic permeates the pedagogical encounter. The dialectics of love and hate are, among other things, about the breakdown of sexual difference (xxix), the inability of the feminine subject *as sexual subject* to exist in the Symbolic order, and the difficulties we have adhering to normative heterosexualities. The refusal to recognize hate in maternal pedagogies of love, employed primarily by white female teachers, parallels the trouble that many have understanding maternal or pedagogical love as erotic. Both love and hate are crucial to understanding what happens between teacher and student in the erotic pedagogical dynamic.

Perhaps no cultural narrative is as pervasive and deeply entrenched as the master narrative of child sexual abuse, which engulfs even the most benign gestures of love and desire between teacher and student. The master narrative is premised on the idea that children are innocent and asexual. Thus it cannot account for intergenerational love, desire, and transgressions that were – at least in part – incited and enacted by the younger party. I focus on the failures of this narrative to account for intergenerational desire in the educational encounter. I also suggest that it is used in the service of heteronormativity as opposed to child welfare in the case studies to be examined in the following chapters.

As I explain below, because the lascivious white female teacher is read as queer, panics erupt about her sexuality in much the same way as they do in response to the sexualities of homosexual and lesbian teachers. This is because there is an intimate cultural association between homosexuality and pedophilia (Sears 1998) that spills over to the lascivious white female teacher. The feminine subject in pursuit of what Lacan called "jouissance" (erotic agency and orgasmic disintegration of and in the Symbolic order) is seen as perverse in much the same way as the homosexual is so identified (Miller 1998). Both subjects fall out of the heterosexual Symbolic and threaten the family. Because the family has a patriarchal investment in the next generation, it sees nonprocreative (pleasure-seeking) sexualities as a threat. As Jan Jagodzinski (2002, xxi) explains, the presence of the queer voice or of the gender variant in education is "especially dangerous or unnerving since they throw the structural logistics of the pedagogical family romance into disarray. [They expose] the suppressed eroticism that already circulates within those boundaries, for surely the fantasy is that gay and lesbian teachers are wildly promiscuous and will 'infect' students with their erotic lifestyle."

I contend that the lascivious, transgressive white female teacher performs the same queer pedagogical disruption as the lesbian or gay teacher. As I argue in Chapter 6, people worry about heterosexuality dying out and about the proliferation of queers in the school. The lascivious white female teacher is seen as a threat to heteronormativity and its reproduction because her desire is not contained within a nuclear-family structure. Her undomesticated sexuality is dangerous because it upsets how we think about adult female sexuality, about teenage and childhood sexualities, and about intergenerational prohibitions on love, desire, and sex in the service of the white heteronormative family. Intergenerational desire, talk of childhood sexualities, and lascivious white female teachers all spark public and professional debate and upset.

Many people do not want to think about how, when breached, these taboos affect our understandings of sexuality, gender, and other normalizing structures. Champions of heterosexual cultures and other normalizing ideals default to the childhood sexual abuse thesis and refuse to acknowledge the symbolic and social consequences that sex scandals involving female teachers have for our ideas about intergenerational desire. The childhood sexual abuse narrative is colonizing, making it difficult – perhaps impossible – to articulate or to remember an intergenerational flirtation, affair, or relationship in terms other than those offered up in the master narrative of sexual abuse.

Through an exposé of the messy underside of the abuse narrative, this book is also engaged with the problem of queer developmental time. Here, the term "queer" refers to an effect that upsets the dominant, normalizing regime of heterosexuality. As Deborah Britzman (1995, 152) argues, queer pedagogies interrogate the "conceptual geography of normalization." Queer theory invites us to "stop reading straight" (151) so that we may cease reproducing a set of heteronormative identifications that depend on the erasure or exclusion of those who are uncomfortable or at odds with its normalizing agenda. In this context, "queer" does not refer exclusively to those who have same-sex desires but includes all who do not live, express, or feel their genders and sexualities in a manner compatible with normative heterosexuality and with the developmental timelines on which it depends.

Queer theorists are deeply concerned about manadatory gender and sexual binaries and about what is considered normal and deviant in Western cultures. Queer theorists, pedagogues, and activists challenge normalcy in ways that are upsetting to those who cannot tolerate incoherence or ambiguity when it comes to gender and sexuality. "Queer activism seeks to break down the traditional notions of 'normal' and 'deviant,' by showing the 'queer' in what is thought of as normal, and the 'normal' in the queer" (Tierney and Dilley 1998, 60). In this book, I identify the queer in sexual relations between female teachers and male or female students and seek to understand the panic to which it gives rise. The teachers and students caught up in the scandals stand in as queer subjects because they upset the intergenerational barriers put in place to ensure reproductive heterosexuality. By challenging the idea that youth are necessarily harmed by intergenerational sex, I show how the scandals are not so much about whether the sex act occurred as about what the invocation of sex between female teachers and their students does to the institution of heterosexuality and its developmental timelines.

To speak of queer time is to draw attention to what we might call a developmental arrest in heterosexual growth. Time is a curious thing. It marks the process by which adolescent gender-identity developments and their asymmetries, sex, and love morph into evidence of abuse, and it recasts teachers into villains in the play of school life. In her discussion of queer time and culture, Judith Halberstam (2003, 328) argues that for queers the "separation between youth and adulthood quite simply does not hold, and queer adolescence can extend far beyond one's twenties." I contend that the reverse is also true: the queer adult can revisit childhood in much the same way as an underage youth can enter into adulthood. In queer time, the adult may be more like a child and the child more like an adult. Those contemptuous of teacher-student sex are panicked not so much by the intergenerational dynamic of the exchange as by its challenge to heterosexual time. Heterosexual time is consistent with developmental growth and life stages that lead to marriage and to human reproduction. Intergenerational desire interrupts heterosexual time and its reproductive, futuristic agenda. As Lee Edelman (2004, 31) writes: "What is queerest about us, queerest within us, and queerest despite us is this willingness to ... insist that the future stop here."

Queers upset narratives of chronological development and show us how life stages are incongruent with psychic life. An adult can have a desire that fits into a teenage flirtation ritual, and a more mature preteen or teenager can love and seduce in ways that our culture reserves for those whom we see as adult. This is the case not only because queers neither fit into nor grow into (nor necessarily grow out of) normative, heterosexual developmental stages, but also because the logic of reproductive heterosexuality (with its chronological and marital divisions) does not apply to the queer. What Halberstam (2005, 314) calls "conventional forward moving narratives of birth, marriage, reproduction and death" do not apply. As Kathryn Bond Stockton (2004) explains, queer youth grow sideways. By this, she means that they refuse to grow up and instead stretch the boundaries of any given developmental stage so that it swells into a queerly defined life moment. The queer child is queer not only because he or she has same-sex desires, but also because chronologies of heterosexual development are transgressed or interrupted. A child who has a crush on his or her teacher may be seen to have a queer desire because the crush breaches normative chronological templates governing taboos on intergenerational desire. A female teacher who flirts with or has sex with a student may also be seen to exhibit a queer desire because she perverts developmental and intergenerational taboos regarding love, desire, and sexuality that the maternal pedagogue is meant to uphold. She also queers maternal pedagogies by exhibiting a desire inhospitable to children's educational or heterosexual development.

As Lee Edelman (1998) argues, the child is hailed as the anti-queer. It is for the good of the child that we censor discussions about the body and its sexual capacities in school. Members of the Christian right campaign against sex education, homosexuality, and premarital sex for the good of the child and of the family in which it necessarily needs to live. The child is an empty space onto which adults project their desires for the future, and all in the name of innocence. Nobody is pitted against the queer with as much rigour as is the innocent child (who is most often imagined to be white). What Edelman (2004) calls reproductive futurism – the mission of the heteronormative family – is accomplished partly through an appeal to the child. The "future is figured by the ubiquitous icon of the innocent child and ... this child is often invoked as a symbol of family" (Bruhm and Hurley 2004, xiii). But the prototype of the student as son or daughter and of the teacher as future (or now) wife and mother conceals the queer composition of the dyad. Such a queer dyad necessarily involves the role of Eros and the potential for intergenerational desire in the pedagogical encounter. As the sex scandals involving female teachers reveal, there is more going on in maternal pedagogies of love than meets the eye. Both parties in the scandals to be discussed throughout this book are ambivalent or in some way resistant to what Judith Butler (1990b) calls the heterosexual matrix.

Butler (151) defines the heterosexual matrix as a "grid of cultural intelligibility through which bodies, genders, and desires are naturalized." She is committed to theorizing about what Adrienne Rich (1980) called compulsory heterosexuality and does so by analyzing how gender is used to regulate and manage bodies in the service of heterosexuality. Butler claims that the belief in "opposite" sex bodies (male or female) is accomplished through the repetition and recitation of gender norms (normative masculinity or femininity) over time. When one performs femininity successfully and reliably over time, ideas about the body of the performer, her skin, her genitals, her physique, her sexuality, become real in ways that produce a truth about the sex of the body. The same is true for masculine subjects. Gender is, as Butler (140) argues, "a construction that regularly conceals its genesis; the tacit collective agreement to perform, produce, and sustain discrete and polar genders as cultural fictions is obscured by the credibility of those productions – and the punishments that attend not agreeing to believe in them; the construction 'compels' our belief in its necessity and naturalness." The idea of sex is consolidated through gender performativity. Heterosexuality, for Butler, is dependent on gender performativity and is thus fragile and vulnerable to subversion. Without two oppositional sexed bodies, normative heterosexuality cannot sustain itself.

The sex scandals involving female teachers thwart reproductive futurism and the heterosexual matrix. The school has been seen as a second home, as a place where boys and girls learn to be gendered masculine or feminine, to adopt a normative heterosexual orientation with age-appropriate love interests. Both are essential for the reproduction of the white nuclear family. Nations depend on "good citizens," which are produced through the regulation of sexuality, gender, family, kinship, race, citizenship, and desire. The school sex scandals are driven by a panic about normative gender identifications and their role in consolidating heterosexual cultures in schools. I consider how ideas about childhood sexual innocence, reproductive futurism, maternal pedagogies, developmental narratives central to hegemonic heterosexualites, and postcolonial investments in racial purity, cultural demarcation, and citizenship are all upset by the revelation of sexual transgressions between teacher and student. Female teachers are supposed to be virtuous and maternal, not lascivious and diabolic. Boys are supposed to pursue girls their own age and to take the lead in such pursuits. They are not supposed to desire and seek out older female teachers charged with maternal care and educational guardianship. Intergenerational desire in school cultures is as taboo as incest is in the family. Both clandestine desires ignite worries of epic proportions in those who cannot tolerate hankerings for something other than white, reproductive, familial, and age-appropriate heterosexuality. Ideas about childhood sexual innocence seem to be upset beyond repair. Female teachers, like mothers, are not supposed to have desires, let alone act on yearnings for underage boys, who are designated innocent.

The scandals remind us of desires and experiences unwelcome in or at odds with heterosexual cultures. They speak to permutations of desire unacknowledged or castigated in the heteronormative mainstream. While some high school students do have sex with teachers and others may want to, there is little room to narrate these wishes or to fit them into the stories that we tell about who we are. Queer desires are not often discussed, and we draw on the more socially legitimate desires when recounting boy- or girlhood school tales. The queer school tales that are told tend to be about gay teen suicide, homosexual teachers and priests recruiting young boys, and pornographers and pedophiles infiltrating the schools. They are unhappy, to say the least.

The stories our culture tells about childhood sexualities (innocent and otherwise) shape and give rise to normative and formulaic accounts of masculinity and femininity and of heterosexuality. The sex scandals as narrated by the mainstream media, likewise, authorize and render legitimate certain ways of being heterosexual (coming-of-age narratives are a favourite) and constitute other ways of being sexually dangerous, deviant, and/or criminal. Given the dominant cultural narratives that constitute intergenerational sex as de facto abuse, it is difficult, perhaps in some instances impossible, to narrate or render intelligible an amorous pedagogical encounter that was not harmful or abusive. Through narrative we constitute and work to solidify our genders and sexualities. But master narratives of abuse make it difficult to tell stories that trouble heterosexual genres. Genders and sexualities are seen to be less than stable and transparent in queer tales. The sex scandal stories told in this book are queer tales not because they involve lesbian teachers or gay students but because they run counter to the mainstream heterosexual genre. As I explain in the chapters that follow, female teacher sex scandal stories signal a developmental arrest in the otherwise seamless narrative of heterosexuality. Consequently, there is a push to recast the female teacher (otherwise the object of student desire) into a dangerous character who perpetuates abuse against innocent children. The master cultural narrative of abuse leaves almost no room to remember an erotic pull (acted upon or not) between a student and teacher in terms other than abuse.

Deborah Britzman (1995, 164) argues that there are "no innocent, normal, or unmediated readings and that the representations drawn upon to maintain a narrative or a self as normal, as deviant, as thinkable, are social effects of how discourses of normalization are lived and refused." Reading practices are central to identity formations, sexualities, and structures of normalization governing school cultures. Sex scandals involving female teachers must be read through a queer lens if we are to unlock structures of normalization employed in the service of heterosexuality. I am in agreement with Britzman, who claims that queer theory must be engaged in the study of ignorance – understood not as a lack of knowledge or as a learning deficit but as an organization of knowledge that prohibits ways of thinking that challenge structures of normalization sustained by the institution of heterosexuality. Queer pedagogies call on us to grapple with ignorance, particularly with our refusals to know about clandestine genders, desires, and expressions of love and hate such as those unmasked by sex scandals involving female teachers. In so doing, we might be able to remember a time when our own genders and sexualities were more ambiguous and less likely to be straitjacketed by the colonizing agendas of normality.

The school sex scandals discussed here are as troubling as they are exciting. The attentions given to the professional transgressions analyzed in this book signal repressed wishes to escape the ordinary and to challenge what we take to be normal. The scandals provide a forum to talk about queer sexualities, desires, genders, and pleasures in school life even as they are couched within moralistic frameworks. As Michel Foucault (1978) reminds us, queer sexualities have not been repressed so much as subsumed into normalizing professional, institutional, and pathological discourses. Intergenerational desires in the school are especially prone to being subsumed into narratives of child sexual abuse. For this reason, queers often choose not to talk openly about crushes on, affairs with, and flirtations with teachers. Queer folk do not want their stories misunderstood or their love objects tarnished (or jailed) by the taint of abuse. Nor do people want their memories to be subsumed into master narratives of abuse or perversion. As a result, school sex stories tend to be confined to whispers and gossip, particularly when they are queer and intergenerational. Consequently, the media-based outing of these stories was scandalous, as it ran what Britzman (1998) calls interference and ignited curiosities.

Sex Scandals in Education and the Mythology of the Innocent Child

According to James Kincaid (2004, 13), the early meaning of the word "scandal" was to "cause perplexity of conscience, to hinder the reception of faith or obedience to Divine Law, to present a stumbling block." In present-day usage, it is associated with a moral wrongdoing and also with the "rage, rumour, or gossip arising from this" (Oxford English Dictionary). In other words, a scandal is not just about an objectionable behaviour but about the intensity of public response to it. The catalyst for any given sex panic is less than obvious. Because female teachers do not really pose a threat to students that is proportionate to the associated press coverage, we must turn our attention to how the alleged transgressions camouflage and thus distract us from the real issue at hand. To properly understand the catalyst for school sex panics, it is necessary to focus on the panic as opposed to the transgressive act per se. Public and professional response to allegations of sexual abuse by white female teachers, sensational media coverage of such allegations, and professional censure and discipline of the involved teachers needs explanation because they are out of proportion to the infractions against which they are mobilized. The sexual misdemeanours are red herrings. The real show is to be seen in the narration of the taboo, in the moralistic responses uttered by those whom we might call champions of the innocent child, and the teaching profession.

Using psychoanalysis as a methodology, I endeavour to uncover what drives the panic. I am interested less in what actually happened than in what we think and how we worry about what happened. I am concerned with the panic itself as a scholarly topic of investigation. This book offers an explanation for how professional administrators in education, the public, parents, child-welfare advocates, and others came to be so concerned about the sexual transgressions of female teachers. Scandals are always more interesting and significant than the clandestine activities themselves. Psychic anxieties about the sexualities of white female teachers are the focus of my investigation, and using psychoanalysis, I endeavour to understand their impact on the genealogy of school-based sex panics.

Scandal is the "enemy of cultural hegemony," and "we are drawn to scandal by a hope to trip up the cultural censors, by a dream of escaping culture or transforming it" (Kincaid 2004, 13). There is something about genders and sexualities, particularly the illicit sexualities of white female teachers, that is scandalously exciting, and we wish to hear more about them. This is why so many newspapers featuring stories of sex between female teachers and their students are sold. We care very much about the desires that we are not supposed to have, about the gender identifications that we are supposed to disavow, and about the intergenerational desires that are not supposed to exist. At the same time, many are driven to punish and ostracize those who dare to transgress societal taboos. Those who are excited and those who insist on punishment are often the same people. In Chapter 3, I consider how this dialectic operates at the level of the unconscious. Segments of the population seek to punish individual teachers, and moralists worry about a whole generation of female teachers tempted by the sexual availability of teenaged boys (and girls). The sexualities of white female teachers in Canada, the United States, and England are now regarded with a new sense of alarm. No longer seen as asexual, the white female teacher is thought to be capable of sexual depravity, impurity, and vice in the pedagogical encounter.

Because the sex scandals involving female teachers reveal gender identifications that are not hospitable to normative heterosexualities, they must be quashed. The panic is not really about the sexual violation of school boys and girls but about the multiple ways that boy- and girl-students and white female teachers are already gendered and sexualized subjects. The panic is also about a moment in which the white female teacher is seen to have failed in her task as a guide or agent in the management of normative heterosexuality. It is no coincidence that use of the white female teacher's body in education is evident when she departs from an ascetic or heteronormative mandate – that is, when she commits a sexually transgressive act involving a student. When she becomes a scandal and is pitted against the innocence of the child and all that is good and white about heterosexuality, the nation, and its commitment to reproductive futurism, she becomes a sensation in the Western world: "The Child ... marks the fetishistic fixation of heteronormativity: an erotically charged investment in the rigid sameness of identity that is central to the compulsory narrative of reproductive futurism" (Edelman 2004, 21). In other words, reproductive futurism is about a dream of the future, an investment in white heteronormativity that has its roots in colonial societies, human reproduction for racial and national betterment, and nuclear-family structures. The white boy-child occupies a pivotal role in this dream, and violation of his innocence shatters the dream along with the configurations of nation to which it adheres. This explains why white female teachers who violate the dream by having sex with or flirting with a teenaged boy-student, otherwise suited for marriage, paternity, and white reproductive futurism, is received with such scorn. She is to prepare and educate the child who stands in as the future generation, not harness him for her own *unproductive* pleasures.

But the futuristic agenda cannot have it both ways. The child cannot be heterosexual *and* innocent. He (or she) cannot be a budding heterosexual without sexual desire of his (or her) own. A curious doublespeak emerges in the print media. The child seduced by his predatory teacher is framed as "no longer innocent," but he is also framed as having his *heterosexual* development thrown off course. In the first moment, the child is innocent, and in the second, he or she is a heterosexual in the making. Normative, masculine gender-identity development is interrupted, so his heterosexuality is also perceived to be under threat. Developmental stages are said to have been interrupted even as the adolescent and teenaged boys are also said to have been pure, virginal, and untouched by adult desires. The doublespeak is even more absurd when we consider that a flirtation between a boy and a girl at school is seen as a normal expression of desire, whereas a similar gesture between a student and a same-sex peer, an adult, or an older child robs the student of sexual innocence – that which was not supposed to be there in the first place. The oxymoronic constitution of the child as asexual and as heterosexual at the same time should alert us to more than a problem of logic. The slippage enables the child to be used in the service of something else, namely the heteronormative, white, and reproductive family. Here, we see a dual usage of the teacher and the student. There is a curious coupling between the student and the white female teacher in how the thesis of childhood sexual innocence is strung together. Both are expected to be devoid of desire in the service of heterosexuality. As such, both are eroticized, as I claim in Chapter 2, but this eroticization remained largely underground until the outbreak of the media-generated sex scandals involving female teachers.

The place of the school, and the role of the white female teacher more specifically, in the management of heterosexuality has not been adequately considered or acknowledged in queer theory or in critical pedagogical studies of the hidden curriculum. Queer pedagogy is a field in curriculum studies that has made important contributions to the study of heterosexuality and its normalizing regimes (Britzman 1995; Cavanagh 2005b; Gallop 1992, 1995, 1997; Pinar 1998). The school is charged with the reproduction of normative heterosexualities, and the sex scandals involving female teachers are seen as violations of this national responsibility. It is important to note that this heterosexuality does not operate in a vacuum. Normative heterosexuality forges dangerous liaisons with postmodern eugenic discourses, as I show in the following chapter. The production of queer racializations provokes panic as well. Developmental psychologies, reliant on normative gender and age templates, render queers, racialized peoples, and transgendered peoples out of time and place. In other words, queer or trans folk who do not grow up to become reproductive citizens – that is, clearly masculine or feminine in ways sanctioned by white heteronormative culture – but who live in opposition (by choice or necessity) to the developmental psychologies that saturate the school are seen as either anachronistic, foreign, or in some way alien to the futuristic agenda. Gays, lesbians, bisexuals, queers, transgendered peoples, transsexuals, racialized peoples, and gender-queers all fall outside of heteronormative templates and, like lascivious female teachers, are the stuff of which scandals are made. Anomalous positions are hard to inhabit, and the threat of scandal is used to discipline those who would live, self-identify, and love in another way.

It should be clear that this book is not meant as an invitation to, or apology for, childhood sexual abuse. My wish is not to grant adults sexual access to youth but to wrest youthful sexualities from the clutches of adult projections, pedophilic fantasies, and paternalistic policies and practices. I make what many might take to be a curious claim: that the student and teacher, together, are being used in the service of normative heterosexuality's futuristic agenda. The perpetrator is the moralist, and the teacher is the scapegoat. The adolescents or teenagers caught up in the scandals are imagined to be victims and are in most instances saddened and/or infuriated by child protectionists who insist on their innocence. Their sexualities are violently erased, and as always this is said to be "for their own good." Childhood sexual agency is not possible in hyperbolic child-protectionist discourse. It is important to separate the abusive and criminal from that which is based on social consent. I offer this book as a contribution to the sorting out process. To ask whether an intergenerational flirtation or sexual relation that has been instigated and chosen by the younger party is ultimately harmful is not to legitimize what some might take to be a harmful pedophilic encounter but to seek to better understand the nuances and complexities of such relationships. Writes Phillips (2002, 101), "One can, and should, disapprove of the sexual abuse of children without denying that it raises some unsettling questions about its uncertain measure in our lives." Most unsettling and pertinent to the discussion here is what happens when the alleged adult seductress is female (as opposed to male) and the youth involved do not see themselves as victims. When the relationship lasts for years, when the two cohabit, marry, and/or raise children together (as they do in some cases to be discussed in this book), the master narrative of child sexual abuse is called into question. We can no longer responsibly vilify those who take part in an intergenerational sexual relationship or flirtation when no harm can be found to have befallen the alleged victim. Such relationships may be unprofessional but not criminal. New questions and examinations are required to unpack the Pandora's box of desires that has been opened in the schools of today.

I agree that we need to think carefully and critically about intergenerational desire and about its many permutations in the educational milieu, but I also think that we must guard against an unwarranted moral panic. People are often moved to panic when there is a worry that cannot be named explicitly. A worry that is real can be dealt with and named for what it is. An unconscious anxiety, one that is socially remiss or in some other way objectionable, goes underground and resurfaces as an attachment to something seemingly more legitimate. The fuel driving the panic about sex scandals involving female teachers is, I argue, misplaced, so we must strive to identify the latent cause for the panic that has been driven underground.

If child protectionism was the actual cause for alarm, we would see evidence of this. We would witness a comparable upset about similar cases involving male teachers, but we do not. We would see more detailed discussion about childhood sexual abuse, how to prevent it, how to detect it, how it hurts children, and what to do about it. In the print media's coverage of the sex scandals involving female teachers, there is little if any discussion about childhood sexual abuse, except to name it and then to talk about the teachers with sensational detail and intrigue. As I show in Chapter 2, there is little if any significant focus on Mary Kay Letourneau's student lover and on his experience of the relationship that he had (and continues to have) with Letourneau. This is largely because he doesn't understand it within an abuse narrative. Newspaper reporters, child protectionists, lawyers, psychiatrists, social workers, and others caught up in the moralism of the case rush to save Vili Fualaau from Letourneau without stopping to take seriously his account of the relationship. Because we lack evidence of harm and because, in some instances, the alleged "victim" vehemently refuses to see him or herself in terms sanctioned by the master narrative of child sexual abuse, we must ask new and unsettling questions about what might be going on.

This book is not meant to incite sex in the school but to enable understanding about the angst surrounding it. Nor should it be read as an attempt to underwrite and thereby sanction a pedophilic encounter that may cause harm. Because pedophilia is a colonizing analytic, it leaves little space in its shadow to ask questions about how heterosexualities in the school depend on the image of the white female teacher as virginal and saintly to enforce and perpetuate itself as a dominant institution. The public, the courts, child protectionists, and those involved and well acquainted with the players in the sex scandals could not show that harm had come to the students who had sex or illicit flirtations with the female teachers, and so I contend that something queer is going on. Even the students, at the time of the alleged infraction, did not see themselves as victims or in any way harmed by coquettish teachers. In most cases, the students sought out the amorous attentions of the female teacher and did not experience remorse, regret, or nullifying side effects. That sexually dissident or queer children often have their "initial sexual experiences with older men or women, experiences they will probably not define as traumatic or exploitative as they reflect on them later" (Bruhm and Hurley 2004, xxvi) does not even warrant commentary when our thinking is straitjacketed by the master narrative of abuse. As Bruhm and Hurley explain, "remembered childhood sexual experiences can be traumatic *or* pleasant; the problem that interests us most here is how to make sense of the child's pleasure without pathologizing it or reducing it to 'trauma'" (xxix, original emphasis). The normative thesis of pedophilic or childhood sexual abuse is not only malapropos, but also dangerously misleading when we try to understand the unprecedented hype and outcry about female teachers' sexual transgressions with all-too-willing students. In these instances, the master narratives of abuse direct attention away from the more legitimate crisis, the latent point of anxiety to which a troubled public is responding. This crisis has to do with what is concealed by the hyperbolic insistence on child sexual innocence and its violation, despite the absence of supporting evidence. The underside of the child-trauma thesis is what this book is about and endeavours to uncover.

The Sex Scandals

In Chapter 2, I discuss the Mary Kay Letourneau sex scandal. The Letourneau transgression is by far the most upsetting and curious of those witnessed by a concerned public. Readers said that they could not comprehend the desire behind a transgression that led to a scandal of international renown. This case not only set the tone for how subsequent sex scandals involving female teachers were received in Canada and England but also reveals, most acutely, how "race" and racialization play an integral role in these scandals. Using the cultural mythology of *Lolita* and postcolonial theories of sexuality, I show how the whiteness of the teacher and the boy's Samoan American background are integral to the panic. As literary scholars of what Elizabeth Freeman (1998) calls the American pedophilic picturesque maintain, the American pedophilic genre performs a pedagogical function: it enables the white colonial – now postcolonial – reader to navigate geography, time, kinship, indigenousness, and gender in ways that legitimate European travel and conquest in what we now know as the United States. The female child stands in as a naive and passive recipient of a colonial advance and, at the same time, legitimates this conquest. What excites the reader of a pedophilic text – and of the Letourneau transgression as well – is how the child (coded as Native) not only welcomes, but also has surreptitiously orchestrated, the clandestine encounter. The child in the literary genre (usually female) perverts time because we are dealing with ages of discovery now past (although psychically real), and she defies a taken-for-granted developmental sequence by outmanoeuvring an older white male adult. She is not really a child but an indigenous "other," *and* she is a child wise beyond her years; both time anachronisms function to legitimize the colonial conquest and to reveal the role of illicit sexuality in the orchestration of this conquest.

The Letourneau scandal involves a reversal of gender roles that upsets the pedophilic fantasy sequence central to white American encounters with space, time, geography, and foreign "others." If the pedophilic seduction (by white males) enables the emergence of a white colonial empire, the seductions of the white female teacher – as the Letourneau case shows – promise to reverse normative identifications with empire, family, heterosexuality, and racial demarcation. Letourneau not only rewrites American cultural mythology associated with conquest, but also abandons her implicit role as white, female, virginal ambassador cultivating Americanness in children new to (or perceived to be new to) the United States. Using pedagogies of love – not so loosely based on pastoral care and missionary zeal – the white female teacher is supposed to govern student enculturation but is also expected to prohibit the kind of sex in school that produces racial hybridization. As Ann Stoler (2000) contends, white women have played a crucial role in maintaining racial demarcation and in managing the eugenic angst experienced by colonialists in the New World. In essence, white women have been positioned as sexual gatekeepers in colonial times.

Today, white female teachers, like Letourneau, are appointed to manage "race relations" between students and to enable patterns of stratification key to perpetuating a vision of racial otherness. The prohibition on sex in school is integral to the professional mandate. Letourneau couldn't have failed more publicly in her mission. Not only did she have sex with a boy from the Samoan Islands, but she also had children by him, thereby transgressing sexual and racial taboos in the white postcolonial imaginary. She became, in some ways, a racially hybrid subject or, at the very least, an advocate for racial hybridity. The teacher fell from grace and ceased to be white in the idealizations of an American public invested in racial demarcation. Her transgression was not just sexual, but also racial. Letourneau abandoned her white family to forge a new alliance with white mainstream America's foreign "others." Through her identification with her boy-student, a subject racialized as black, Letourneau positioned herself as a sexual subject despite her cultural alignment with the asexuality of the white female teacher. This is the stuff of which scandals in American-style education are made.

In Chapter 3, I explore the Canadian scandal involving former teacher Annie Markson. In this case, the teacher was subject to sensational press and professional censure as well as publicly villified for having written to – and having received sexually suggestive love notes from – an underage boy-student in the school where she worked as a temporary supply teacher. Unlike the Letourneau transgression, there were no sex acts in the case. Although the case was thrown out of court for lack of evidence of indecent assault involving a minor, Markson was subject to unusually harsh professional reprimand. To understand the gravity of the panic surrounding the Markson transgression, I draw on psychoanalysis to theorize about the panic over Eros in the pedagogical encounter. I use the concept of maternal erotic countertransference, developed by psychoanalytic theorists, to provide an organizing frame for erotic desires that teachers almost invariably have for their students at some point in their careers.

Using postcolonial theories of sexuality and feminist film theory informed by psychoanalysis, I interpret the sensational press coverage and presentation of Annie Markson as a dangerous, femme fatale–like creature. The femme villain in film noir threatens to undermine and erode normative heterosexuality's investment in the stable divisions on which the nuclear family is based, such as those between inside/outside, home/street, good guys/bad guys (and girls), adults/children, white/black, masculine/feminine, heterosexual/homosexual, and good/evil. She is gendered and racialized as a dangerous sexual subject, so it is telling that Markson was invested with a similarly evocative and diabolic persona. That the legendary femme fatale is a sexual subject makes it even more worrisome that the white female teacher would be seen to embrace a similarly potent and dangerous sexuality. The symbolic positioning of the white female teacher (coded as mother) in the re-enactment of the incest taboo is vile for news readers. What happens to white schoolboy innocence and budding masculinity is the anxious question that acts as a catalyst in the panic. Not only does the teacher promise to castrate the Father, but she is, seemingly, also willing to have sex with the son – thereby feminizing him – without guilt, remorse, or apology. Drawing on culturally specific anxieties about intergenerational desire and the incest panics that they invoke, I show how the lascivious teacher poses a symbolic threat to the white, heterosexual, nuclear family and its empire.

Chapter 4 relies on a close reading of the school sex scandal involving Amy Gehring, which, like the Letourneau case, made international headlines. Appointed to teach in Guildford, England, Gehring found herself subject to sensational press coverage, drawn-out court proceedings in England, and unduly harsh professional reprimand in her native Canada. In essence, Gehring was accused of having sex with two boy-students, brothers, and of cultivating close interpersonal relations with students. Although she was not found guilty of having sex with boy-students, she did cultivate flirtations and what some reporters called hedonistic relations with students. What made matters worse is that Gehring did not express remorse for her salacious activities – however unconsummated they might have been – but proudly proclaimed a sexual preference for younger boys (of age to consent). The proclamation shocked the moral majority in England, and child protectionists insisted that innocent male students – despite their teenage years – would be harmed by the unapologetic sexuality of the newly imported white teacher. She was consequently fired and barred from any mode of employment (including teaching, of course) that involved work with children.

Using sex-positive feminism and queer theories of gender and power, I show how the Gehring transgression upsets conventional ideas about the sexualities of good female students and white female teachers in the school, how it disrupts heterosexual bifurcations of gender, and how it challenges the predominance of normative (i.e., vanilla) sexualities in the school and in British culture more generally. Further, the Gehring transgression exposes the pedagogical problematic of moralism and censorship by revealing it as an example of the very thing against which it stakes a claim: punishment for pleasure. Using Freudian psychoanalysis, I show how the moral panic about Gehring's sexuality is a technique of pleasure: the media-reading public punishes Gehring and is perversely pleasured through the enactment of punishment (professional censure). Those in the moral majority are revealed to have an investment in transgression even as they insist that they are opposed to it. This revelation positions child protectionists and those who insist on the sexual innocence of children (and of teachers) in the same economy of desire as the sexual outlaws with whom they would do away.

Chapter 5 builds on the technique of punishment adopted by the moral majority and uses Freud's analytic of A Child Is Being Beaten to theorize gender formation and heterosexuality in the school sex scandal involving Heather Ingram. The British Columbia teacher entered into a sexual relationship with a male student aged seventeen and a half. At the time of the affair, she was unaware that the relationship was illegal (Canadian law now prohibits sex with persons under the age of eighteen when in a position of care or trust) but knew that it was unprofessional. Ingram was found guilty of gross indecency involving a minor by the courts and consequently sentenced to house arrest and community service. She also lost her licence to teach. Despite having a long-term consensual relationship with the former student, a child with him, and the approval of the young man's mother, Ingram was condemned as a sexual predator.

What is unique about this case is that the good-girl teacher Heather Ingram, bent on rescue and salvation, is seduced by a bad-boy student rapper said to have a machismo and bravado beyond his years. The case enables us to acknowledge an erotic component in the pedagogy of salvation, but it also enables us to witness an erotic appeal central to pedagogies of discipline and punishment – much like that seen in the older caricature of the spinster-teacher as tyrannical battle-axe fixated on rebellious boys. Maybe the older boy-student who "asks for punishment" is – like the teacher – asking for an alternative or queer economy of desire? Using the Freudian analytic of A Child Is Being Beaten, I show how the Ingram sex scandal is related to the wish for punishment (and the desire to give it), I expose the romance between female teacher and boy-student (masked as pedagogical incitements to care, love, and rescue), and I discuss the will to violate those laws of the Father that have to do with sexual and generational difference. The vicissitudes of sex, powers, and pleasures in this case, including those seen in the media reports, speak to a wish to alter the white, heteronormative, patriarchal Symbolic that governs school cultures. A beating (or seduction) is never *just* a beating, so the re-enactment, or consummation, of this fantasy in the realm of the sexual must not escape queer, psychoanalytic, and feminist inquiry.

Chapter 6 focuses on a sex scandal involving a lesbian teacher that is, in many respects, out of place and time. Jean Robertson was accused in 1993 of lesbian seduction dating back to the 1970s. Although the female student was a willing participant at the time of the affair and even though the two cohabited and the teacher gave her financial assistance, offered support in dealing with her turbulent family, and encouraged the alleged victim to continue with her studies, the teacher is remembered as a predatory viper and dangerous seductress of young white girls. Using queer and postcolonial theories, I argue that the case is not so much about child protectionism as about the problem of knowledge, secrecy, disavowal, and shame. The problem of lesbianism in the school is about the proliferation of queer subjectivities in the school. The heterosexual future may stop here, but the proliferation of queers is an anxious beginning. The concern about the proliferation of queers must be read as postmodern angst about sexual contagion, infection, and contamination originating not with the "darker races," as early-modern eugenic thinkers maintained, but with white teacher lesbianism. The worry about the survival of heterosexuality (which is often subsumed into the domain of whiteness) is akin to the panic over "racial" interbreeding in early eugenic discourse, so I wish to examine the panic occasioned by a white lesbian teacher as one instance of a larger fear of the white race's (i.e., heterosexuality's) suicide.

Taken together, Chapters 2 through 6 consider the social and psychic implications of queer and transgressive female teacher sexualities in the pedagogical encounter. I argue that the moral panic about female teachers' sexuality is less about child protectionism than about preserving heteronormativity in the school, safeguarding the white nuclear family, and maintaining the hegemonic bifurcations of gender on which the nuclear family depends. Champions of heterosexuality cannot tolerate the reproduction of anything but idealized innocence and dormant heterosexuality in school children and white female teachers. My overarching question concerns the impact of these scandals on thought about Eros in the pedagogical encounter. Might these scandals be queer, and could we imagine a queer pedagogy based not on sex between teachers and students but on illicit wishes and non-normative identifications with these wishes? In other words, could we embrace a pedagogy opposed to reproductive futurism, normative heterosexuality, and the categorical gender binaries that the latter inscribes? Could we use desires not yet colonized by heterosexuality as a means to stop thinking (and teaching) straight (Britzman 1995)? What nuances of desire and identification are afforded by refusing the master narrative of sexual danger predicated on fantasies of budding heterosexuality and the sexual innocence of school-aged youth? How can we imagine an alternative sexual Symbolic – one that does not adhere to the dominant regimes of heterosexuality; to white postcolonial power structures and their racist identifications; to gender templates that erase the complexities of life as we know it; and to the normative family with its insistence on order, status, formulaic Oedipal resolutions, and monogamous sexualities? This book is an invitation to ponder the pedagogical possibilities of scandal and to unearth queer desires, which are otherwise masked by the master narratives of danger and professionalism that govern school life.

2

Teacher's Pet: Mary Kay Letourneau and Her Fall from Grace in White America

> It may seem odd that our culture could conceive of an ordinary classroom as a bordello, a place charged with exotic passion (rather than with the smell of wet wool, peed pants, and old uneaten lunches). But most of us take care to know next to nothing about what actually goes on in classrooms ... and erotic suspicion finds its best food in ignorance. Thus we both glamorize (as we ridicule) and resent (as we depend on) the teacher who seems to be "reaching" the child, teaching her and actually gaining her attention. We might imagine that there's only one way this could be happening, and that way is sinister ... We are concerned, let's pretend, about teaching being a haven for pedophiles. (Kincaid 1998, 218)

In 1997 Mary Kay Letourneau was arrested for having sex with one of her sixth-grade students, Samoan American Vili Fualaau. Letourneau gave birth to two daughters following the love affair – by all accounts Fualaau is the biological father – and was forced to relinquish them to Fualaau's mother, Soona, because of her seven-year jail sentence. Both Fualaau and Letourneau professed to being in love, and the former student married his teacher upon her release from prison. At the time of the affair, Letourneau was married to Steve Letourneau and they had four Caucasian children who were invariably described by the tabloids as beautiful, blond, and impeccably dressed. The Letourneau family appeared to be a model family, but difficulties lay beneath the façade of happiness. Mary Kay Letourneau was not in love with her husband and was being physically abused by him, the family was in dire financial straits, and increasingly, the college beauty queen was spending time away from home, allegedly neglecting her children. Steve Letourneau was also having an extramarital affair of his own. Perhaps because of the difficulties at home, Letourneau spent unusual amounts of time with her sixth-grade students and, over time, befriended and seduced the precocious sixth grader named Vili.

The teacher was found to have had sex with the boy in the classroom, in the school gym, in the girls' bathroom, in her van while parked at a marina, and also in her place of residence in Normandy Park. The affair was abruptly brought to an end when one of Steve Letourneau's relatives called the police and reported the sexual impropriety. The teacher was placed in protective custody. Teachers, parents, school administrators, friends, neighbours, and relatives were all shocked that the beautiful blond teacher and mother of four had engaged in a sexual affair with a twelve-year-old boy. By all accounts, Letourneau was a much-loved and devoted teacher who was regularly sought out by parents who wanted to place their children in her class. Her principal considered Letourneau to be one of the best teachers in the school. What happened? How could the teacher of the year have become the protagonist in the most sensational sex tabloid story of the decade?

Fualaau did not launch a complaint against his homeroom teacher and insisted not only that the affair was consensual, but also that he was in love with her. "Both families pleaded with police and the Washington State Attorney-General's office to allow them to deal with the matter within their own families ... It was agreed by everyone that Fualaau had been a more than willing partner" ("Remnants" 1999). Despite their pleas, Letourneau was sentenced to prison in August 1997, three months after giving birth to Audrey, the infamous couple's first child. The sentence was suspended on condition that she undergo psychological treatment and cease to have contact with Fualaau and his family. Letourneau could see her children only under supervision. Upon release, Letourneau resumed contact with her former student, becoming pregnant again within thirty-two days of her release. Because she had broken the court order, Letourneau was sent back to jail for seven years to complete a total of seven and a half years in prison.[1] Unapologetic and unrepentant, Letourneau insisted that this was a "pure, spiritual love she had been waiting for all her life" ("Remnants" 1999). She believed that jail time was worth the love that she and Fualaau so cherished. Although Fualaau hadn't seen his teacher/lover from 1997 to 2004 – the duration of her prison sentence – upon her release, he married Letourneau with the blessing of his mother. The media-induced scandal rocked the nation, and white female elementary school teachers came to be regarded with a suspicion once reserved exclusively for male teachers.

Certainly, male teachers had been imprisoned for sex crimes against underage female students, but the Letourneau story triggered a public outcry and intrigue far exceeding the usual response to male sex criminals in the school. The attention given to the Letourneau sex panic in the media suggests that there is something unusual or perhaps troubling about the idea of the *female* sexual predator. There was an obvious preoccupation with Letourneau's gender as a white heterosexual daughter of a flamboyant, ultraconservative California politician (who, as we shall see in subsequent sections, endured a sex scandal of his own that shocked the nation and ruined his career). People whispered, and reporters speculated: Was the crime really that serious given that she was a woman? Did the teacher really harm the boy who was said to be mature beyond his years and sexually savvy? Is Letourneau a pedophile or an immature thirty-five-year-old who had more in common with her sixth graders than with her adult peer group? Do women have the same aggressive, predatory sexual impulses our culture attributes to men? Must we send her to jail? Do we need to protect our children from the white female teacher who purports to love children?

In this chapter I use postcolonial and psychoanalytic theories to understand why the sex panic was so acute in the Letourneau case and how the two lovers were racialized in the print media. I also draw heavily on Vladimir Nabokov's *Lolita* and on postcolonial literary analysis of Nabokov's text to properly situate the Letourneau sex panic in a long tradition of writing on intergenerational desire in the school. A central part of my argument is that the Letourneau sexual transgression upsets the white nuclear family with its investment in successive generations. The dream of reproductive futurism, as Lee Edelman (2004) conceives of it, is intimately related to whiteness and techniques of racialization. The Letourneau sex panic upsets the dream because it is founded on a set of identifications that seem to be inhospitable to white American reproductive futurism. The "child" in the Letourneau story, characterized by Vili Fualaau, stands in as a substitute for something else in the American imaginary. The postpubescent student is not innocent as much as he is a curious vehicle through which the protagonist (Letourneau) can escape adult time and place in the heterosexual landscape. Lolita was, similarly, coded as a substitute for geographical landscapes and seemed to invite the white man to perform colonial and imperialist manoeuvres through her adolescent savvy and coquettishness.

The Letourneau story, by contrast, is founded on a gender-role reversal that upsets postcolonial powers and imaginaries intimately related to heterosexual futurity. We may account for the panic, in part, by attending to this role reversal. The white female schoolteacher seduces the boy-student and usurps the white adult male in the pedophilic narrative. I show how Letourneau's sexual transgression threatens to undo the identity-based divisions on which reproductive futurism in the United States is founded. The genders of the sexual interloper and the surrogate victim are as significant as the techniques of racialization through which the American pedophiliac picturesque, so-called by Elizabeth Freeman (1998), is established.

Before I develop the specifics of my argument relating to the American pedophiliac picturesque, reproductive futurism, and the mutually entangled identifications with gender and race in the establishment of each, I first show how the Letourneau story is a popular tabloid and cultural sensation. Using Freeman (1998) and James Kincaid (1992, 1998), I examine the white American obsession with the pedophile. Through my examination of pedophilic panics, I trouble the thesis of childhood sexual innocence. Particular attention is given to the techniques of racialization that underpin our images of innocent children. To insist on childhood sexual innocence and to obliterate youthful claims to desire, as hyperbolic child-protectionist discourse sometimes does, is a colonizing move – one not unrelated to how the sexualities of white female teachers and of male and female students are sanitized. I then show how white female teachers have been positioned as colonial mothers and guardians of children who stand in as representatives of the white nation. As Lee Edelman (2004, 75) explains, a fascism attaches itself to the whiteness of white children. I consider how the white female teacher of today and yesteryear has been positioned as a guardian of this white child, who symbolizes heterosexual futurity. White female teachers are charged with the responsibility of arbitrating sexual (i.e., foreign and undomesticated) encounters, whether they be interracial, intergenerational, or, in any respect, un-American. Mary Kay Letourneau refused this positioning and failed miserably in her role as an arbitrator of social difference. Consequently, she ignited worries, moralisms, and panics of epic proportions in the educational milieu. The panic surrounding Mary Kay Letourneau is, as I argue throughout this chapter, incited by deep-seated anxiety about the status of the white, heterosexual, nuclear family in an increasingly multicultural and diasporic culture. The concern is whether the future, as marked by heterosexual time, stops here.

The Child Sexual Trauma Thesis

I begin by making the troubling argument that Vili Fualaau was not traumatized by teacher sex. He was not a victim, and the master narrative of child sexual abuse is less than adequate for those who wish to understand the nature and significance of the Letourneau transgression. The Letourneau affair cannot be compared to the sexual assaults that we see most often in cases involving male teachers. It is not because Letourneau is female that the charge of child rape is unwarranted and malapropos but because the affair was consensual (not withstanding the legal definition of consent); because no measurable harm by any account can be seen to have befallen the boy-student; because the normative pedophilic power imbalance (between older man and younger girl-student) was arguably offset by the gender-role reversal; because the boy initiated the encounter, pursued his teacher, and, even after seven years, married her; because the boy's family and friends did not see him as an injured party or in any way traumatized by teacher sex; and finally, because he went to extreme lengths to convince the press, the school community, and child protectionists that the clandestine affair did him good. This profile does not fit the one often attributed to female students who have been sexually assaulted, which needs to be distinguished from sexual contact that is sought out and/or agreed on by all parties involved. Children and teenagers who are subject to coercion and sexual exploitation report feeling traumatized by the event and seek out legal retribution or distance from the assailant. I agree that boys, like girls, can be sexually assaulted or harassed and that this type of abuse can be perpetrated by male *or female* teachers in positions of care, trust, and authority. Although the latter is rare, it is serious. My point is that the template of childhood sexual abuse cannot account for intergenerational sex based on social consent – as distinct from legal consent, which has nothing to do with what the younger party actually wants or does not want – as opposed to coercion, duress, or physical force. The thesis of childhood sexual abuse is not only inappropriate, but also misleading, when we seek to understand the cultural significance of the Letourneau transgression.

If we can suspend our moral judgment for a moment and agree that Fualaau was not harmed by the illicit affair – except in so far as it led to the imprisonment of his teacher/lover/girlfriend, a media fanfare, and a hound of reporters tracking his former teachers, family, and friends for pictures, interviews, and trivia about the clandestine affair and the two individuals involved – it is curious that the public at large could be so troubled by what might have been more amicably dealt with by the involved families and the school community than by the courts and the international press. The relationship is certainly unusual, and critics are right to question the harm that might have befallen the boy given his age and Letourneau's role as a professional trusted with the care of underage youth. There is a long and upsetting history of child sexual abuse in North America, as outlined in the previous chapter. In no way do I challenge this truth or suggest that sex without consent is not a problem confronting North American youth.

The Letourneau sexual transgression is, however, peculiar because it is based on a crime with no victim. A crime without a victim is a worrisome formula for moralists. Without a victim, we must look elsewhere to account for the source of panic surrounding the case. Using psychoanalysis as a methodology, I argue that the cause of the panic is latent, not obvious or manifest in newspaper reports. I contend that the *alleged* victim (Vili Fualaau) is a stand-in for a psychoanalytic developmental crisis. Heterosexual time is upset. Reproductive fantasies of colonial succession are troubled, and the white female teacher (coded as mother) is a catalyst for the trouble. She cannot be relied on to discipline and punish queer permutations of desire that are anti-Oedipal. She does not rebuke but encourages the sexual manoeuvres directed at her by a boy-student (coded as son). Along these lines, she seems to invite intergenerational relationships that are otherwise forbidden and antifoundational to the institution of heterosexuality.

Childhood developmental sequences are supposed to unfold along a linear, predictable path. If the child is to grow up straight, he or she must adhere to heterosexual time. Heterosexual time tells us something about who we are and must be. Queer time, by contrast, cannot tell developmental time. To queer heterosexual timeframes is to upset taken-for-granted distinctions between homo- and heterosexual, male and female, masculine and feminine, adults and children, and other binaries through which Western cultures enact structures of normalization. In queer time, bodies, genders, desires, and racializations do not make identifications with reproductive futurity. As Lee Edelman (2004, 16-17) writes: "Queerness should and must redefine such notions of 'civil order' through a rupturing of our foundational faith in the reproduction of futurity." The panic is about a rupture to the imaginary structures on which we base our investments in heterosexual futurity, racial demarcation, and postcolonial territorial divides.

By flaunting the prohibitions against intergenerational and interracial love, the teacher ignited a scandal of epic proportions. As a sexed body, Letourneau is stripped of the pedestal on which "good" white mothers and women are placed (Finateri 1999). She can no longer be entrusted to disavow undomesticated sexualities, those that trouble the normative heterosexualities central to the monogamous family unit. White futuristic agendas committed to positive eugenics – that is, to the reproduction of the white race – are troubled by sexualities that aren't reproductive, especially when engaged in by white women. In the public eye, such sexualities are seen to be un-American. The relationship between the white female teacher and the insistence on childhood sexual innocence is key to understanding the Letourneau transgression and its threat to reproductive heterosexualities. To refuse Fualaau's claim to sexuality (however worrisome to child protectionists) is to colonize the child and insist on his domestication. This domestication is about the imperative to abide by familial protocols and developmental templates leading to marriage and paternity in heterosexual time – which, as discussed in the previous chapter, runs counter to queer time. Domesticated sexualities are those that are based on and that instruct us in identifications with monogamous, marital, reproductive, and age-appropriate heterosexualities. They are in keeping with older, missionary dreams of civilized society in colonial America. White female teachers, as I demonstrate in this chapter, occupied an important position in the management of these dreams and in the sexual regulations on which they are founded. By contextualizing the Letourneau story as a fantastical wish for racial purity and as a libidinous desire for American imperialism and patriarchal succession, I expose the socially disavowed content of the sex panic. I remove the pedophobic mask shadowing the pedagogical transgression.

The American Pedophiliac Picturesque

Because Fualaau was a preteen, the Letourneau affair became a tabloid sensation – but not for the reasons that we think. The injunction against pedophilia is not about child protectionism. The taboo on pedophilia is set in place to ensure a particular relationship to nation, empire, and social reproduction within the confines of the white nuclear family with its insistence upon heterosexuality, monogamy, and what Lee Edelman (2004) calls reproductive futurism. As Elizabeth Freeman (1998, 865) argues in her discussion of Vladimir Nabokov's *Lolita,* the mythology of pedophilia "works to contain what eventually become nationalist concerns about space, family and cultural assimilation." She argues that the character of the pedophile operates to manage anxieties about social difference in American literature. There is, in other words, a long tradition of writing on pedophilia that does not invoke upset so much as it manages difficult memories about colonization in what we now call the United States. Because the Letourneau story fits within a long American literary tradition of what Kincaid (1992, 1998) calls pedophilic stories, I contend that we must read against the grain. We need to consider how what we take to be queerly perverse – the pedophile – is used in the service of white American nation building with its investment in what Judith Butler (1990b) calls the heterosexual matrix. By invoking the story of *Lolita,* I mean to consider how the idea of the pedophile in the literary genre performs a pedagogical function: he is used to consolidate a fantasy about the United States built on heterosexual, reproductive, and postcolonial investments in white racial demarcation.

Through her analyses of American and British literature in which the male pedophile plays a key role, Freeman (1998) contends that intergenerational love and sex are literary tropes and metaphors functioning to legitimate histories of colonial expansionism and imperialism in the United States. In what she calls the American pedophiliac picturesque, there is an ever-present "foregrounding [of] age difference rather than racial difference, thereby distorting the developmental logic that ostensibly separates adult and child sexuality, the pedophiliac picaresque suggests that pedophilia, travel, and the transformation of men into 'Americans' are deeply imbricated, and that the expansion of American territory and identity has depended upon the energies of the most taboo of 'perversions'" (865-66). Freeman makes the argument that the sexually precocious child – otherwise known as "Lolita" – stands in for a racially coded (usually indigenous) "other" who would otherwise be displaced by colonial expansion into, and exploration of, foreign (presumably virgin) lands. The child – coded as natural, innocent, and all that is good and pure – grants the colonial male permission to conquer "foreign" lands precisely because she is lascivious and invites his colonial advances. There is, of course, a whole body of postcolonial literature dealing with the centrality of sex and sexuality to the colonial encounter (Eng 2001; Gilman 1985; McClintock 1995; McClintock, Mufti, and Shohat 1997; Nagle 1997; Patton and Sanchez-Eppler 2000), but less has been written on the child's positioning in colonial and now, for many cultures and peoples, postcolonial power structures. It is the paradoxical construction of the child as both innocent and seductive that legitimates the colonial narrative central to the discovery of America in the Western imaginary, as several scholars who theorize about Nabokov's *Lolita* contend (Freeman 1998; Power 1999; Rothstein 2000; Tweedie 2000; Whiting 1998).

A peculiar reversal is at play in the Letourneau story, which undermines the imperialist and heterosexualizing manoeuvre of the colonial enterprise. Man-girl love, so often portrayed in fiction and popular culture, manages colonial angst about the desire to penetrate foreign lands by neutralizing the wrongdoing of the interloper and the sexual transgressions involved in forging liaisons with people of non-European lands. But woman-boy love flaunts the pedagogy of the white colonial pedophile and transgresses the boundaries set in place to demarcate the nation, the family, and the empire, as I argue in this chapter. If a socially "sanctioned form of racially pure pedophile sexuality ... manages nationalistic concerns about how to imagine [indigenous] North Americans (wipe them out)" (Freeman 1998, 873), then the racially mixed pedophilic encounter (with a gender-role reversal to boot) ignites white, nationalist concerns about racialized and sexualized "others."

The Mary Kay Letourneau Story as a Tabloid Sensation: A Pedophile in the Making

> We are instructed by our cultural heritage to crave that which is forbidden, a crisis we face by not facing it, by writing self-righteous doublespeak that demands both lavish public spectacle and constant guilt-denying projections onto scapegoats. (Kincaid 1998, 20-21)

As Kincaid (1998, 21) argues in his now-famous book *Erotic Innocence*, pedophilia is a nationwide story of incitement: "The trouble is that these stories of protection are also stories of incitement; the denials are always affirmations. The stories we tell of the monsters are also stories of home and family (our home and our family)." Speaking of the media publicity surrounding Mary Baxter, a female teacher who had sex with a seventeen-year-old student at Van Buren High School in California, Kincaid considers how it is that we are now "willing to see [female] teachers as predators, enemies of the family and deadly rivals for our control over children" (45). That the "boy" was seventeen and not a child or even an adolescent does not enter into the public equation: "A smart and active older adolescent is shrunk into a child, a generic 'essence-of-child,' by this cultural story, remolded as passive, innocent, and guileless. His actual age, activities, particulars are melted away to fit our needs" (31). The same dynamic is at play in the Letourneau story: the boy (although twelve and post-puberty) is infantilized and rendered mute, incapable of speaking intelligently on his own behalf because he has been presumably brainwashed or deeply traumatized, and the teacher is seen as an enigmatic, diabolical threat.

As in the Baxter case, the media publicity surrounding the Mary Kay Letourneau story was reactionary, moralistic, and hyperbolic, but most of all it was excessive. Beginning in 1996, the North American headlines read as follows: "The Law Must Protect Young Boys from These Women Sex Perverts" (1998); "Teacher charged with sex assault: Woman may be pregnant by boy, 13" (Rendon 2002); "Teacher Who Pled Guilty to Two Counts of Rape after Having Sex with Her Sixth-Grade Student Will Be Sentenced Today in Seattle" (Lauer 1997); "How a very unusual romance has ended in a court battle" (Fryer 2000); "Sentence for teacher angers child advocates" (1997); "An Equal-Opportunity Vice: More Female Sexual Predators Are Being Exposed, though the Phenomenon Is Not New" (Ward 2000); "A teacher's obsessive teen love" (Givens 2000); "Teacher's dad had affair, too: Conservative politician lost career" (Fitten and *Seattle Times* staff reporters 1997); "Raped dad 'can't wait to see my baby'" (1998).[2]

People want to know about the Letourneau story, about the minute details of her seduction, about the clandestine interludes, about the unseemly underside of the beautiful blond teacher, her family, and the all-American school. To manage our own interested fascination in the case, we too often vilify the teacher and insist that our interest in the case is about child protectionism. Others insist that Letourneau is morally bankrupt, a pedophile, and a danger to society. Reporters gesture to the boy's sexual savvy but then, in a moment, reverse the gesture by defaulting into an angry and moralistic pedophilic narrative. A columnist with the London *Daily Telegraph* wrote that "Experts in ... sexual abuse all agree that Letourneau's actions are those of a pedophile and that she should be treated just like a man." Quoting Florence Wolfe, co-director of the Northwest Treatment Associates in Seattle, the reporter reiterated her question: "Lots of 13-year-old kids are physically mature, very intelligent. But this business of a 35-year-old woman making a love commitment with a 13-year-old boy is hard to fathom. What 13-year-old has the capacity for that kind of love?" The expert also said that even if the feelings are genuine, there is no "context for a relationship like this to be normalized" (Beveridge 1998).

People complain that seductions by female teachers are erroneously seen as benign. For example, Cathy Young (2002), a reporter with the *Boston Globe,* wrote that female teachers were given less severe sentences than male teachers: "In 1993 in Virginia, a male teacher who had sex with three teenage female students was sentenced to 26 years in prison – while the next day, a female swimming coach who had an 'affair' with an 11-year-old boy and sexual encounters with two others got 30 days." The question of social consent did not enter into Young's discussion of "political correctness gone mad." Another reporter, quoting an "expert," wrote that "a lot of people wouldn't believe a woman would attack a boy, or a man, or a child ... They think that women are feminine, delicate, motherly. But it does happen" (Bell 2003). One caller to the online show *Today* said, "I say there's a double standard here. Men rape, jail 'em forever. Women rape and give 'em a break" ("Teacher" 1997).

A moral panic about lascivious and predatory female teachers in North American and British schools began after the Letourneau story hit the international news. One columnist wrote: "Twenty years ago, barely 100 women were in state prisons across America for rape or other sexual offenses, according to the US Justice Department. In 2000, the nation's prisons held 1,200 women for sex crimes" (Bell 2003). Another writer with the British, conservative magazine *Male View* insisted that it is "clear that new legislation must be introduced as a matter of urgency by the British Government to protect young boys from the rising number of women sex perverts who are increasingly active in this country ... Soft sentences are not the answer to the rising tide of female violence and child abuse ... The boys ... attacked by these vicious women might never be able to enjoy a normal relationship with another woman for the rest of their lives" ("The Law" 1998). One reporter cautioned the parents of America: "Don't sit by and let it happen. Don't let your child's life be ruined by an adult who should know better, but doesn't give a damn – Prosecute!" (Hayes 1997).

Never before had so much publicity been given to a female teacher convicted of a licentious crime against youth! Child advocates worried about a generation of female teachers who seemed to be as capable of child corruption as lascivious male teachers. Others were convinced that Fualaau was under the spell of a diabolic and rapacious teacher and that his testimony could not be taken at face value. Anxieties led people to question whether "middle-aged, married women [are] increasingly targeting teens as sexual partners" (Ward 2000). Parents worried that their children were no longer safe under the supervision of sexually active and promiscuous women appointed to teach the nation's youth. The Christian right blamed sex education, sexual promiscuity, and lax moral codes. Principals and school trustees imposed new restrictions on teacher-student interactions and cautioned staff against touching or being seen with students outside school hours. Reports were issued to investigate what many thought to be the escalating problem with teacher-student sex. Harsher penalties were instated to deal with teacher malpractice, and sexual transgressions (consensual or not) between teacher and student were severely punished with unprecedented urgency.

After the sex scandal made national headlines, the teachers at Shorewood Elementary School (the school at which Letourneau met Fualaau) were warned by their administrators against touching students and urged to display extreme caution in all interactions with students. "Gone were the hugs to comfort a child in need. Gone were any displays of friendly affection. Nothing like that was appropriate. This hurt many teachers, especially those with younger students who might, on occasion, need a hug" (Olsen 1999, 274). According to Gregg Olsen, who wrote a book about the Letourneau story, most teachers at Shorewood refused to do lessons involving the media, current events, public opinion, or anything that might lead students to discuss the Letourneau sex scandal (275). A cloak of silence fell on the now-famous elementary school, and relations between students and teachers were subject to extreme scrutiny and surveillance.

As Kincaid (1998, 76-77) contends, the panic, the doublespeak, and the moral indignation accompanying the obsessive worry about pedophilia in the United States has had "no apparent effect on the statistics on child maltreatment, which continued to climb rapidly." The effect is detectable in other areas. Adults are afraid to touch children, to hold them, and to love them. Children are sometimes drawn to pedophilic love because the family is increasingly ill-equipped to provide care, love, and affection (not to mention food, clothing, and shelter, as statistics on childhood poverty show). Love for the child, the subject of Walt Disney movies and age-old fairy tales, is a worrisome spectacle, and always, however deeply buried in the recesses of one's mind, there is a question about the nature and boundaries of this love. But the forfeiture of all adult-child expressions of love is not only about setting boundaries on what can and cannot be done, shared, and expressed in the school, the family, and other legitimate institutions for the sake of the child/teen, but also about the management of illegitimate love. Love and sex that cross boundaries into what is commonly thought to be un-American territory (whether homosexual, interracial, or intergenerational) is threatening to the reproductive family and, by implication, the nation.

Reconsidering the Master Narrative of Child Sexual Abuse: A Feminist Taboo or a Sex-Positive Intervention?

In the last decade, scholars have written about the moral panics surrounding childhood sexuality (Heins 2001; Jenkins 2001; Levine 2002; Miller 2002), but little has been done to understand the obsessive worry about childhood sexuality in relation to the nation, Western imperialism, cultural hybridity, racialized sexualities, and non-normative gender identities. Families are, of course, understood in the literature to be implicated in the taboos surrounding what Freud called the sexual enlightenment of children. But the taboos are, as I argue in this book, about a more fundamental set of anxieties about the Western nation and its diasporic and culturally hybrid citizenry.

Although second-wave feminists have been loath to consider childhood sexuality as anything but innocent and in need of protection, there have been in recent years a few attempts to question the legitimacy of the master narrative of child sexual abuse (Reavey and Warner 2003). Lindsay O'Dell (2003), for example, considers how stories of child sexual abuse and harm are structured by assumptions about normative child development embedded in other dominant narratives about sex, gender, sexuality, race, and power. Ann Levett (2003) claims that there is a suspicious relationship between the late-twentieth-century worry about child sexual abuse and the use of professional discourses to regulate workers. Educational theorists have likewise argued that the latter half of the twentieth century witnessed the professionalization of the teaching force in an increasingly conservative educational climate. The preoccupation with teacher accountability and ethical codes of conduct are, in part, legitimated through a public panic about the state of the school, the teacher, and sexual morality. As I show in subsequent chapters, the panic about female teachers' sexual immorality has functioned to legitimate new regulatory codes of conduct and unusually harsh punishments for professional infractions of a sexual nature, even when they are not, according to the courts, criminal or otherwise illegal.

The anxiety about female teachers' sexual deviance and immorality is not, by any means, confined to a few isolated regions or school districts. The media hype about the Letourneau case sparked a host of other sensational stories about female teachers throughout the Western world. In the United States, there have been many well-publicized sex scandals involving female teachers since the national debut of the Letourneau story. For example, Pamela Diehl-Moor, a former teacher, had "sexual relations with a male student when she was 40 and he was 13" (Young 2002). Diehl-Moor was sentenced to probation, and at least one reporter – Cathy Young (2002), with the *Boston Globe* – was aghast at the closing remarks made by Judge Bruce Gaeta: "It's just something between two people that clicked beyond the teacher-student relationship ... I really don't see the harm that was done, and certainly society doesn't need to be worried." Tammy Chmela, a substitute teacher in the Crystal City School District in St. Louis, was caught having sex with two boy-students, one fourteen and the other fifteen. "She allegedly videotaped some of the acts while her toddler was in the same room of the apartment" (Bell 2003). Also in 2003 Janet Medley, a special-education teacher in the Grandview School District in Jefferson County, St. Louis, was charged with having sex with a sixteen-year-old boy-student (Bell 2003). Susan Charmaine Franklin, a Houston elementary school teacher, was given an eight-year suspended sentence for having a sexual affair with her son's fifteen-year-old friend. The judge said that the Franklin case had "eerie parallels" to the Letourneau case (Rendon 2002). Liza Zuniga was accused of aggravated sexual assault of a thirteen-year-old boy-student enrolled at a Pasadena Christian school in 2002 (Zuniga is now pregnant, and as in the Letourneau case, the boy is the paternal father). Tanya Hadden was given life in prison for kidnapping a fifteen-year-old boy-student and sexual seduction of a minor, also in 2002. The teacher and boy were – as in the Letourneau case – involved in a consensual relationship and decided to take a trip to Las Vegas as boyfriend and girlfriend. The judge, who was said to have imposed an "overkill" prison sentence, reported that he was concerned about a "Mary Kay 2" (Hockenberry, Thompson, and Lauer 2002).

The Letourneau sex scandal also ignited a nationwide panic in Canada, as I show in the chapters that follow. In fact, the scandals involving Canadian-born or -employed teachers from the late 1990s to the early twenty-first century were all, despite their differences, read through the lens of the Letourneau transgression – even though most were thrown out of court due to lack of evidence supporting accusations and rumours of child sexual abuse. It is therefore important to understand how ideas about the predatory sexualities of white female teachers and the mythology of childhood sexual innocence are linked to more fundamental concerns about the status of the nuclear family and its reproductive responsibilities, racial purity in multicultural societies, binary gender-identity formation in a postcolonial context, and the heterosexual matrix.

Childhood Sexuality and Its Pedagogical Possibilities

Childhood sexuality in modern, industrial nations has been taboo, as everyone from Sigmund Freud to Alfred Kinsey would attest. There has been an insistence on childhood sexual innocence. Consensus holds that children do not have sexual desire, are unable to exert sexual agency, and so must be protected from predatory adults. Children and teenagers are too young and inexperienced to have sex, to want sex, or to think about sex. Even age-appropriate sexual touching between children is cloaked within a discourse of sexual danger. Despite evidence suggesting that youth are in fact sexual and often capable of negotiating age-appropriate sexual relations with their peers, adults often default into an almost manic insistence on the thesis of childhood sexual innocence. The Letourneau case, like other sex scandals involving female teachers and their sexually savvy, teenaged boy-students in the Canadian context, begs us to re-examine what we take to be true and natural about postpubescent and teenaged youth subsumed into the generic category, "child."

In his discussion of child pornography and the Internet, Philip Jenkins

(2001) reminds us that in most traditional societies, it is puberty that marks a child's entry into adulthood. Following adolescence, a girl or boy is considered a sexual subject able to partake in sexual activity (within the bounds of community codes of conduct, mores, and religious practices). From colonial times until the late nineteenth century, the legal age of consent in the United States was set at ten years of age. The intent of this legislation was not to protect children from harm but to guard the virginity of young girls, who were thought to belong to their fathers: "In the thirteenth century, a father's right to his daughter's virginity was unquestioned. She (like her mother) was chattel, and if he suspected somebody of trespassing on his property, he could haul the culprit before the magistrate like a horse or a thief" (Levine 2002, 77). Laws on statutory rape were thus about claiming children as property of their fathers and, by extension, of the nation. "Over the next century, the American age of legal consent rose steadily, commonly to sixteen or eighteen, while the physical and sexual maturity fell equally dramatically, from fifteen to twelve or thirteen" (Jenkins 2001, 26). The age of consent allegedly rose to protect children, but as scholars critical of childhood sexual-danger narratives suggest, raising the age of consent can more accurately be seen as a way to regulate sexuality, desire, and pleasure in North American youth.

Until 1981, the US Supreme Court saw it as an offence to have sex with a female minor but not with a male minor. "The justices noted the greater risk of sex to a girl because of pregnancy but not the greater discrimination against a girl in assuming she never wanted sex" (Levine 2002, 71). Recently, state statutes recognized boys as potential victims of statutory rape. But almost invariably, it was an adult male who was seen to have allegedly forced the young man into a homosexual liaison. Cases like the Letourneau crime are rare not only because boys tend not to be seduced by adult women and not only because, if they are seduced, such "crimes" tend to go unreported, but also because a successful prosecution usually "needs a victim willing to testify against her [or his] lover, and few [male] teens are [willing]" (72). The concept of statutory rape is oxymoronic because it depends on the insistence of a rape that is sometimes – according to the alleged legal victim – consensual. The so-called victim doesn't usually see him or herself as having suffered from a crime, so it is often the case in the United States, England, and Canada that suits are filed by the parents.

Westernized nations in the present day cannot agree on what the age of consent should be, and even in the United States, where puritanical moralism surrounds talk about child sexuality, there is a significant difference in age-of-consent laws between states. In some states, the clandestine affair between Letourneau and Fualaau would not have been illegal. Levine points to and validates a Dutch law that decriminalizes sex between an adolescent (aged twelve to fifteen) and an adult. The law does allow adolescent youth and their parents to press charges if the sex was in any-way coercive or harmful. Challenging the presumption of sexual danger, Levine insists that preteens should be seen as having sexual agency and given rights to sexual self-determination, a right denied to youth in the United States. Levine also outlines the problem of using statutory-rape laws, which are designed to govern and ultimately to punish adults who have sex with teenagers. Just before the Letourneau transgression reached the Washington court, the state had changed the statutory-rape law (which, as Levine points out, is often based on what I call "social consent" between an adult and a teenage or preteen minor) into a child-rape law. Speaking of girls, who are usually denied agency in matters relating to sexuality, Levine (2002, 72) rightly points out that "statutory-rape is not about sex the victim says she did not want. It is about sex she did want but which adults believe she only thought she wanted because she wasn't old enough to know she did not want it." In the Letourneau case, the statutory-rape law is about the sex that the postpubescent boy claimed to want (and went after) but to which the American public thought him incapable of consenting.

Although teenaged girls and boys are more likely today to be sexually active (given their physical and sexual maturity), their activities are also more likely to be criminalized. Judith Levine (2002, xxv) agrees that even though children today are more likely to be sexually active than their predecessors, the statistics are not galloping upward: "Despite the less-than-electrifying facts [about child sexual activity], almost every major report [in North America] on teen sexuality is pitched with the staples of sensationalism – the shock of what the story will reveal and the reproachful dismay that the readers don't know it already." The criminalization of sex with a minor is dependent on the thesis of childhood sexual innocence, which itself is a relatively recent invention (Heins 2001).

Conflating a prepubescent child with a more mature teenager is central to the modern panic. There are significant differences between a prepubescent child, a preteen, and a more developmentally mature, older teen. Differences also exist between youth of the same chronological age with respect to sexual maturity, partly depending on when they go through puberty. The pedophilic discourse erases these differences, as Kincaid (1992, 1998) argues, and treats all youth under eighteen years of age as children (devoid of power, agency, and desire). In 1997, Fualaau, then fourteen, expressed frustration with this collapsing of discrete stages in what is otherwise a very significant developmental maturation sequence. Focusing his frustration on the media and particularly on child protectionists, Fualaau refused to be positioned as a child who was entrapped by a lascivious, predatory teacher. "He said he realizes that people are trying to protect him but that, as a result, he has not been given a voice in all that's happened ...

'I want people to stop seeing me as a victim ... My life is going to be fine. Mary didn't harm me in any way. Who are they to say I'm too young to know anything when they don't even know me?'" (Fitten, Bartley, and *Seattle Times* staff reporters 1997). Upon the birth of their second child, Georgia, Fualaau said he was "overjoyed ... very excited and can't wait to ... see my ... baby," reunite with my girlfriend, and get married. The same newspaper article reported that Fualaau was upset that Letourneau was again jailed following the birth of their second daughter and that it "bothered him to have Letourneau separated from her newborn girl ... I wish that the mother could spend time with her baby and her other kids ... She's a victim at the same time they say she's a criminal" ("Raped dad" 1998). Fualaau's mother and relatives told the press that they would welcome Letourneau into their family if, upon her release, the two followed through with their desire to marry.

Alarmists and child advocates alike positioned Fualaau as a casualty of what child psychologists call "grooming" (a process whereby an adult predator prepares the child for an eventual seduction), but it became clear through detailed media reports that the so-called victim "bet a friend $20 he would have sex with Letourneau" at age twelve, before Letourneau even considered having him as a sexual partner (Frankel, Nolan, and Hardy 1998). It was not Letourneau, but Fualaau, who pursued the affair and seduced the teacher. Soona Fualaau testified in court that Letourneau was not strong enough to resist what her son wanted and that she did not hold her responsible for the affair. By all accounts, Fualaau initiated the original seduction, and some commentators conjecture that he had more power in the relationship than did Letourneau to determine the nature and frequency of their illicit meetings, the kind of sex that they had, and what would become of their relationship.

Kincaid (1992, 25) speculates that as a culture, we refuse to acknowledge a place for childhood sexual power and prowess for much the same reason that we hate the pedophile: "Perhaps power hates pedophilia so because it actually threatens to grant power to the child, placing the adult in a weakened, sometimes dependent position." Even in Vladimir Nabokov's book *Lolita,* and in its various Hollywood film adaptations – which, like the book, have been censored, scorned, and held in contempt for allegedly advocating pedophilia – we confront depictions of an older man losing control of his pedophilic fantasy (as it becomes enacted) as well as control of the actual girl whom he adores. The pedophilic narrative (in *Lolita*) – with its penchant for anachronistic time, geographical displacement, and vertigo (as we shall see in a later section) – upsets the binary logic and linearity of the Father. There is something queer in and about *Lolita.* "Adults and children are separated by puberty; men and women are separated by – well, everything ... Child-loving demands a release or displacement of our habit of creating oppositions, slides us toward a paradigm that does not make things distinct but blurs them" (Kincaid 1992, 13). In the pedophilic narrative, gender roles, in particular, are blurred, and masculine and feminine scripts are turned upside down. Gender trouble is on the horizon, and reproductive futurity is at stake. According to Elizabeth Power (1999, 116), who offers a feminist reading of the now-famous story of *Lolita,* Humbert (the adult male pedophile) is "domesticated, even feminized, and the Lolita figure becomes conversely masculinized." Gender roles are reversed, and age, which is central to familial organizations of power, is irrelevant. "Pedophilia is remarkable for melting down gender difference in the same way it abolishes distinctions between ages" (Kincaid 1992, 14-15).

Pedophilia (as a cultural narrative) confuses and queers gender. Although many pedophiles are consistent in their desire for young boys and are themselves usually heterosexual, white, and male, others are indeterminate with respect to the gender of the children in whom they are interested. As well, after the Letourneau scandal made international headlines, pedophilia can no longer be seen as a preoccupation exclusive to adult males. "We are confused about the nature or location of gender in both the child-lover and in the child being loved" (Kincaid 1992, 189). The heterosexual matrix, which depends on clearly delineated and oppositional gender demarcations, is troubled by the pedophilic narrative. The powers of parents, teachers, cultures, and white nations are subject to question because the pedagogy of pedophilia (dependent as it is on a recognition of the child as a sexual subject) is capable of reversing the hierarchies through which subjects and nations confer meaning on themselves and others. Patriarchy and white America are seemingly under attack because the social and legal regulations governing sexual encounters – most often regulated and sanctioned by marital vows between a man and a woman of similar ages and racialized social positions – are being flaunted and transgressed. Something queer is happening to what many took to be naturalized forms of powers, relations, and identifications with American nationalism. "Pedophilia emerges as a basic and subtly embedded threat to the power of parents, to the institution of the family, and to implicit hierarchies within the culture" of the United States (Kincaid 1992, 26). Reproductive futurity is at stake. This is not because woman-boy love cannot lead to human reproduction but because it is based upon desires that are taboo and anti-Oedipal. The liaison is coded as incestuous (teacher stands in for mother, student for son) and thus runs counter to the classic, Oedipal resolution sequence. The sexual relationship is transgressive because it exposes the incestuous prohibitions upon which normal, heterosexual, adult desires and identifications are based. The transgressive liaison is antifuture because it reveals a wish to regress, to go back to a time in which the mother was a primary object of desire. The clandestine relationship is also transgressive because it produces racially hybrid children: not clearly white or black. For those panicked by the sexual and interracial transgression, the future is at stake. The babies in the Letourneau-Fualaau affair are racially hybrid and were produced through a symbolic breach of the incest taboo – the taboo upon which the heterosexual, nuclear, monogamous family is based. Because the teacher (coded as mother) and the boy-student (coded as son) formed a union, the contents of our own national unconscious and disavowed fantasies (Oedipal, homosexual, intergenerational, and racialized) have been aired for all to see.

As Lee Edelman (2004) argues, the queer stands in to receive the projections of these troubling fantasies. I contend that the lascivious white female teacher who leaves her socially legitimate and normally reproductive family to pursue a boy-lover is queer because her identifications, desires, and activities are antithetical to those issued by heterosexuality's normalizing structures. Speaking of the trouble that comes by forfeiting one's manifest destiny to love normally and to reproduce white American babies, Edelman writes: "If, however, there is *no baby* and, in consequence, *no future,* then the blame must fall on the fatal lure of sterile, narcissistic enjoyments understood as inherently destructive of meaning and therefore as responsible for the undoing of social organization, collective reality, and, inevitably, life itself" (13). The queer is a holding tank for disavowed fantasies and is thus pitted against the white child, who represents the future in all its glory. "For the only queerness that queer sexualities could ever hope to signify would spring from their determined opposition to this underlying structure of the political – their opposition, that is, to the governing fantasy of achieving Symbolic closure through the marriage of identity to futurity in order to realize the social subject" (13-14). The queer, who is also by Edelman's definition the sinthomosexual – a Lacanian identification with narcissistic pleasure, jouissance, and ego-based destructive impulses that trouble normalizing, linear, and rational accounts of the Symbolic order – is aligned against the child: "Sinthomosexuality ... affirms a constant, eruptive jouissance that responds to the inarticulable Real, to the impossibility of sexual rapport or of ever being able to signify the relation between the sexes" (74). The homosexual (despite his or her actual investments in normalizing regimes, reproductive families, and the like) is seen as a sinthomosexual by the heterosexual majority. The homosexual, like the sinthomosexual, is seen to be a subject in pursuit of carnal lust that bears no responsibility to the reproductive family. The white female teacher whose lust appears to be out of bounds is similarly taken to be a sinthomosexual. Representing death and all that stands against and outside of the white reproductive family, the nationalisms of white America, and sexual difference, the sinthomosexual teacher can be seen to trouble what Lacanian psychoanalytic theorists call the Symbolic order. The white female teacher who refuses to domesticate her desire, like the sinthomosexual, is regarded by conservatives as a "child-aversive, future-negating force" (113). Conservatives imagine the "wholesale rupturing of the social fabric" (14) and the end of heterosexual time with its hold on the future.

Judith Halberstam (2005, 1) also contends that "queer uses of time and space develop, at least in part, in opposition to the institutions of family, heterosexuality, and reproduction." Life schedules and childhood developments are thrown off course. Queer folk grow up not in but out of heterosexual time. Adults regress and children grow up before their time. It is thus not surprising that Letourneau, an adult, a mother, a teacher, and a professional in the heterosexual Symbolic order was infantilized through her construction as a sinthomosexual. By bedding a man-boy, she fell out of adulthood and was consequently infantilized through mainstream media and popular tabloid reports.[3] As Gregg Olsen reminds us in his telltale account of the nationwide scandal, the vilified teacher frequently lost track of time. Referring to the Letourneau family, Olsen (1999, 87) writes that their biggest difficulty was their "inability to make it anywhere on time." He claims that Letourneau's children waited long hours at home for her to return from school (110). Her colleagues at Shorewood wondered "what was so terrible about home that kept her [Letourneau] from her own babies" (111). The teacher was said to cook dinner for her family at midnight, to sleep only a few hours in the evening, to arrive at school late on a regular basis, and to be indifferent to report-card deadlines, school time-schedules, and staff-meeting times. Her relation to time was incompatible with professional and familial protocols, so her status as a responsible adult mother, teacher, and wife was called into question, and she was constructed as juvenile, irresponsible, and queerly erratic.

She was infantilized and, along with her student lover, seen to have re-entered adolescence. This was another queer permutation in time. For example, Gregg Olsen (1999, 82) quoted a family friend who said: "I always thought she [Letourneau] was really young in how she looked and acted. She always made us [the children] feel older when we talked to her." Upon befriending Fualaau, Letourneau began to dress like a teenager instead of an older, more mature adult: "Instead of a classic pleated wool skirt and blouse, Mary wore tennis shoes and layers of T-shirts – sometimes as many as three or four at once. She also wore tights" (139). The clothes belied her chronological age. A fellow inmate and former friend said that after Letourneau had served part of her sentence, her maturity began to slip away, leaving a "gleam of infantile madness in her eyes" (Dress 2004, 209). On *Good Morning America,* Barbara Walters compared Letourneau to Alice in the famous Walt Disney movie: "She's sort of like Alice in Wonderland. She's got this little voice ... this innocent face, the long blonde hair" (Gibson 2004).

Letourneau's gender presentation as childlike and feminine seemed to mock and, at the same time, undo binary gender and intergenerational prohibitions governing school and family life. The teacher was read as a queer subject who parodied heterosexual cultures and the generational divisions integral to the family and to the school. She was also read as hysterical and thought to suffer from poor mental health. Although I am in agreement with Jane Gallop (1985) that hysteria does not necessarily contest the social order, it does, as David Eng (2001, 176) argues, "mark a tear in the patriarchal order" because it upsets the presumed linearity and coherence of identities and identifications on which patriarchies, heterosexualities, and nationalisms depend. Hysteria, to follow Slavoj Žižek, is a failed interpellation. To adopt a hysterical gender and age formation is to point to an inability to satisfy the patriarchal, symbolic mandate of binary gender without harm, excess, and/or psychic confusion. "Refusing – or unable – to occupy her proper social position, the hysteric points to interpellation's failure" (Eng 2001, 176). By flaunting society's inability to police and manage a categorical gender binary, hysterics, like Letourneau, upset the heterosexual Symbolic and expose a messy underworld of disavowed identifications, desires, and chronological developments. We disavow objects and desires that are not congruent with cultural mandates on gender, sexuality, and a host of other specifications governing race, nation, home, citizenship, parenthood, and reproductive futurism. To be a gender or sexual hysteric is to have "reneged upon the paternal [or maternal] responsibilities of the Oedipal contract" (177) and to have "abandoned to some degree the here and now – or, in short, to have failed to live up to the demands of the Oedipalized world" (Smith 1988, 109). Like Eng's hysterical subject, Letourneau failed to live up to the demands of the Oedipalized world with its insistent delineations of gender, age, nation, kinship, sexuality, race, and racialization.

To further upset the Oedipal developmental sequence, Fualaau was depicted as wise and mature beyond his years despite being in the sixth grade. For example, one woman interviewed about the case contended that Fualaau was "not a little boy playing Legos and G.I. Joe [action figures] and wearing little Ninja costumes and running around the neighborhood ... [he] was not in the same league as other kids that shared his chronological age" (Olsen 1999, 219). According to a prison friend of Letourneau's interviewed by Olsen, the teacher constructed Fualaau as a Zeus-like figure who would dominate her [sexually] "in the most masculine way that any man, any leader could do" (368). Letourneau also claimed that Fualaau went through "puberty at age nine, he was certainly a man by age thirteen ... Steven, my son, is thirteen and hasn't gone through puberty yet" (Dress 2004, 147). The comparison between the two boys was also racially coded. Letourneau's son was white, while Fualaau was Samoan American, and the cultural difference seemed to enable the public to see the latter as sexually mature and savvy. As Olsen (1999, 317) writes: "The boy was Samoan, and, in 1998, people began to focus on that aspect. Was it cultural? Was he some man-child from the island?" The racialization of the boy enabled the public to imagine that Fualaau, somehow, defied an otherwise normative maturation sequence by becoming a man at thirteen. Accounts of Fualaau's sexual experience – even before seducing Letourneau – were widely reported in the media, which added credibility to the argument that he wasn't your average twelve- or thirteen-year-old. The mainstream public was also shocked (and titillated) to learn that Fualaau had an "uncle who had started getting involved with an older girl when he was twelve. The uncle married the girl and they were still married" (254). The story suggested that Fualaau had witnessed intergenerational sex within his family, thereby becoming accustomed to intergenerational sexualities.

The elasticity of the pedophilic narrative affords other conceptual slippages besides that of chronological age. Woman-boy love is also, curiously, coded as outside the bounds of normal reproductive heterosexuality. It is queered. For example, the same prison friend who spoke of Letourneau as infantile hinted that the former teacher may have been having a lesbian affair. Christina Dress (2004, 210-11) wrote that the former teacher had made a new prison "friend" who was "young, very young, [with] dark hair, olive skin – as a matter of fact, she kind of resembles Vili." "They [Letourneau and the new friend] were exactly like two giddy schoolgirls talking about boys and smoking in the bathroom." Interestingly, the pedophilic narrative also became about lesbianism in Olsen's (1999, 147) account, wherein he quotes a relative who did not, at the time, know of the affair that Letourneau was having with a schoolboy: "I think she's having an affair and it's not with a man. Either she's a lesbian or something worse." At the end of the book, Olsen also gestures to outside-the-family rumours that Letourneau is a lesbian (373), and other tabloid references are made to her alleged hypersexuality. For example, medical "experts," quoted in the media, contend that her manic-depressive state (a diagnosis contested by Letourneau, her family, and others who know her) leads to hypersexuality and that this explains her bizarre sexuality. In one media report, Letourneau's defence attorney refused to see Seattle (Letourneau's hometown) as a city of sex, particularly of homosexuality, as San Francisco is thought to be. The attorney stammered when asked if Seattle was like San Francisco: "I have to defend Seattle, and we're a great city ... It's a beautiful city, but you know the [public] mentality out there" (O'Reilly 2004).

The pedophilic panic is not, as I explain above, so much about child welfare as a holding tank for social anxieties about non-marital and alternative sexualities threatening to the traditional all-American family, the sanctity of the "white race" in the face of global migration and cultural hybridity, American nationalisms, and the vicissitudes of gender. The master narrative or discourse of pedophilia colonizes multiple worries and crystallizes them into one overriding panic about the child. This is a process that Freud refers to as condensation, wherein a series of worries are centralized into one discrete point of anxiety and preoccupation. Both the innocence of childhood and the whiteness of those in need of protection speak to the racialized politics of childhood protectionism. The pedophilic master narrative – and its colonial capacities – are most visible when taken outside North American borders. For example, feminist scholar Ann Levett argues in her discussion of imperialism and narratives of childhood sexual abuse that Western anthropologists' assumptions about abuse have led to what she calls cultural appropriation and misinterpretation. By naming a girl of a non-Westernized nation abused because she has had intergenerational sex or a more subtle or complex version of what the West imagines intergenerational sex to be, the Western anthropologist misses the more subtle nuances and relations at stake in cultural interpretation. The narrative of childhood sexual abuse is therefore colonizing. She also suggests that the presumption of harm (originating from intergenerational sex) determines the evidence of abuse that is found. It is not possible to find, for example, that a child has benefited from relations with an adult lover, as is sometimes the case. Levett (2003, 67) explains: "Rules of behaviour render talk about child sexual abuse difficult, constrained or taboo – except in relation to those other than oneself, preferably strangers, reported in newspapers or professional journal articles. The belief that experiences of sexual abuse causes psychological damage helps maintain the taboo (even among feminist researchers) and also makes it difficult to study." Levett offers the tentative conclusion that narratives of childhood sexual abuse are themselves imperialist and that non-English-speaking communities (in and out of North America) are, interestingly, not talking about an abuse epidemic. For her, this suggests that the panic about intergenerational sex (which disregards the politics of social consent) might be a Western cultural problem and preoccupation.

So it follows that child protectionists who insist on a master narrative of childhood sexual abuse may in fact be imposing a regulatory and coercive narrative independent of a particular circumstance – one that undermines children's sexual agency, independence, and autonomy. The narrative of danger and child victimization renders youth less able to articulate their own physical boundaries and to define, for themselves, what is good and bad touch or what is sexually age-appropriate and age-inappropriate. Because power "cannot imagine a desire that is not intent on fulfilling itself, on ending itself in a grand and destructive act of orgiastic violence, extinguishing itself and annihilating the Other" (Kincaid 1992, 32), we cannot yet imagine an age-appropriate intergenerational sexual liaison that does not cause harm. This is not a problem because we should endeavour to make children available to adult seduction but because the taboo colonizes what are so often human and otherwise inoffensive and benign activities. It also denies power to young people and creates a climate of fear and sexual danger that denies those younger than the legal age of consent a right to sexual freedoms that many heterosexual adults take for granted.

The panic about childhood sexuality, and the refusal to talk openly and honestly about what an age-appropriate, youthful sexuality might look like, creates a climate of danger for students. It is not easy for children and teens to articulate and negotiate a sexuality that they are not supposed to have and cannot talk about. Hyperbolic child-protectionist discourse, with its insistence on negation (children are not sexual but innocent) creates, as Kincaid argues, the conditions under which it is possible for adults to eroticize the child. It is, therefore, the will to silence and negate childhood sexuality that produces the very danger against which child protectionists see themselves protecting children. Theorizing about child sex that involves illicit liaisons with adults in a position of trust and care, as I do here, should not be read as an attempt to validate without question the Letourneau transgression. My wish is to open a pedagogical space for critical and reflective thought about the vicissitudes of teacher and student desire, the politics of intergenerational consent, and queerly gendered identifications and desires that fall outside of heterosexual futurity.

Erotic Innocence and Postcolonial Fantasies in White America

> The linkage between sexual control and racial tensions is both obvious and elusive at the same time. While sexual fear may at base be a racial anxiety, we are still left to understand why such anxieties are expressed through sexuality. (Stoler 1997, 346)

Kincaid suggests that the nationwide panic about pedophilia is not just an attempt to guard children against the dark and racially coded – although, ironically, white – pedophile lurking in the bushes, but also a seemingly compulsive need to invest children with erotic innocence. Strangely, media-driven fanfare about child molestation, abduction, incest, pedophilia, and child-pornography rings (the latter of which are frequently attributed to the male, homosexual mass allegedly infiltrating the American family, the school, and the nation) is committed to a sanitizing impulse that envisions children as pure, chaste, and unencumbered by carnal desire and sins of the flesh. This vision endangers children, as I have said above, but it also depends on whiteness as a literary trope. Kincaid (1998, 17-18) explains: "Baby-smooth skin is capable of inciting desire; unsmooth, or contoured skin is not: is this because flatness is innately more titillating than texture, or because flatness signifies nothing at all and thus doesn't interfere with our projections? In the same way, desirable faces must be blank, drained of color; big eyes round and expressionless; hair blond or colorless; waists, hips, feet, and minds small. The physical make-up of the child has been translated into mainstream images of the sexually and materially alluring." To sanitize children is to colonize their desires, fitting them into an all-American, heteropatriarchal culture that depends on a racially unmarked category (whiteness) to perpetuate a territorial entitlement to children's bodies. Assumptions are made that children belong to their parents and are, by their very nature, committed to heterosexual growth. To insist on their innocence and also on their budding heterosexuality is to justify protection and adult intervention. The child stands in as a boundary or an access point for foreign, queer, and nonreproductive invasions. By getting at the child, it seems as though the pedophile, the queer, the perverse can undermine heterosexual orders to reproduce the white nation.

Of central importance is the idea that pedophilia is no longer an act per se. It has become a trope for worries about cultural, racial, and sexual dispersion as well as an incitement to expunge what the white postcolonial subject cannot incorporate. "The 'pedophile' is the place where a host of current revulsions are relieved; it is perhaps our most frequented cultural and linguistic toilet" (Kincaid 1998, 88). Reading between the lines, we see that Kincaid, without overtly acknowledging the racialization of the pedophilic cultural narrative, is pinpointing a crisis of whiteness. This crisis centres on the matter of how to both have and repudiate familial and interracial desire at the same time, of how to live with the guilt associated with the knowledge that one has a desire that is inhospitable to reproductive futurity. To have an "uncivilized" desire (pedophilic, homosexual, incestuous, interracial, intergenerational, or otherwise nonreproductive) and to obsessively refuse, repudiate, and attach it to another is not unlike what critical race theorists refer to as white guilt – that is, guilt that comes from having benefited from one's origins or participation in a cultural heritage that has enacted colonial conquests and contemporary racisms.

The national crisis surrounding pedophilia is about white children, but in this case, it is the transgression of the white *woman* that is central to the panic. Letourneau's departure from her original, white, normative, and all-American family is of foremost concern. As her husband told reporters, Letourneau's transgressions had been "like taking a picture of our family and throwing it to the ground" (Hewitt 1998, 44). The nuclear family – and white women's position therein as wife and mother – is central to the colonizing legacy of the United States. As Christians and Republicans alike claim, the family is the backbone of the nation. The pedophilic transgression is not about child welfare but about an interracial boundary crossing enabled through a pedophilic engagement. That Fualaau is of Samoan descent adds to the white female teacher's transgression not because we worry about the use and appropriation of non-white children but because the American fantasy of a racially pure, consensual pedophilia – so eloquently portrayed and reviled in Vladimir Nabokov's *Lolita* and other books central to the child-bride genre – is subject to exposure in an unexpected reversal. In the Letourneau story, the pedophile is a woman (not a man), and the allegedly sexually innocent and racially pure child is a Samoan American.

By sanitizing the child and insisting that she or he is sexually pure, innocent, and untouched by carnal desire in the hegemonic pedophilic narrative, we are also, according to Kincaid, involved in a subterranean and covert plot to eroticize the child. The erotic child is an unmarked terrain, a mirror for colonizing desires. "Purity, it turns out, provides just the opening a sexualizing tendency requires; it is the necessary condition for the erotic operations our cultures have made central" (Kincaid 1992, 13). But how, in a postcolonial context, North American cultures depend on an empty, racially pure image of white childhood innocence is still in need of explanation. What precisely is at stake in the story of the pedophile? To what extent does the child perform a pedagogical or national function? Is the dominant pedophilic narrative involving white men and white boys and girls a fantasy on which the American empire is forged? Might the cultural obsession with pedophilia and the unusually excited response to the Letourneau affair be about something other than child protection?

The Pedagogy of Lolita and the Postcolonial Encounter

In her discussion of pedophilia in literature, Freeman sees the child as a mirror for colonial desires but argues that the use of the child is also about the establishment of nation, the mediation of time anachronisms in an industrial age, the negotiation of racial purity in the colonial enterprise, and geographical displacement. Freeman contends that the Lolita phenomenon in literature is linked to the expansion of the American empire through its representation in travel narratives. Speaking of Nabokov's novel *Lolita,* she claims that the protagonist's "attraction to female children appears indirectly as a pedagogical technique for encountering American space" (Freeman 1998, 868). Traversing a new geographical terrain is not only about displacement and entry into foreign territory, but also about "becoming differently sexualized" (868). Through child seduction, the colonizer forfeits guilt and anxiety by learning how to please and sex an allegedly all-too-willing child.

Focusing on child-bride novels, such as *The Scalp-Hunters,* Freeman (1998, 869) argues that in the age of exploration, European colonial manoeuvres are legitimated by and follow a "logic of an imperialist heterosexual desire

– here explicitly imagined as pedophilia." The child, like the indigenous person of what we now call the United States, is not a victim of violence but of a love that exists but that cannot be fully recognized as existing. The child is a stand-in for the original inhabitants of the colonial landscape. That the racialized child is willing to be seduced (penetrated) is central to the narrative structure along with its success as fiction. For example, Lolita, like many other children in the pedophilic literary genre, is of Anglo descent but racialized through her association with Monte Cristo (her place of conception) and her residence with people referred to as "Mexican trash" (870). While the illicit love enables colonial expansion without guilt – the child, a stand-in for a racial other, consents to and, in fact, encourages colonial penetration – it also maintains the separation between the white male colonizer and the racially coded child in the service of white racial purity.

Similarly, when the child of the pedophilic narrative is racially coded as white, the pedophilic liaison enables the white European to dominate the land (and indigenous persons on it) by forging a new claim to nationality, citizenship, and identity. The child is no longer a stand-in for a First Nations or indigenous "other" but a companion who, through her association with virgin lands, can guide exploratory (and colonizing) travels. "Acquiring the competence necessary to have sex with a child inaugurates a kind of political and cultural legitimacy that goes beyond juridical citizenship" (Freeman 1998, 875). The land (and its original inhabitants) remains primitive and savage, while the newcomer is – with his child bride – coded as racially pure, neutral, and entitled to his manifest destiny. The pedophilic encounter, like the expansion of empire, is heterosexual and racially pure: "The child-bride, rearticulated as whiter than white, comes to represent the synthesis of Anglo superiority and democratic idealism in an 'America' defined in opposition to both European monarchism and all other races" (875).

Speaking also about the pedophilic narrative in American literature, Frederick Whiting (1998, 834) contends that the publication of *Lolita* "raised a traditional anxiety about monstrous births, namely, their relation to the illicit desires that conceived them." Focusing on the postwar worry about the family and traditional gender roles, Whiting examines how the spectacle of the pedophile in legal, popular, and literary culture incited nervous apprehension beginning in the postwar period: "Although the emergence of pedophilia as a distinct form of sexual subjectivity had, like homosexuality, its roots in a variety of conceptual transformations during the latter half of the nineteenth century, its legal codification in the United States awaited the intersection of two phenomenon in the mid-twentieth century: sex panics before and after World War II and the explanatory theories, which had only recently become available in American psychiatric circles" (837).

The pedophilic panic must, therefore, be read against the backdrop of

American imperialism, colonization, postwar militarism, and white American anxieties about being conquered (penetrated) by a superior power. "In much the same fashion that political enemies threatened to penetrate the government, sexual others threatened to infiltrate the home. At its center, both symbol and synecdoche of private life, was the child" (Whiting 1998, 836). The horror of pedophilia was not really about the child but about a more deep-seated set of American and Western imperial anxieties and preoccupations with international relations, racial purity, and family formations with roots in the McCarthy era.

The pedophilic anguish must also have a central relationship to place and time if it is charged with the responsibility of policing borders in a postcolonial context, as I suggest. In Nabokov's story, "Europe and America aren't only geographical ... they're historical" (Rothstein 2000, 27). As in the story of Lolita – where the reader is introduced to an anachronistic landscape in which the boundaries between Euro-American and indigenous "others" (including Mexicans and other displaced peoples) threaten to collapse – the Letourneau story is about geography and social and cultural dispersion. In his telltale story of the Letourneau sex scandal, Olsen (1999, 66) describes the teacher's home as a "suburban city [with a] bland mix of old and new Ticky-tacky apartments along I-5 and view homes overlooking the Kent Valley and Mount Rainier ... It was by far middle and working class." Given Letourneau's class background (higher pedigree), she was out of place, and by marrying Steve, she had disappointed her parents: "Her family had expected better things of her. A better husband. Someone more in line with their socioeconomic status" (71).

Because the American suburb has been associated with normative heterosexuality and because it is also racially coded as white and middle-class, the geography of Letourneau's family home, notably her place of birth in a more pristine California neighbourhood, is of crucial significance to the sex scandal story. Much like the protagonist in *The Graduate,* Ben, who is seduced by a sexually savvy adult female neighbour, the infamous Mrs. Robinson, Letourneau is caught in a restrictive, heteronormative suburb: "Ben's search, at the dawn of his 'manhood,' for an identity apart from what he sees as the constricting, spirit-crushing world of his parents' generation, an unreflective, blandly material existence [is] best symbolized by their ersatz suburban landscape" (Beuka 2000, 14). Mrs. Robinson is the quintessential seductress of young boys in popular Hollywood culture: her character was associated with unusual powers of sexual conquest, and like Letourneau, she was less than satisfied in the heteronormative, middle-class, white, nuclear-family unit.

Frederick Whiting, in his discussion of the monstrosity of the pedophile in *Lolita,* notes that by making the pedophile a mutant, a freak of nature, the integrity of the American home, the suburb, and the nuclear family is secured as part of a natural (and national) landscape. The birth of the monster signals a departure from home, and he (in Letourneau's case, she) enters into an un-American, racially, and working-class–coded space, often thought to be vile and loathsome. Although the all-American teacher was seen to have fallen from her pristine, California, sunshine-girl roots, Fualaau's family was seen to reside in the place where people hit rock bottom. Fualaau lived in the white Center, a place known for rat infestation and described by Olsen (1999, 93) as a "world of jacked-up cars, liquor bottles, and water-stained curtains ... Seattle's version of the hood. Rap and hip-hop pulse in headsets and from boom boxes." The white Center, according to Olsen, is composed of "Cambodians, Russians, Samoans, and African-Americans [who] run the restaurants, go to the storefront churches, and their children stake-out the Taco Time and Dairy Queen on Ambaum Boulevard ... drug use is so common deals are done in the light of day" (93-94). As one public relations officer is alleged to have said about the white Center: "This is the land that time forgot" (94). The Center is said to be a kind of anachronistic space untouched by waves of progress associated with upward mobility, gentrification, economic growth, and urban development. "Locked in time, [racialized peoples] are pre-individuals and mal-developed groups, undeveloped and undevelopable" (Eng 2001, 7). The people who live at the Center never seem to leave or to be changed by the prosperity and development of the city itself. Much like the image of "primitive man" in the narratives of European colonial explorers and in contemporary stories about atavistic time and thwarted attempts to civilize white America's racial "others," the multicultural community of the white Center is depicted as stagnant.

But it is not only Letourneau's displacement from her socioeconomic background that signals anxieties about geographical displacement. Her position at Shorewood Elementary School as a white woman of an affluent background also sets the scene for illicit border crossings. The school is located in a neighbourhood that

> hasn't changed all that much since the 1950s when the school was a bastion of middle-class homogeneity. The homes are tidy and the yards clean. No autos growing moss on blocks in the front yards. Shorewood remains far enough from the white Center [Fualaau's home neighbourhood] and Burien to feel safe at night, though not as many would walk its streets as they did in the past. Today, the school draws students from a larger area, going far to the east to pick up children who live in low-income housing ... Almost a third of the children enrolled at Shorewood are eligible for the free-lunch program. (Olsen 1999, 78-79)

Olsen also tells us that more than forty languages and dialects are spoken in the school district: "At Shorewood, twenty percent of the students are

Asian and Pacific Islander; six percent black; four percent Hispanic; and the other two thirds, white" (79). Despite the multicultural composition of the school, the teachers are uniformly white. The teachers at Shorewood were employed to educate and to lead the culturally hybrid student body to salvation. Employed with the task of cultural assimilation through education, enculturation, and pedagogies of love, the teachers were charged with the responsibility of polishing the otherwise rough boundaries between new and old Americans and between the working poor, the unemployed, and the middle classes. As white onlookers familiar with and sympathetic to Letourneau insisted: "She's helped that boy. She's given him the best of life. That boy would be one of the teenagers who commits suicide" (316). As a white female teacher in the late twentieth century, Letourneau was charged with the task of salvation – much like a Christian missionary who does God's work abroad.

Both in the media and in court, Fualaau's family was depicted as unfortunate and in need of help, and even Olsen (1999, 113), who sees himself as offering a relatively balanced portrayal of the Letourneau scandal, gives a less-than-flattering racialized portrait of the Fualaau family: "At thirty-eight, Soona Fualaau had plenty of problems. With an ex-husband in prison, and bills and eviction notices in the mail, the heavyset woman with long black hair streaked in gray lived stoically in a burdensome world. She'd worked dead-end jobs at everything from taking orders at Taco Bell to cashiering at the Roxbury Texaco." The imprisoned father had assaulted Soona. And Fualaau, having witnessed the abuse, was deeply affected by the violent attacks. The father also allegedly had eighteen children with five women. But "when the Fualaau house caught fire it was Shorewood teachers and students who collected clothing to get the family of five going again. Soona was poor, but her sons and daughter could transcend all of that because they were stellar in different ways. The teachers at Shorewood [Letourneau in particular] saw their potential very clearly" (113). The boy was, in Letourneau's eyes, from a "troubled home, being raised by a single mother in poverty with a father in prison" (126). She believed that she could save him, encourage his talent in art, and lead him to a better life. The quest to save Fualaau, however, took an unexpected sexual turn, and the boundaries demarcating teacher (white female missionary) and student (cultural "other" in need of help) crumbled into a mosaic of un-American tensions and transgressions.

The Fall of Mary Kay Letourneau: Race, Desire, and Transgression

The media-reading North American public (not to mention the courts) struggles over how to understand the lascivious, all-American, *female* teacher, but this can account only for a proportion of the apprehension and foreboding surrounding the case. As I suggest in the above section, the panic about the Letourneau sex crime is ignited by the gender and whiteness of the beautiful blond teacher and by her seeming departure from her traditional role as wife and mother. Postcolonial scholars have argued that the family is an important site of racial formation (Dyer 1997; Hartigan 1999; McClintock 1995; Stoler 1997, 2000): "The 'meaning' of race depends to a large degree on whether particular families reproduce homogeneous or heterogeneous racial categories" (Hartigan 1999, 184). The institution of the family is not only the site on which racial formation is enacted, but also the sphere in which gender and sexuality are constituted in order to ensure the reproduction – or fantasy – of the all-American (i.e., white) nation and its citizenry. Letourneau reneged on her responsibility to the motherland and in so doing unleashed a pandemic anxiety about the state of the reproductive family, the nation, and permutations of gender, desire, power, and pleasure central to postcolonial American society.

White, middle-class, heterosexual women have been responsible for maintaining the sanctity and the tradition of the family from colonial times to the present. In her discussion of empire, race, and sexual morality in twentieth-century colonial cultures, Ann Stoler (1997, 355) contends that European colonial women have acted as "custodians of family welfare and respectability and as dedicated and willing subordinates to, and supporters of, colonial men." With their allegiance to the colonial enterprise, white women in previously colonized countries worked to ensure that the colonial family was "racially" pure and unmarked by racial degeneracy. As agents of colonial morality, nation, and empire, white European women were in charge of policing interracial encounters and were, in many instances, seen to be the arbitrators of sexual and racial transgression. "European women were essential to the colonial enterprise and the solidification of racial boundaries in ways that repeatedly tied their supportive and subordinate posture to community cohesion and colonial peace" in the name of the colonial family (355). This imagined, racialized cohesion was dependent on a fantasy of racial demarcation. White families – and their offspring – had to be clearly distinguished from colonized "others." Postcolonial angst about racial hybridity, undomesticated desire, and the health of the nation is triangulated in a primal worry about the state of the all-American family.

If it is true that sexual prohibition is and has been essential to maintaining colonial orders, then we may assume that sexual transgressions, of various kinds, upset the coherence of the imagined, racially pure, white family, relations between formerly colonized peoples and colonizers in the present-day context, and the binary gender templates used to sustain the heterosexual and patriarchal order of things. In twentieth-century colonial cultures, "changes in sexual access and domestic arrangements have invariably accompanied major efforts to reassert the internal coherence of European communities and to redefine the boundaries of privilege between colonizer and the colonized" (Stoler 1997, 366). I argue that the same can be said for sexual transgressions in the present-day postcolonial North American context. Contravening sexual moral codes is political because the felon is seen to upset the postcolonial, heterosexual, white familial order; "Race and gender are ineluctably intertwined, through the primacy of heterosexuality in reproducing the former and defining the latter" (Dyer 1997, 30). To forge a sexual liaison out of wedlock is threatening to the North American Christian right. But to cross generational and racial boundaries in such a liaison when one is appointed to act as a keeper of those boundaries – as white female teachers (often coded as missionaries) and mothers are routinely expected to do – is to commit a transgression of a higher moral order.

The Letourneau transgression is upsetting partly because she gave birth to Samoan American babies, thereby confusing the racialized boundaries set in place to ensure a fantasy of cultural demarcation. While neighbours believed that the Letourneaus and their white children were "nothing short of a beautiful family, all golden" (Olsen 1999, 86), the daughters born of the clandestine affair raised anxieties about racialization, beauty, and culture. The two Samoan American baby girls to whom Letourneau gave birth are at once sites of anxiety and objects of cultural struggle because racial demarcation between white Euro-American peoples and Samoan Americans threatens to collapse and because the golden family is "tarnished" by Samoan blackness. But the hybrid racial demarcations associated with Letourneau's interracial and carnal sin must be read within a long history of European colonial worries about the whiteness and sexuality of bourgeoisie children.

In *Race and the Education of Desire* (2000), Ann Stoler argues that "knowledge and control of servants within middle-class homes [many of whom were non-white], and the seductions attributed to them, were part and parcel of the normalizing regime of that discourse [of child sexual abuse]" (138). The child's sexuality was, paradoxically, seen as both innocent (endangered) and dangerous (in need of containment). Children were to be "protected against exposure to the dangerous sexuality of the racial and class Other, not because their sexuality is so different, but because it is 'savage,' unrestrained, and very much the same" as that of the racialized (adult) "other" (141). The sexuality of the child (its containment and its education) is, as Stoler contends, intimately connected with ideas about white racial purity and with American colonial fantasies about the survival of the master race. To keep white children safe (and to curb their polyamorous and otherwise un-American sexual desires), colonial and working-class "others" (those outside the middle-class or bourgeois, white family) were subject to surveillance when touching, caring for, and interacting with children.

The imagined boundaries, set in place to demarcate racialized positions, like those demarcating white and Samoan American, are threatened by sexual and maternal boundary crossings. As Stoler (2000, 145) illustrates in her discussion of domestic servants in early-modern Europe: "European discourses on the dangers of wet nurses and nursemaids for the identity formation of noble and middle-class children have a long genealogy, suggesting that nursemaids were seen to enjoy a special power over their charges. A baby was thought to absorb the 'personality traits' of his nurse when he drank her 'whitened blood.'" A similar anxiety about racialized boundary crossings can be seen in the present-day postcolonial context. The boundary crossing in the teacher sex scandal is orchestrated not only at the level of an interracial birth, but also through Letourneau's upset about Soona, Fualaau's mother, and her maternal presence (wet nurse stand-in). Because of her prison sentence, Letourneau was forced to relinquish custody of her newborn baby girls to Fualaau's mother, who cared for the infants. Consequently, two culturally distinct, maternal relations to the newborn babies came to be a focus of interest to a mass American audience. For example, readers of Olsen's (1999, 243) telltale story about the Letourneau transgression learned that the blond teacher rolled her eyes at the "little red Samoan dress that Soona had given [the first-born baby girl]." She didn't like the dress but agreed to have her first baby wear it in a photo to please Soona. Letourneau was also, reportedly, disgusted by the grease that Soona put on Audrey's hair. The friends of the family listening to Letourneau's complaints "gathered that it was some kind of Samoan style. Soona had used some kind of oil to slick up the hair before twisting it into shape ... Soona was dressing and grooming that baby the way she would any of her children. When Mary Kay got out of jail and could raise the baby [herself], the grease, the stretch pants, the hideous red dress, would be history" (272). As we can see in the above examples, there is a kind of turf war between the white and Samoan American mothers. The racialized bodies of the baby girls, their cultural affiliation, and their kinship relations are at stake in the narrative, but it is also the recognition of the "legitimate" mother that is at stake.

The Letourneau transgression also created a space to ponder white female desire in the pedagogical (and maternal) encounter and the desire of boy-students for white female teachers in the same pedagogical encounter. The white female teacher has been, in North American popular culture, positioned as an asexual paragon of virtue, as a maternal force of nurturing love who is devoid of desire. Her wants are channelled into an almost obsessive care and protection of students, coded as children, in the name of the American nation. This positioning is not without its impossibilities: How can the white female teacher love and not love children at the same time? How can she wish for their success and, in a multicultural school, their cultural assimilation without having (post)colonial desires herself? If the teacher is to be something more than a conduit for a child's desire, developmental and educational progress, or enculturation into American ways of life, she must acknowledge a claim to something more than a desire to facilitate a benign pedagogical encounter.

But it is not that white female teachers do not have desire. It is that this desire has taken refuge in the child. In *The Ego and the Mechanisms of Defense,* Anna Freud defined altruistic surrender as involving a process in which women, usually mothers and teachers, project their wishes onto others (usually a child, a close friend, or relative) in order to abide by feminine social scripts (insisting on virtuous asexuality) and, as I would argue, to channel their instincts into a desire to service the nation. Satisfaction is gained by seeing others have what the altruistic personality (i.e., white lady-teacher) originally wanted for the self. Referring to a governess under analysis, Anna Freud (1966, 125-26) explains: "It looked as if her own life had been emptied of interests and wishes ... Instead of exerting herself to achieve any aims of her own, she expended all her energy in sympathizing with the experiences of people she cared for ... The patient did not dissociate herself from her proxies but identified herself with them. She showed her sympathy with their wishes and felt that there was an extraordinarily strong bond with these people and herself." Letourneau was – before her arrest – seen to be an unusually devoted and loving teacher who over-identified with her students. The problem was that she placed the needs of her multicultural student body above those of her immediate white family. Her family came second to the needs of the children in her class, and the teacher's social life became entwined with the students whom she taught. While teachers at Shorewood saw her commitment to, and entanglement in, student lives as unusual, they never suspected that she may have wanted something more than their well-being.

The underside of the defence mechanism – altruistic surrender – is that the altruistic personality is aggressive in her identification with the object of care; to refuse the love, as a child, student, or close friend or relative might, is to incite rage and resentment. Letourneau shocked the nation because she exposed the altruistic role of the white teacher as involving an instinctual composition, but she also set off alarm bells when she wrote Fualaau a letter from prison threatening him with castration if "he even looked at another girl" (Olsen 1999, 361). The letter was entitled "Test Time," and it was written because Letourneau was reportedly upset that her former student had been dating other women during her prison sentence. Fualaau told reporters that he wasn't threatened by her letter but excited and glad to know that she still cared. When questioned about the aggressivity of the letter, Letourneau insisted that the reference to castration was a joke, something the illicit lovers understood to be part of their flirtation.

Members of the white American public were shocked and outraged not because they perceived Fualaau to be under threat but because the female teacher (coded as passive, nurturing, altruistic, and devoid of desire) revealed a libidinous and aggressive predilection. The Letourneau transgression upsets the cultural mythology associated with the positioning of the white female teacher as ascetic and virtuous by revealing an otherwise disavowed wish that American fantasies involving teachers deny. Maternal pedagogy is no longer seen to be unencumbered by illicit desires and personal investments in the child. To forge a desire in the face of an ascetic mandate is the ultimate transgression in the Letourneau story, not withstanding the illicitness and unprofessionalism of the encounter with Fualaau. The Letourneau story reveals a wish, on the part of the white female teacher, to be something more than a pedagogical space (a maternal holding tank) for the student (coded as daughter or son), and this is not a desire easily reconciled with the colonizing educational missions of Western civilization. The Letourneau transgression is foreign and undomestic because it acts on a forbidden desire (aligned with non-European peoples and non-Western nations) and pairs white femininity with carnal excess.

Film theorist Richard Dyer (1997, 29) contends that there are "special anxieties surrounding the whiteness of white women vis-à-vis sexuality" in film and American culture more generally. Women bear children, but they are, as Dyer maintains, caught in a polemic. Women are divested of sexuality in Christian discourse (permeating American culture) in order to occupy a position of asexuality and cannot – without breaking the sacrament – give birth to children without engaging in carnal sin. "The model for white women is the Virgin Mary, a pure vessel for reproduction who is unsullied by the dark drives that reproduction entails" (29). The whiteness of white women is thus a racial paradox. Reproducing the race is "white women's duty but it is what white women are least able to do and still be white" (29).

The white female teacher – positioned as missionary, saviour of lost souls, virgin (let us not forget that until the mid-twentieth century in most North American school districts, female teachers were forbidden to marry), and ascetically pure in her love and commitment to children and the school as a whole – is perhaps most frequently caught within the sexual polemic that Dyer describes. (As I discuss in Chapter 3, the question of what the white female teacher wants is both controversial and enigmatic.) Because sexual desire has been projected onto the dark races (Dyer 1997; Gilman 1985), the white female teacher, the protagonist in the interracial teacher sex scandal, now has a dubious relationship to an idealized image of whiteness in the imaginary of middle-class (white) America.

By foregoing her positioning as asexual and selfless in the tradition of the "good" teacher, Letourneau enters a racialized space. For example,

Sonny Grosso, an executive producer of the made-for-television movie featuring the story of Mary Kay Letourneau, was quoted as saying that the maligned teacher was "articulate, intelligent. She had great looks. Her father ran for the presidency of the United States [after serving in Congress]. She could walk into a party and walk out with the quarterback every single time. She had great breeding. She had a very religious background" (Givens 2000). That Letourneau, a woman of good breeding, political stature, and class, had sex with a working-class Samoan American boy from a broken family (his father was imprisoned in Samoa, and his mother resided in the United States) is central to the media hype and related anxieties about lax moral codes.

The boy is coded as a racial "other," and the teacher's racial identification is rendered invisible (and normative, as whiteness in the United States and Canada typically is), but this invisibility does not preclude the colonizing practice of attributing dreams of racial purity to an unmarked category. As Angie Chabram-Dernersesian (1999, 114-15) contends: "Whiteness is partnered both with structures of domination and with the effects of domination. Such effects include different types of loss: of one's nation of origin, one's territory, one's barrio, one's social location, as well as a 'perceived threat' to one's national ethnic or regional identity and economic well being." The loss of which Chabram-Dernersesian speaks can also be understood to explain the media uproar about the clandestine affair. White heterosexual dreams about racial purity, heterosexual familial structures, and racial hierarchies in a culturally hybrid nation are thought to be lost, and the Letourneau story symbolizes the collapse of all that is American. For example, the storytellers never forgot to remind readers that the "Steven and Mary Kay Letourneau marriage was a gorgeous package with nothing inside. They seemed to want the world to see them for what they had a right to be – pretty, handsome, and with money to spare" (Olsen 1999, 101). In another passage, Olsen describes the now-famous, former teacher as being the "California girl with the stylish hair and the figure of a model. He [Steve Letourneau] was the square-jawed Dudley Do-Right; all blond and broad shouldered ... Their children were perfect, too" (102).

Letourneau's sexual and reproductive transgression crystallizes age-old American fears about white women in the colonies "going Native." It is also reminiscent of a fear of black men stealing white women. The association of sexuality, carnal excess, and lust with the dark races is worrisome to the white, heterosexual, masculine, postcolonial imaginary because it is the racialized "other" who is associated with sexual prowess and machismo. That a white man – Steve Letourneau, Mary Kay's legal husband and college sweetheart – could be upstaged by a Samoan American boy is both humiliating and shocking to the normative, white, heterosexual, male imaginary. In his telltale book *If Loving You Is Wrong: The Shocking True Story of*

Mary Kay Letourneau, Olsen (1999, 201) explains that Steve Letourneau was humiliated by his wife's seduction of an underage boy and that her subsequent pregnancy led him to violent outbursts: "Normandy Park police officers responded to a 911 call from Mary Kay on May 9. They found the pregnant woman with a red mark two inches wide and four inches long across her stretched stomach. She said her husband had hit her." On the same day, Steve Letourneau hit her with the family car. The police report stated that "Steve suddenly pulled away and she felt the vehicle bump her and knock her down ... She said she struggled to crawl toward the house and at some point [a neighbour] came and took her to the hospital" (201). Doctors found that Letourneau's pelvic bone had separated and that she had suffered additional bruising and scratches. According to Olsen, Steve said that "he wished he had killed her and the baby" (201).

When Audrey, the first baby born of the intergenerational affair, was seen to have black hair and olive skin, Steve Letourneau, who valued appearances (like his wife), continued to assault Mary Kay. Even Steve's mother was quoted as saying that an "ordinary man would have had her killed" (Olsen 1999, 292), thereby justifying her son's attacks on Letourneau. The beatings can be read not only as attempts to regain a sense of masculine entitlement and control over an unfaithful wife, but also as a response to a fear of the racial "other" usurping his status as white patriarchal father and husband to the beautiful blond mother (and lover) of children. Samoan blood had entered into his familial lineage. The attacks on Letourneau by her husband are driven in part by a fear of racial infiltration, boundary violation, and familial pollutants. If it is true that postcolonial powers – like the United States – maintain an image of the nation as pure, patriotic, and of course all-American by policing sexuality as an engagement that gives rise to multiple, interfamilial ties and entanglements, then it is understandable that the violent attacks on Letourneau by her husband are attempts to reinstate a semblance of white, patriarchal, heterosexual order. America, as a nation, is of course founded on policing sexuality to ensure that the patriarchal fantasy of succession and racial purity is maintained.

However, this is not to say that extramarital relationships have not been central to American cultural formation from colonial times to the present, only that they have been disavowed and driven underground. The cornerstone of the Letourneau sex scandal was that John Schmitz, Letourneau's father, had also had a clandestine affair, which had brought his political career to an end and upset the nation. Schmitz was a member of the ultraconservative John Birch Society, a state senator who became president of the American Independent Party in 1972, a staunch Christian, and a champion of conservative family values. Ironically, his "finest achievements were in curtailing sex education in the classroom and limiting the availability of condoms where young people might get their hands on them"

(Olsen 1999, 17). Schmitz was known to move his "children out of their Catholic schools if the curriculum was not strict enough to meet his own exacting standards or – heaven forbid – if they offered sex education" (Beveridge 1998). He was also known for his racism, his extreme homophobia, his antiunion stance, and his antiabortion advocacy, the latter of which was also supported by his wife, Mary Schmitz (Letourneau's mother). His racism and homophobia were almost unprecedented. As California State Senator, Schmitz issued a press release in 1981 entitled "Attack of the Bulldykes" (Olsen 1999, 36). Schmitz also made offensive remarks at the time about Jews, Hispanics, Chinese, and other racialized groups in the United States. His hate for minority groups was so extreme that he was eventually asked to leave the already conservative John Birch Society.

The nation was shocked to learn that the ultraconservative senator had been leading a double life. He had been having a long-term, extramarital affair with a woman named Carla Stuckle (ironically, a former student of the senator's at Santa Ana College), he had fathered two children out of wedlock – one boy and one girl – and he had refused to pay child support or hospital bills for his unacknowledged son, who needed life-saving surgery. Even though Stuckle was in dire financial straits, Schmitz would not offer assistance until the courts instructed him to pay $275 a month in child support. The financial disparity between the Schmitz and the Stuckle families was stark; one lived in a Tustin trailer park, while the other lived in the "splendor of Spyglass Hill" (Olsen 1999, 52). Even upon Stuckle's premature death, the former senator refused to look after his children born out of wedlock; they are now living in an orphanage (55).

Getting Out of Jail Free and the Paradox of Time in the Pedophilic Encounter

On 4 August 2004, Letourneau was released from prison after serving seven and a half years for statutory rape. Shortly after midnight, she left the prison gates and was "met by a crowd that included dozens of media outlets and a group of rowdy teenage boys waving signs that said 'I'm 18, Baby!'" (Ko 2004). As one sex-crimes prosecutor said, most people see boy-woman love as a "right [sic] of passage ... He [Fualaau] hit the jackpot: an older woman and a younger guy" (Napolitano 2004). Still, Letourneau is registered as a sex offender. The American public wondered with baited breath: "Will she resume the relationship [with Fualaau]?" (O'Reilly 2004). In 2004, Fualaau was twenty-one, well above the age of consent.

Shortly after Letourneau's release, Fualaau successfully petitioned the courts to remove the court order banning contact between him and his former teacher/lover/girlfriend. Ten minutes after the ban was removed, Fualaau reportedly cried because he was so happy. As one broadcaster with MSNBC said: "My take – this was the right call. He is an adult. She served her time. They have two children together. No one benefits from them being apart at this point." In the same interview, Anne Breminer, a friend of the former teacher, said that Letourneau still loves Fualaau and that, to her, this has been "Romeo and Juliet. She is the Joan of Arc of forbidden love and she absolutely does want to see him. To her it's eternal and seven years didn't make a difference" (Abrams and Williams 2004). Fualaau told interviewers with the *Today Show* that he was "looking forward to seeing if they [Letourneau and he] will be able to live together as a family" ("True Crime Book Watch" 2004).

Although public opinion supported the Seattle judge's decision to remove the court-ordered ban separating the two lovers, psychologists interviewed said that Fualaau is still "under some type of psychological brainwashing and what's happening is that he's just reliving the traumatic experience that he experienced when he was younger." Most mental-health professionals are allegedly upset by the removal of the ban. Die-hard child advocates insisted that Fualaau's wish to reunite with his lover/teacher was akin to a scar that children who have suffered childhood sexual abuse are forced to carry around with them (Abrams and Williams 2004).

One psychologist said on television that if Letourneau is "truly a pedophile, he is 21, she won't be attracted. Now if she's not and this was just an aberration, the relationship should move on" (Abrams and Williams 2004). The paradox of pedophilia is that it is time-sensitive. One is a pedophile not because she or he desires those below the legal age to consent but because she or he desires them as an adult. Most children desire other children; having a youthful desire above a certain age is what makes one a pedophile. Similarly, desiring a particular child – as a pedophile – is possible for only a brief moment in time; the child matures and is inevitably no longer a child. Moreover, as the above-mentioned psychologist suggests, the adult is no longer a pedophile if the desire for the coveted person (no longer a preteen in this case) is sustained. The age transgression, as opposed to an essential kind of desire, is what makes one a pedophile. Otherwise, children (who desire and are curious about other childlike bodies) would be pedophiles.

As Tweedie (2000) explains in his discussion of the pedophilic desire in *Lolita,* there is a perversion of time in the pedophilic fantasy. As the protagonist in Lolita acknowledged: "I knew I had fallen in love with Lolita forever; but I also knew she would not be forever Lolita" (quoted in Tweedie 2000, 160). Pedophilia also short-circuits and undermines normative adolescent maturation sequences; confuses gender, as I demonstrate above; and in some ways, is diasporic or otherwise displaced in its erotic trajectory. The normative pedophilic gaze of the white male adult in his desire for the white girl or boy traverses geography and, as argued above, has performed a national – if fantastical – colonizing function.

The Letourneau transgression, by contrast, disrupts the normative pedophilic narrative. The story of the white, pedophilic, all-American *female* teacher perverts heterosexual time and upsets adolescent growth and maturation sequences. The narrative undermines gender binaries, normative sexualities, and racialized demarcations in the United States. The Letourneau story rewrites the normative pedophilic fantasy on which the post-colonial United States is based. The gender-role reversal breaks apart and thus challenges any re-entrenchment of institutional boundaries organizing our various hierarchical relations to nation, state, family, gender, and heterosexuality. Stallybrass and White (1986) define transgression as the capacity to override "binary structures, [and to move] into an absolutely negative space *beyond the structure of signification itself*" (18, emphasis added), which is what the Letourneau transgression enables us to do.

In the chapters that follow, I consider Canadian-based school sex scandals involving white female teachers and underage students to better understand the problematic of female teachers' sexuality in the educational milieu. I focus on how the transgressive desires of white female teachers are upsetting to binary gender-identity formations, to reproductive heterosexualities, and to the white normative Oedipal family in a postcolonial context. In Chapter 3, I examine the sex scandal involving Canadian Annie Markson, an elementary school supply teacher, and allegations that she sexually abused an underage boy-student. Using this case, I examine the problematic of desire in professional education and endeavour to theorize the role of Eros in the pedagogical encounter.

3
Upsetting Desires in the Classroom: Annie Markson and the Queer Pedagogy of the Femme Fatale

> The next person to target your child for sexual attention, especially if your child is male, may not be the stereotypical disheveled man in an overcoat lurking at the playground. She might be young, attractive, married and possibly even your son's schoolteacher. (Ward 2000, 45)

> Like other professions, the teaching profession has its share of "bad apples." (Robins 2000, 18)

In the late 1990s and through to the twenty-first century, a rash of school sex-scandal cases hit the mainstream Canadian media in the wake of the Letourneau sex panic. These sex scandals involving white female teachers and students (several lesbian-teacher sex scandals are discussed in Chapter 6) received unprecedented media coverage and ignited widespread curiosity, debate, and anxiety in educational cultures. Most prominent in the Canadian context are the cases involving Jennifer Elizabeth Allan (2004), Sharon Lee Brown (2002), Heidi Franziska Coleman (2001), Amy Gehring (2002), Dale Gosselin-Taylor (1995), Leanne Carla Haselman (2000), Suzanne Marie Herbin-Baker (2001), Heather Ingram (2000), Joyce Jaster (2001), Elizabeth Ann Jeffrey (2002), Billie Jo Johnson (2001), Annie Markson (2001), Paola Queen (2007), Jean Robertson (1993), Laura Sclater (2000), and a number of other teachers whose names were withheld from the public due to court-ordered bans.[1]

The female teachers were accused of licentious behaviour, debauchery, and having predatory sexualities dangerous to male youth. Although it is difficult to determine how many teachers – male or female – involve themselves sexually with students or whether the numbers are on the increase in Canada, the media publicity and teacher-federation records available do suggest a rise in number or, at least, a heightened public awareness and suspicion (founded or not) of child sexual relations with adults. For example, an unnamed teacher of English as a second language in Vancouver was alleged to have had "kinky sex" with a thirteen-year-old male student. The two were said to have engaged in "bondage, urination and ... [used] a number of objects as sex toys" (Ivens 1998). Another British

Columbia teacher was accused of having sex with up to fifteen male students, most of whom were on her senior boys' volleyball team (Humphreys 2000b). A Toronto teacher's aide was said to have had sexual relations with up to five male students (Cantin 1998), and although all the boys were old enough to legally consent, child protectionists insisted that this involved an abuse of professional power. Laura Sclater of Barrie, Ontario, wrote more than sixty-four sex letters to an eighth-grade male student and reportedly called him a "big stud and a hottie" (Gray 2000) in one such letter. Billie Jo Johnson, a former Vancouver teacher, was said to be "highly controversial as she zipped around town in her sports car with her favourite student in tow, a good-looking boy ... They were spotted everywhere – in shops, in restaurants and on the ski hills" (Steffenhagen 2001), and she was consequently fired for her public indiscretions and outings with the teenaged male student.

As discussed in the previous chapter, sex scandals involving female teachers seem to have reached epic proportions in the Western world over the last decade. The very well-publicized case of Mary Kay Letourneau in the United States has its counterparts elsewhere. In the British context, Renate Williams admitted to getting drunk and swimming nude with several of her male students during a school outing. In Australia, Karen Ellis had a sexual relationship with a fifteen-year-old male student, and although it was said to have been socially consensual, parents, child advocates, and school administrators alike constructed the woman as a dangerous pedophile. As Helen Birch (1993, 1) comments in her sociological study of women, murder, and representation in the British press: "A casual observer might be forgiven for thinking that something very strange had happened to the female of the species. Suddenly, the newspapers were full of reports of women killing spouses, lovers and each other with a variety of weapons and in a number of different circumstances; feature articles, drawing together quite disparate cases, inquired whether the traditionally passive, gentler sex was indeed becoming more violent." I contend that the same can be said for female teachers in the Canadian context and in the Western world more generally. However, it is not that they are becoming more violent but that they seem to be more sexually potent and risqué.

Teacher federations, Ministries of Education, professors, policy analysts, professional bodies regulating teacher conduct, and other concerned parties in the Canadian context have been worried about what seems to be an increase in the number of teachers (male and female) forging erotic liaisons with students (Doctor 1999; Dolmage 1995; Matthews, Raymaker, and Speltz 1991; Robins 2000; Trocme and Schumaker 1999; McCrae, Voet, and Nye 1994). For example, the *Ottawa Citizen* published a story about teachers as sexual predators entitled "Sexual predators lurk in Ontario schools" (2000). The Ontario College of Teachers, the professional body responsible for disciplining teachers' professional misconduct in Ontario, now publishes the names of teachers found to have committed sexual crimes and professional improprieties involving students. In 2004, an amendment was made to section 18 of the regulation under the Ontario Teaching Profession Act, requiring teachers to report other teachers suspected of engaging in sexual improprieties without having to notify the accused teacher of the complaint filed.

In 2000, Sydney L. Robins wrote a report entitled *Protecting Our Students: A Review to Identify and Prevent Sexual Misconduct in Ontario Schools* for the Ontario Ministry of the Attorney General. The report offers tips to recognize and identify sexual abuse committed by teachers against vulnerable students. It also categorizes male teachers prone to abusive behaviour: the pedophile, the "romantic/bad judgment" abuses, and the "narcissistic" or "opportunist" offender motivated by power, control, and sex (Robins 2000, 123-24). Female-teacher abuser – to the shock and horror of the concerned reader – are said to "believe the sexual behaviour is an expression of love, do not recognize the negative impact on the youth, and have difficulty seeing the 'relationship' as wrong" (126). Even a cursory review of the child-protectionist literature and of associated studies of sexual-misconduct cases involving teachers reveals a new concern and intrigue with female teachers as sexual perpetrators. The trouble with these studies is that they fail to provide evidence of the harm presumed to befall teenaged boy-students caught up in a sexual flirtation or sexual relationship with female teachers, particularly when the flirtation and/or relationship is sought out and chosen by the teenage boys themselves. We might agree that such flirtations and relationships are less than ideal for educational development (and not professional), but this position should be framed as a pedagogical, and not a legal, issue. As well, these studies ignore the testimonies of the young men who, allegedly, had intergenerational sex with female teachers. Male-student testimonies are rendered illegitimate by the courts, ignored, or interpreted as evidence of abuse unless they are compatible with the harm-to-minors thesis. There is also no attempt to distinguish between what I called socially consensual above and coercion. The failure to distinguish between consent and coercion is what enables the public and the profession to read all female teacher sexual improprieties through the master narrative of child sexual abuse. In adopting an undifferentiated reading, the public and the profession fail to distinguish the cases to be examined in this book from more legitimate instances of abuse (based on coercion and a more blatant disregard for student welfare).

The Annie Markson Sex Scandal

In this chapter, I focus on the Annie Markson sex scandal. Markson is positioned as a dangerous femme fatale–like creature who is seen as threatening to the reproductive family. The media portrayals of the case incite a maternal horror that psychoanalytic film theorists have analyzed in their writings on film noir. For this reason, I use psychoanalytic and feminist film theory to better understand Markson's framing in the media coverage as a diabolic threat to Oedipal life narratives, to what Jagodzinski (2002) calls the normative family romance in education, to schoolboy masculinity, and to the divisions between adult and child that the incest taboo is meant to uphold. I also draw on postcolonial theory to understand the racialization of the teacher as femme fatale and her alignment with all that civilized educational cultures in Western, imperial contexts disavow. Using queer theory and psychoanalysis, particularly what is called the maternal erotic countertransference, I consider why the Markson transgression ignited moral outrage and alarm far surpassing its actual seriousness and threat to child welfare. Reading the Markson case through the lens of queer and psychoanalytic theory, I expose the underside of the sex panic enshrouding the teacher. The underbelly of the sex panic is, as I will argue, not about a monstrous teacher but about the queer desires, investments, and identifications that heteronormative and professional school cultures cannot tolerate.

Annie Markson, the supply teacher formerly employed at a Catholic elementary school in Unionville, Ontario, was gendered as a dangerous sexual subject in a way that is suggestive of popular anxiety and discomfort with the sexualities of white female teachers in the school. The worry about illicit sexualities is also tied to unconscious anxieties about the borders demarcating normative gender binaries, age-appropriate heterosexuality, the nuclear-family unit with its investment in monogamy, and worry about racial hybridization. As Kelly Oliver and Benigno Trigo (2003, xiv) argue in their discussion of film noir, the audience experiences a "primal anxiety over borders and boundaries that manifests itself in specific fears and phobias of race, sex, maternity, and national origin." It is not a coincidence that Annie Markson was depicted as a femme fatale–like seductress with diabolic motives and sexual inclinations. The Markson transgression was reported through the use of literary techniques, tropes, metaphors, and other devices and images reminiscent of and akin to the production of the legendary femme fatale in Hollywood film noir. It is thus important to consider how the female protagonist in the sex scandal – Annie Markson – was gendered and racialized as a threat to the mythical white Canadian family in the news media.

In the following sections, I first outline the specifics of the Markson transgression. Second, I provide an overview of current psychoanalytic writing on clandestine desire in the analytic encounter to provide context for theorizing about the Markson transgression in the pedagogical encounter. Third, I show how an anxiety about the female psychoanalyst, in the analytic setting, can be compared to anxieties about the sex scandal under analysis in this chapter. Because worry about the desire of female psychoanalysts is pervasive in clinical discourse, I use it to better understand societal preoccupations with the sexual subjectivity of white female teachers in the school. Finally, I draw on queer, postcolonial, and feminist film theory to show how the sexuality of female teachers is associated with an ancient fear of and modern cultural fascination with the racialized Medusa figure (the omnipotent mother wielding her powers of seduction, and destruction, over young boys and men). I consider how the anguish about the maternal horror is primarily about the instability of non-normative genders and sexual identifications in the present-day Canadian context. The Markson story is also coded as an incestuous infraction that upsets contemporary discourse and policy (laws of the Father) on professional education. The white female teacher (coded as Mother) threatens to destroy (through her incestuously coded transgression) the foundations of binary gender, normative heterosexuality, and racial demarcation that the incest taboo enables.

To be clear, I am not endorsing sex between female teachers and boy-students but trying to understand the uproar about what – by all accounts (including those of the courts) – is a relatively benign infraction. There was no sex in the Markson case. I am asking how we may conceptualize and respond ethically to an erotic pedagogical moment that must be distinguished from a more overt and coercive instance of sexual assault and/or harassment that is not based on legal *or social* consent. Markson did not have sex with the student, and the illicit flirtation *was* based on social consent. The former teacher flirted with the boy, kissed his forehead, and wrote him love notes. She was, consequently, dubbed a sexual criminal and dangerous pedophile with a constitution befitting the legendary femme fatale. Focusing on what psychoanalysts call the maternal erotic countertransference – the desire that mothers have for their children or, in this case, the desire that female teachers have for their students – I consider what is at stake in imagining an amorous and consensual pedagogical liaison in professional education. The overarching question in this chapter is how to understand and grapple with Eros in the pedagogical encounter in ways that neither cause harm nor contribute to a master narrative of sexual danger in the school.

The desire of the white female teacher has always been problematic. Education folklore has implicitly acknowledged the heterosexual dimension of the pedagogical encounter – boy-student falls in love with older but virtuous, usually celibate, and unmarried white female teacher – but the love in this model is unilateral in direction, benign, and uneventful with respect to sexual border-crossings. The child brings the female teacher a shiny red apple; she lovingly receives it as a grateful and recipient mother figure should. That the maternally endowed white female teacher could return the desirous gaze is almost unfathomable in the dominant pedagogical narrative. Yet, in the late twentieth century and into the twenty-first century, we observe an excessive preoccupation with a series of sexual-misconduct cases involving illicit flirtations and/or clandestine affairs between white female teachers and boy-students in the mainstream media. While male teachers are complaining that they can no longer touch children for fear of inciting suspicion, female teachers seem to be all too ready to enlist underage boy-students in sexual exploration.

It is not surprising that in an era of "political correctness," female teachers, like male teachers, have been designated sexual predators. On the one hand, the traditional construction of the white female teacher as an ascetically pure and sexually repressed sacrificial martyr is being overturned. At the same time, it is important to understand that the media coverage continues to be gendered in ways that conform to traditions of heterosexist gender stereotyping. The media reports of the lascivious female teacher are sexualized in ways that parallel reports of male teachers are not. Because the white woman-teacher, as discussed in the previous chapter, is not supposed to have an active sexuality, the teacher (however white she may be) is racially coded as non-white because it is people of colour who are, most often, associated with sexual excess, carnal sin, and all that is sinister and threatening to civilized (i.e., white) society. The white unconscious is filled with illicit impulses projected onto its racialized "others." When the white female teacher is seen to embody carnal desires, the defence mechanisms used by the white (moral) majority to distance itself from antisocial desires are undone. The process through which Annie Markson is sexualized and subject to racialized signification is of great import to sociological studies of gender and queer theory, to what Judith Butler (1990b) calls the heterosexual matrix, and to what Lee Edelman (2004) calls reproductive futurity.

Annie Markson as Lascivious or Queer Pedagogue?

> When we deliver our children to our teachers, male or female, we expect not only that they will teach them but that they will ... not be their romantic admirers. (Macdonald 2001a)

In February 1999, Annie Markson found herself confronting allegations of sexual misconduct for having written to and receiving romantic letters and e-mail correspondence from a fourteen-year-old male student in eighth grade. Although this real-life flirtation was not unlike the unconsummated crush between motherly teacher and adolescent boy-student long depicted in love stories and adored by audiences invested in the ethos and culture of budding heterosexuality, it was deemed unprofessional by the Ontario

College of Teachers, the provincial body responsible for imposing codes of professional conduct and disciplining teachers, and illicit by reporters covering the case in a contemporary context.

Markson's relationship with the student at the Catholic school, in which she occasionally worked as a supply teacher, was said to be a "boundary violation" in the Canadian newspapers. As Robins (2000, 123) explains in his study of sexual misconduct in Ontario schools, a boundary violation is typically committed by young female teachers who use bad judgment, have "poor interpersonal boundaries, poor understanding of adolescent development and sexuality, or social or emotional immaturity." The "boundary violator" is to be distinguished from the pedophile, who, more overtly, preys on young children. Despite this rather sensible distinction, and even though Markson's advances were gentle and relatively cordial, she was branded a pedophile in the media. Forgetting that she did not teach the boy (who was not enrolled in her classes), the mainstream press used the ambiance of the elementary school to set the seduction scene. However cordial and salubrious the school scene might have been in real life, the press used it to add intrigue to the few out-of-school meetings and babysitting encounters of import to the case. Markson's legitimate contact with the student was through her role as his babysitter and through occasional interactions in the school when she was there on temporary assignment.

These formal associations and secretive meetings were designated problematic because they exceeded Markson's legitimate role as both teacher and babysitter. In a letter, excerpts of which were published in the *Kitchener-Waterloo Record,* Markson confessed her adoration for the young boy: "You are sexy. You are hot. You have sexy biceps" ("Mom tells" 2001). The student also wrote a number of letters to Markson professing his love. In one, he wrote that there were "three spots [that] are able to be touched by your loving hands. I'll probably have a slight erection ... I think I want to touch your breasts, butt, and ... um ... I don't know" (Macdonald 2001a). On occasion, he telephoned Markson and the two would rendezvous in secret. Although the romantic liaison was platonic, the enamoured teacher said in a letter, "I don't want you to get any other or more experience except through me," and "Just the thought of you kissing/talking/breathing with another female except me drives me crazy" (Small 2001). In another correspondence, she wrote: "I love you ... I miss you ... I need you ... Good night sweetie ... I'll be thinking and dreaming of you as always" (Macdonald 2001a).

According to the media reports, the teenager admitted to having had a crush on Markson but explained that the liaison did not include sexual touching; he only fantasized about it. He also admitted to encouraging Markson's sexual attention. With the exception of the occasional hug and kiss on the cheek initiated by the alleged victim, the romantic liaison was a textual and imaginary affair, in all respects unconsummated.

I do not suggest that there are not ethical questions to be asked about the clandestine flirtation or that we do not need to grapple seriously with the problem of sexual abuse in Canadian schools. However, the presumption that the media coverage of the Markson case is driven by a concern about child sexual abuse, coercion, and/or harassment is unfounded. By all accounts, the boy-student enjoyed and initiated the erotic encounters with Markson. Like Fualaau in the Letourneau case, the boy in the Markson case refused to be positioned as a victim. He had sexual agency in the romantic liaison. The flirtation games were not only consensual, but also to his liking. It is also important to note that Markson was not found guilty of sexual misconduct with a minor in the court of law, although she was found guilty of professional misconduct by the Ontario College of Teachers. Consequently, her act was designated unprofessional as opposed to criminal. But the case lends support to public and professional worries about the rising numbers of female-teacher sexual predators.

It is curious that the mainstream press does not cover the sexual transgressions of male teachers with the same moralistic zealousness that it covers cases involving white female teachers. The cases involving male teachers (many of whom *have* had criminal charges laid against them) are consistently underreported when compared to the highly graphic, detailed, and sensational coverage given to the sexual misdemeanours of white female teachers. The latter are eroticized as they are condemned, whereas the cases involving male teachers receive minimalist and factual coverage at best.[2]

It is therefore reasonable to speculate that there is something more at stake in the stories of sex scandals involving white female teachers than a belief that the child is at risk. If the concern were with child welfare, we would see detailed coverage of the sexual misdemeanours of both male and female teachers. We do not. In this chapter, I argue that the manifest accusation of abuse in the Markson case – and the compulsion to talk about it endlessly in the numerous reports published in the newspapers – masks a latent preoccupation with the desire and sexual subjectivity of the single white female teacher in the pedagogical encounter and with the status of hegemonic white boy-student masculinity in the heterosexual mainstream. Normative masculinity appears to be at stake because people worry that boys will be feminized through romantic liaisons with older female teachers in positions of power, care, trust, and responsibility.

The professional uproar surrounding the Annie Markson case, like the Letourneau case, masks a more systemic anxiety about the masculinity of white boy-students (i.e., Oedipal sons) in a generation of students seemingly unaffected by normative gender hierarchies once central to the heterosexual culture and ethos of the Canadian school. The rigid focus on the lurid details of the Markson case directs attention away from the larger intrapersonal anxieties that construct her as a contemporary femme-fatale figure. I argue that preoccupation with the case should be read as social commentary on the development of white hegemonic masculinity in a heteronormative cultural context. The state-appointed teacher who refuses to domesticate her sexuality to a professionally sanctioned ascetic dream of virtuous (i.e., white) motherly love incites anxiety in persons invested in normative white-boy masculinity, age-appropriate heterosexuality, and a patriarchal wish for succession in white nuclear-family structures. The media-generated panic about Annie Markson is not unlike homophobic anxieties about homoerotic encounters in the school (as I argue in Chapter 6), which suggests that the lascivious white female teacher enamoured with a young boy is threatening to configurations of age-appropriate heterosexuality. Heterosexual bifurcations of gender are often organized around comparatively narrow templates prescribing who it is – masculine or feminine subject – that can desire and be desired. In fact, sexual difference is very much about how one can love, be loved, and grapple with obstacles to love in the heterosexual Symbolic order. Female sexual potency tinged with an intergenerational advantage that enables the teacher-as-mother to adopt a position of power over the male student (coded as son) triggers Oedipal anxieties and incestuous fantasies involving the mother. Psychoanalytic theory maintains that boys and men often fear desire by and identification with the maternal subject. At the same time, the story of Oedipus is a cultural fixation and fantasy. There is something tempting and uncanny about the Oedipal transgression. I argue that the Markson case can be read as a contemporary Oedipal myth embodying a moral cautionary tale for those invested in a categorical gender binary, in normative heterosexuality, and in the prototypical white nuclear-family unit.

Eros in the Pedagogical Encounter

Since the publication of Plato's *Symposium,* an exposé on the nature of love in Western philosophical thought, we have asked questions about the place of Eros in education (Alston 1991; Burch 1999, 2000; McWilliam 1999; Muir 2000; Todd 1997). In his introduction to the Penguin edition of Plato's commentary on love, Christopher Gill (1999, xxxvii) writes that erotic-educational love is imagined to be necessary for the cultivation of ethics: "the lover [as teacher] develops the ethical character of the boyfriend [beloved student] in return for sexual gratification." Eros is understood to be the driving force behind the quest for knowledge. Kal Alston (1991, 385) writes, "To dissociate knowledge and its pursuit from love seems almost natural in the context of current talk about the 'science' of education, but that naturalness is sheer illusion." Echoing the Platonic dictum, Alston concludes that love and knowledge are dialectically related; one can't exist without the other. Desire incites the will to know. Using Socrates as a case in point, Alston argues that "Eros is an occasion for growth" (389). In a similar vein, D.P.E. Muir (2000, 246) suggests that the metaphor of teacher as lover enables us to understand the attraction that teachers feel toward their students. But this attraction is not purely physical. It is based on a teacher's desire to "aid in the transformation of the student's soul through increased knowledge of the good."

Although we continue to question the relationship between Eros and education in academic circles, the idea of the desirous female teacher remains contentious in contemporary discourse about professional education. Writes Alston (1991, 386), "In a litigious society in which teachers have found themselves subject to suspicion as well as prosecution on the basis of their relation to desire, encouraging Eros may be seen as irresponsible." Such was the case in the notorious sexual-harassment scandal involving Jane Gallop, a distinguished professor of English and comparative literature at the University of Wisconsin. Two female graduate students accused Gallop of sexual harassment. Although the complaints couldn't be substantiated, Gallop *was* found guilty of participating in a "consensual amorous relationship" with one of her students and of sexualizing the classroom (Gallop 1997). Not coincidentally, this case, like the Markson case, received an incredible amount of sensationalist media coverage that focused not on an alleged abuse of pedagogical power but on the erotic relationship between teacher and student, even though both were found not to have engaged in coercion or exploitation of any kind. The media focus, however, is understandable when we consider that it is not the predatory and rapacious nature of the dynamic that is of public concern but the idea that the white female teacher (or professor) can act as a sexual agent and upset normative heterosexual courting rituals.

Grappling with Desire: The Teacher as Analyst

Although the attraction that a female teacher feels toward her students has only recently been addressed in educational and queer theory (Gallop 1992, 1995, 1997), critical psychoanalytic thought has a longer history of grappling with the desire of the analyst in the therapeutic setting (Benjamin 1995; Bollas 2000; Gabbard 1996; Orbach 2000). I use the example of the clinical setting to better understand the pedagogical setting because there are important parallels between the two. Psychoanalytic theory is also helpful because it enables us to understand the development of normative masculinity and the anxieties that it engenders as they pertain to the clandestine affair between teacher and student.

In his introduction to *Love and Hate in the Analytic Setting,* Glen Gabbard (1996, ix) claims that "the analyst is no longer viewed as a dispassionate interpreter of the patient's intra-psychic conflict. We now realize that analysts [like teachers] are likely to experience feelings such as love similar to those that stir the patient [or student] and often with the same degree of passion." Not only does the client project feelings of love and desire onto the analyst, but the analyst herself is also capable of desiring the client. I argue that the same dynamic is at play in the pedagogical encounter. Using the term "erotic counter-transference" to refer to analyst desire, Gabbard suggests that the countertransferential relationship is centred on the moment in which the "patient [or student] becomes the projected idealized object- or self-representation that will rescue the analyst [or teacher] from despair" (34). That the teacher and student have a transferential relation (like the analyst and analysand) has only recently been acknowledged in educational writing (Alston 1998; Baumlin 2000; Bell and Iverson 1998; Britzman and Pitt 1996; Higgins 1998; Jagodzinski 2002; Robertson 2000). Public and professional refusals to acknowledge the teacher as capable of acting in the transference, however, has yet to be fully understood.

According to Gabbard (1996, 82), "the perspective that the countertransference represents a joint creation that involves contributions from both analyst and analysand is now endorsed by classical analysts, modern Kleinians, relational theorists, and social constructivists." In other words, the erotic connection between analyst and analysand is now recognized as a collaborative effort that involves both parties' personal histories, desires, and feelings of love and hate. Freud first claimed that love in the transference was a prerequisite for cure. He was, however, less comfortable with the desire of the analyst in the psychoanalytic encounter. Today, psychoanalysts tend to agree that it is incumbent upon the analyst to analyze her own erotic projections under supervision (by senior training analysts), just as it is necessary to analyze the client's desire in the therapeutic setting.

A problem emerges when the analyst's desires are left unanalyzed. Her refusal to recognize her desire poses an ever-present danger that she will act in the countertransference and fail to recognize the client outside the confines of his or her own yearnings and projections. A violation occurs in this instance; the analyst, caught up in her own projections, cannot see the autonomous will of the analysand. In more extreme cases, the analyst crosses sexual boundaries and violates the prohibitions on intimate physical contact that are imposed to enable analytic work (or education) to take place. Sexual violation, however, is not a necessary product of a countertransference left unanalyzed, although it is obviously understood to be a violation of the analytic relationship. A teacher may misdirect her desire onto the student and spend too much time "helping" him or her, trying to "reach" him or her, or otherwise trying to discipline or incite ambition in him or her beyond what is needed or sought out by the student.

The countertransferential relation accounts for over-involvement in student life and well-being *as well as* for sexual misdemeanours. It is something that all good and bad teachers must grapple with because they are positioned within a constellation of what Jan Jagodzinski (2002) calls the family romance in education. Without Eros, there would be no incitement to learn or to teach. By virtue of their positioning *in loco parentis,* teachers cannot escape the transferential relations of teaching and learning. As Jagodzinski explains, Eros permeates the pedagogical encounter, and it cannot be otherwise. He regards pedagogical desire as a "symbol for the transference of knowledge between teacher and student" (xiv). Focusing on the transferential relationship (had by the student), as opposed to the countertransference (had by the teacher), Jagodzinski argues that the "proper response of the teacher [to student desire and erotic intrigue in and with the teacher] under the Lacanian suppositions is to insist there is *nothing* in him or herself that is worthy of love" (xxi). In other words, Jagodzinski states that it is the job of the teacher to channel Eros into a love of the subject, into a love of the pedagogical process: "The teacher must *refuse* love since the object that is perceived in him/herself is a pure nothing, an emptiness. It is to be found elsewhere. The student misperceives where his/her desire lies. Hence the teacher must try to retain this emptiness since the student's transference usually emerges *only when s/he does not want to encounter his or her own desire*" (xxi, original emphasis). While this position is professionally prudent and ethically sound, questions remain about the actual location and object of student desire. Certainly, and I think Jagodzinski would agree, the so-called "misperception" had by the student about his/her desire is not necessarily about a "will to learn" an officially sanctioned curriculum (although it might be the teacher's job to redirect student desire to officially sanctioned subject-matter). The desire had by the student might be about a wish for an alternative Symbolic, a wish for an anti-Oedipal or queer resolution to social prohibitions on love and binary gender identifications. The teacher's role in arbitrating this hidden curricular wish is not yet well conceptualized in educational theory or pedagogical studies. I suggest that we must not disregard student investments, and troubles, with heterosexuality, normative gender identifications, and futurism (with its commandment to "grow up") in our rush to apply professional prohibitions to transgressive pedagogies and transferential relations between teacher and student. By transgressive pedagogies, I am here referring to instructional practices that acknowledge or leave room for students to express (not act upon) professionally "illegitimate" desires, and claim allegiance to non-normative sexualities, genders, and anti-futuristic agendas.

The trouble with learning is that one is often ambivalent about what is to be learned and about the heteronormative foundations upon which learning is to take place. Students have difficulties learning math, English, history, physical education, etc., that are not always about the manifest subject-matter. The conditions and relations of learning structure and give rise to heterosexual bifurcations of gender and desire that are latent yet central to sanctioned curricular materials, and dominant pedagogies and teachings. Student resistance (or impulse) to learn may take the form of an erotic transference onto the teacher. But student transference should not be seen as an erroneous or injudicious response to the "official curriculum." I suggest that students (and teachers) caught up in an educational transference are grappling with a higher order of learning that has much to do with heteronormativity, gender, and futuristic mandates imposed on students by the public and the profession. There is nothing asexual about learning, maternal pedagogies of love, and officially prescribed curriculums in school cultures. Perhaps it is through sexuality that one is able to learn at all? As Jagodzinski (2002, xxi) points out, queer voices – gay, lesbian, and/or gender-variant teachers – "expose the suppressed eroticism that already circulates within [the pedagogical family romance in education]." Such teachers (like queer and transgender students) are dangerous not because they are prone to seduction (or to being seduced) but because they reveal and interrogate the otherwise unacknowledged heteronormative order structuring the dominant educational milieu. As well, queer and transgender students and teachers reveal new ways of being in the world that aren't beholden to heteronormative bifurcations of gender, its educational and futuristic mandates.

I therefore contend that the proper – or, rather, queer – response of the teacher to a student's transferential love must not only be repressive. Keeping one's hands to oneself and one's mind on the subject-matter of the curriculum or pedagogical task at hand, as Jagodzinski argues, is only part of an ethical response. The teacher must also seek to validate (if not incite) identifications, investments, and desires that the heterosexual and future-oriented curriculum does not yet have on offer. In other words, the teacher's task is to make a place for what conservative child advocates, champions of heterosexuality, and those uncomfortable with queer permutations of gender cannot tolerate: queer childhood proclivities. Children (and teenagers) are often queer, not necessarily homosexual but unbounded and fluid in their object choices and in the various relations that these choices engender. As such, they are perceived to be a threat to heterosexual futurity. The moral majority does much to deny this threat and to displace the worry about unbounded and queer childhood sexualities onto a nearby adult who may more easily be seen as culpable. The child or teen must not be seen as an agent or as having chosen queer or otherwise non-normative expressions of desire. The "child" (despite his or her actual age) must be seen as in need of protection within the master narrative of childhood sexual innocence. Christopher Bollas (2000) claims that there is an aggressive imperative behind the insistence on human innocence. To say that someone is innocent is to refuse to acknowledge his or her relationality. In other words, the thesis of childhood sexual innocence is based on a series of denials. The advocate of this thesis denies youthful desires for and relationships to adults, who are sometimes teachers. More important, however, the advocate obsessively insists that children and teenagers cannot see or understand themselves in relation to adult or non-normative desire. The refusal to acknowledge that those designated underage do and can comprehend adult and queer desires allows us to project whatever we want onto students without guilt or fear of reprisal; they will never know. The idea and insistence upon child and teen innocence is perhaps the most aggressive and insidious technique for indoctrinating heterosexuality in Western educational cultures. Little is known about how adults take possession of child and teen sexualities and translate them into normalizing heterosexual narratives. Paradoxically, as I explained in the introductory chapter, the child, adolescent, or teen is seen as a heterosexual in the making as he or she is also seen to be innocent (and hence vulnerable to the seduction of adults). Little room is left in this narrative to validate and give voice to the sexualities of young people in education.

The repressive mechanisms and negations through which youth are interpolated into discourses of innocence and heterosexuality are in need of examination, and it is through scandal that such processes are subject to scrutiny. Although I support the carnal rules of teacher professionalism and psychoanalytic training that guard against sexual misdemeanours, I am interested in what breaching such protocols reveals about the operation of heteronormativity and its injuries. How does heterosexuality with its insistence on childhood and teen sexual innocence injure or violently erase the queer and non-normative genders and sexualities of students? I offer up a queer reading of the Markson sexual infraction and call for a queer pedagogy based on a recognition, as opposed to a disavowal, of childhood queer and non-normative sexualities. Queer pedagogy must be about what the insistence on innocence negates: queer desires and gender identifications that are not intelligible to the heterosexual matrix, and queer developmental or educational templates that disrupt and unnerve heterosexuality and its futuristic agenda.

Annie Markson and her boy-student were caught up in an unanalyzed countertransferential relation parallel to that of the analyst and analysand. Thus the case offers a means to theorize about the disavowed erotic content of the pedagogical engagement. Markson was not the boy's teacher and did not cross legally sanctioned sexual boundaries, but these facts did not save her from public scorn in media representations of the case. I suggest that what is at stake is not an allegation of sexual abuse but a larger public fear of the white female teacher acting in the *maternal* erotic countertransference. The moral majority worries about what such an "acting out" does to heterosexuality and to its normalizing imperatives. The white female teacher has a long history of being coded as mother and as lover of children, and until now her activities have been employed in the service of white heterosexual reproductivity. The maternal transferential relationship between son/student/analysand and mother/teacher/analyst is characterized by the latter's response to a psychic dynamic that evokes a "baby's earliest sensual contacts and [is] manifested in concrete loving and hateful erotic wishes towards the real parts of the body of the therapist, as well as their symbolic counterparts" (Welles and Wrye 1991, 93). The *female* analyst, like the female teacher, is most likely to trigger such primal wishes and accompanying anxieties in the analysand/student. The female teacher is therefore subject to a particular kind of erotic gaze and disdain that signals, on the part of the student, an attempt to manage the anxiety resulting from the primal scene exemplified in the media portrayals of the case.[3]

According to Welles and Wrye (1991, 95), a "patient's maternal erotic transference elicits powerful and primitive wishes and defenses in the analyst, including manic, depressive, obsessional, schizoid and paranoid elements." Female psychotherapists have been subject to unusually perverse and psychotic portrayals in Hollywood film (Samuels 1985), suggesting a larger, societal fear of such grandiose countertransferential responses in the analytic setting. There are, of course, very real concerns about the analyst or teacher acting in the maternal erotic countertransference. She may refuse to notice the analysand/student's emotional and educational development, thereby infantilizing him or her and prohibiting growth that would threaten the pre-Oedipal bond.

The magnification of such a possibility is central to the sensational spectacle of the "devouring mother" portrayed in Hollywood horror films such as *Psycho* and pathologized in the newspaper coverage of the Markson case. The countertransferential relationship may also incite an "impulse to rebirth and remake the patient" (Welles and Wrye 1991, 96) or pupil. In the now-classic film *The Prime of Miss Jean Brodie* (1969), the teacher boasts: "Give me a girl at an impressionable age and she is mine for life." In this moral cautionary tale, the female students do not exist as autonomous agents in the pedagogical encounter. Rather, the female teacher attempts to manage the differentiating process by demanding that her female students create themselves in her own image or that they identify with images of her own projection – in short, that they reproduce the family romance and the heterosexualities on which it is founded.

An unchecked maternal erotic countertransference is an ever-present concern in the analyst-analysand relationship, but so, too, is the associated risk involved in the refusal to acknowledge or act in the erotically charged encounter (Benjamin 1995; Bollas 2000; Gabbard 1996; Kristeva 1995). The analyst must acknowledge the erotic dimension of the encounter and locate herself within it. In fear, analysts sometimes repudiate the erotic component of the analytic exchange, as do teachers in the pedagogic exchange, subsequently jeopardizing the creative use of the countertransferential relation (Welles and Wrye 1991, 96). When Eros is blocked, the analysand/student cannot act in the positive transference and flourish as a "good student"/responsive analysand should. As explained by Muir (2000, 246) – referencing an idea taken from Bloom (1993) – in the erotic educational ideal, "not only does the educator find pleasure in the potential of youthful souls, but the student is also deeply moved – perhaps shaken – by the encounter with one who introduces him to the means to pursue answers to important questions. There is an excitement for the student in meeting a person in whom there is 'the beautiful overflow from a generous nature that addresses the essential perplexities' of his existence." When the teacher disavows the erotic dimension of the pedagogical encounter, the educational outcome is less than ideal. In a therapeutic setting, "this is seen when the analyst colludes with or phobically avoids the patient's sexual impulses, particularly perverse wishes. Similarly, the analyst may unconsciously structure the situation in order to protect herself (or himself) from such unflattering or noxious projections as the incestuous arachnid or vampire mother" (Welles and Wrye 1991, 96-97). It is not uncommon for the female teacher to employ similar strategies in the educational context out of fear of being recognized as a desirous sexual subject. By disavowing the erotic content of a pedagogical encounter, the teacher is also refusing to acknowledge queer permutations of desire that are not intelligible to normalizing heterosexual cultures.

By refusing to validate the erotically charged relationship, the teacher or analyst, as mother figure, commits an act of aggression. The professional teacher committed to a renunciation of Eros refuses to acknowledge childhood or teenage desires and identifications that may involve her. This erasure is painful and injurious to the subject and to the student. The teacher or analyst committed to an asexual or heteronormative pedagogy leaves the student open and exposed to the reigning narrative of heterosexuality, which usurps all that remains unspoken or disavowed. Markson may be read as queer not only because she forged an alliance with a queer or deviant desire – she had a crush on a young boy coded as her son – but also because she did not insist on the boy's sexual innocence. She did, however, allow herself to be pulled into an erotic exchange that was un-professional and inconsistent with a queer pedagogy that forges *only* identifications with clandestine desires. Nor was it consistent with psychoanalytic protocols and the mandate to subject these desires to analysis. A countertransference that is well analyzed engenders creative potentialities that remain to be tapped. The same can be said of the pedagogical encounter: it can benefit from teachers' professional self-analysis. Markson's transgression does, however, offer up an opportunity to understand how heterosexuality is upset by the expression of taboo or otherwise queer desires. Intergenerational taboos that are acted on do not in and of themselves always cause harm to the child or teen allegedly in need of protection. The harm that child protectionists and lawyers were not able to find in the Markson case was not of a material but of a symbolic order. Heterosexuality felt itself to be harmed because a taboo on which it is founded was foisted into public consciousness through an amorous textual and nonnormative pedagogical exchange.

Psychoanalytic theories conceptualize the dangers of an unanalyzed countertransferential relation and also of a rejecting mother or father figure who is inattentive and ultimately withholding in her or his love of a child/student/analysand. In her manic insistence on asexual love, the white female teacher is in danger of disappointing the student and undermining his or her investment in the learning process. While this negation is consistent with professional protocols, it hurts. More important, it enables an unspoken adult-based heterosexual code of conduct to map itself onto the pedagogical scene. Although Markson acted in the maternal erotic countertransference (as opposed to keeping her desires in check, as professional protocol demands), she did not *grossly* violate the boundaries set in place to facilitate learning, so her actions were not criminal. But they were seen as unprofessional because the protocols of contemporary teacher professionalism, being founded on negation, repression, and abstinence, demand an absolute repudiation of the erotic. Despite her refusal to abide by what many of us would agree to be appropriate boundaries, she can, to some extent, be read as a "good mother" (in the pscychoanalytic sense) for not having aggressively disavowed her desire for the child, coded as son. She upset the family romance because she did not deny the intergenerational desires that underpin normative heterosexual orders. There was no negation for the good of the family or for the sake of heteronormative teaching and learning. Markson allowed the student to speak of his desire for her and attempted (however unsuccessfully) to act as an age-appropriate container for his sexual yearning. She did not deny her associated response and allowed the erotic exchange to continue within legally sanctioned boundaries. Even though Markson respected the legal boundaries governing her relationship to the boy, she could not escape social castigation and reproof – on par with that directed at actual sex offenders – because she committed a *symbolic* violation. The symbolic violation upset a heterosexual, and generationally specific, normative order. Consequently, she was the target of intense moral outrage, parental loathing, disgust, and professional reprimand.

Markson was, in effect, caught within an age-old; western-European gender polemic. She could not withhold sexual gratification without being a rejecting mother (asexual, sacrificial martyr, bitch), and she could not gratify the boy (coded as son) without inciting the horrific image of the devouring, engulfing Medusa figure, who threatens white masculine autonomy and individuation with her perverse and racially coded sexual potency. The culturally shaped incompatibility of the white female body – as symbol of heterosexual male desire and maternal bliss – and her authoritative positioning in the public sphere as rational subject further complicate the binary. In a heterosexist culture, the white female teacher begs the question of the commensurability between the anatomical sex of the white female teacher and her authoritative positioning over boy-students. The white female teacher cannot be straight and innocent *and* an autonomous professional. By queering her relation to the boy-student (consciously or unconsciously), Markson upset the binary and heterosexuality's investment in sexual difference. In Lacanian psychoanalytic theory, sexual difference is not so much about anatomy as about how men and women as desirous subjects form a relation to a dominant (I would say conventionally gendered and heteronormative) Symbolic order. "For Lacan, sexual difference is the Real of a fundamental antagonism. Masculine and feminine – *as logical positions* – are irretrievably separated and deadlocked, defined as different kinds of relations to the Symbolic order" (Jagodzinsky 2002, xxvi, original emphasis). The Symbolic order is the nucleus of the heterosexual matrix and the core of reproductive futurity.

As Jagodzinski (2002, xxv) writes, the "practice of pedagogy is also a question as to how much 'cross-dressing' and 'cross-sexing' is allowed when the fundamental antagonism between masculine and feminine is taken into account." In other words, what can education and professionalism tolerate? What is permissible with respect to gender and its messiness in the pedagogical domain? The sexually lascivious white female teaching subject is frightening not only because she upsets our stake in sexual difference, but also because she reveals object choice (sexual orientation) to be less important than a relation to desire or loss in the heterosexual Symbolic order. This relation is the organizing feature of gender in the Lacanian schemata. Markson's sexual transgression can be read as what Jagodzinsky calls a "non-phallic *jouissance*" (xxvii), a desire "*not* concerned with or disregarding the phallic order" (xxvii). Markson's desire for the boy seemed to be out of Symbolic order and incongruent with heteronormativity.

Like the caricature of the femme fatale, who is unapologetic about her diabolic and unfeminine desires, Markson is positioned as a schism in the dominant heteronormative and Symbolic order. As such, she risks "symbolic death" (Jagodzinsky 2002, xxvii) and enters into an ontology not of this world, or of what Lacan calls the Real (Campbell 2004). The female subject is thought to be feminine because she refuses an active claim to her sexuality. The femme fatale is not a "normal" woman in the Symbolic order because she has entered into what is taken to be a masculine domain. She is not intelligible to a heteronormative order. Teacher professionals and their advocates insist that they cannot understand the desire that led to the Markson infraction. The erasure of such a queer desire seems to be comprehensive in range and scope, but there is, at the level of the unconscious, a niggling suspicion that the transgression is not altogether "out of this heteronormative world." As film theorist Lisa Gornick (1986) explains of the psychoanalytic setting: "Given the cultural proscriptions against men's erotic relationships with women in either authority or maternal positions, a male patient who fell in love with his woman analyst would not be like *'any other mortal man'*; to the contrary, relationships in which women are in some way in the dominant position are pathologized and set apart from what any 'normal' man might encounter" (271, emphasis added). For a male student to openly proclaim sexual desire for a white female teacher – historically coded as a dignified model of maternal sobriety, ascetic purity, and asexuality – is to risk making himself vulnerable to an all-powerful mother figure. But more than this, he is at risk of falling outside heterosexual time. While a pre-Oedipal toddler may openly love and desire his mother, a fourteen-year-old boy who proclaims an erotic attachment to a female subject in a position of power evokes castration anxiety and the incest taboo. Heterosexual time is at stake because the heterosexual order counts chronological age based on calendar years. Psychic and queer times are associated with a developmental arrest. The circularity and boundlessness of our desires and relations to loss do not compute. Although we have queer desires and our psychic lives are not measured in time with heterosexuality's futuristic clocks, we have difficulty knowing what to do with non-normative desires and memories of loss because they are out of heterosexual place and time. Heterosexual orders depend on a repudiation of queer desires. Time anachronisms and atavistic desires are worrisome, and developmental life-courses must remain on track if reproductive futurity is to remain intact.

Heterosexuality does not want to be reminded of the forfeitures on which our adult lives as normative subjects are based. Psychoanalytic theorists from Robert Stoller (1975) to those of today who are invested in heterosexual time and its developmental sequences contend that young boys must repudiate their love and desire for their birth mothers to achieve a normative identification based on masculine subjectivity. Because boys and men are said to be deeply ambivalent about this socially imposed separation, they have an ever-present desire to return to the mother. However frightening the prospect of maternal engulfment, boys and men yearn for maternal connection according to this prototypical narrative. Psychoanalytic theorists committed to object relations also contend that boys unconsciously hate their mothers because they cannot possess them. Read in these terms, the Markson case evokes painful memories of maternal separation; it also exposes the disavowed content of a normative masculine, heterosexual subject in the making. The transgression exposes the defence mechanisms employed by young heterosexually identified boys and men to fulfill their longing for intimate connection with the mother. The public revelation of this longing is both risky and humiliating for the male subject. Having been made vulnerable, the men who champion heterosexuality can either express hatred, intolerance, and scorn for Markson and the illicit love or identify with the young boy and presume that he is in control of the erotic encounter. Male readers of the popular press often opt for the latter strategy and say of the boy involved in the Markson affair that he was a "lucky bastard."

The Story of Annie Markson: A Contemporary Oedipal Drama

> What is more interesting than the film's representation of femininity in its woman characters is the feminization of the male characters throughout the film. (Oliver and Trigo 2003, 30)

> At the margins of masculinity, film noir liberates alternative types of masculinity ... The association between femininity and danger or evil displays an anxiety not only about women's potency but also men's impotency. Insofar as femininity and masculinity are seen as opposites, not only is femininity a threat to masculinity, but ambiguity itself is a threat to the two poles that keep identity fixed. (Oliver and Trigo 2003, 34-35)

Although the "erotic transference can serve to alter in fantasy the structure of the analyst/analysand relationship – undoing the shame-evoking power of the woman therapist by restoring the man to a fantasized dominance in the sexual encounter" (Gornick 1986, 275) – it continues to be regarded as an unacceptable psychic risk to normative, white, masculine, heterosexual subjectivities. In a pedagogical relation, the boy-student who acts on his desire for the female teacher experiences the "erotic contact [as] undoing her authority and [this] restores ... [him] to the dominant position" (279). To him, the encounter fits into a narrative not of abuse but of empowerment in which he is able to imagine that he can love and conquer the omnipotent mother.[4]

Lisa Gornick (1986, 278-79) identifies the same phenomenon in her discussion of Hollywood films depicting female therapists and male clients: "As in all relationships that involve significant power disparities (parent-child, teacher-student, employer-employee, therapist-patient), it is men, by and large, who abuse the power differentials for sexual ends. In these films, however, the eroticization of the therapeutic relationship does not take on the meaning of abuse of power by the woman professional, who is allegedly in a dominant position. To the contrary, the erotic contact undoes her authority and restores the man to the dominant position." By investing the parent/teacher/employer/therapist with *hetero*sexual allure, the child/student/employee/patient, coded as male, is able to imagine himself in a dominant position and, in so doing, also able to undermine the authority of the female subject in a position of power. As relayed by a reporter speaking about the Heather Ingram sex scandal (discussed in Chapter 5), boys or "men will sort of nudge, nudge, wink, wink at it a little more, but it is sort of male bravado that males use to indicate to each other, to imply they have sexual prowess, a way of maintaining masculinity" (Humphreys 2000a).

Elaborating on the same strategy of sexualization, feminist film critic E. Ann Kaplan (2000b, 135) writes that the "domination of women by the [heterosexual] male gaze is part of men's strategy to contain the threat that the mother embodies, and to control the positive and negative impulses that memory traces of being mothered have left in the male unconscious." Here, Kaplan describes a pornographic technique central to white Oedipal fantasies in film and popular Western cultures. The heterosexualization and subsequent debasement of the desirous white female subject is a longstanding patriarchal strategy, strikingly evident in the media coverage of the Annie Markson case. The reader is first titillated by the lewd descriptions of the female teacher and then encouraged to partake in her condemnation.

Heather Bird (2001), a columnist for the *Toronto Sun,* described Markson as a "plump, blonde Annie ... [who had] voluptuous breasts and thighs." Explaining that "teenage boys ... spend large proportions of their high school years lusting after shapely teachers" such as Markson, Bird suggested sarcastically that "it must have taken [a] Herculean effort not to give in to these yearnings during those secret assignations which took place in parks and cars over the summer of 1998." Bird also relayed the fantasies of an unnamed man who joined his classmates in urging their former third-grade teacher to "bend over their desks in the hopes of a fleeting glimpse of cleavage."

The idea that the body of the white female teacher is available to the hyperhormonal adolescent boy serves to quell castration anxiety in male-identified, heterosexual readers: the all-powerful mother figure, posing as state-appointed teacher, really exists for adult-male (and boy-student) pleasure. As Benjamin (1995, 188) explains: "Sadistic erotic fantasies, which may then attract adult men to pornographic sadism, usually represent a retaliatory reversal of the omnipotent control suffered at the mother's hands.

The impotent rage that the child has split off, unable to express or encompass, reappears in the sexualized fantasy – fueled not by Eros but by aggression." In essence, the pornographic tellings of the Markson case are about a white, adult-male, heterosexual wish to reverse the feelings of infantile helplessness and to restore the masculine subject to authority.

In his psychoanalytic discussion of romantic love, Stephen Mitchell (2001, 205) suggests that "it is very difficult – perhaps, Freud thought, ultimately impossible – for the boy to fully reconcile his sexual wishes toward mother as sexual object with the mother who protects and preserves him." The same impossibility is at play in the erotic dynamic between the boy-student and white female teacher involved in an erotic pedagogical encounter. The female teacher is caught between her desire for the boy and her wish to attend to his developmental – or educational – needs as a responsible mother figure. The analytic space, like the classroom, is sometimes imagined to be a maternal holding space in which the client or student can grapple with his developmental or educational progress. According to Mitchell, "this relationship in which subjectivity develops is predicated on certain kinds of activity by the [maternal] other, variously described as recognition, attunement, holding" (55). Because there is desire in recognition and because maternal holding is ultimately pleasurable, there is always an incestuous dynamic to the mother-son relationship in the set-up of the white, Western, Oedipal nuclear family. The son's access to the maternal body is legally prohibited by law; this prohibition, consequently, ignites desire. The mother, for Freud, is the ultimate seductress: she offers her body as a developmental container and then enables the child to locate his desire in relation to her physicality. Given this realization, Erica McWilliam (1999, 33) poses the question: "Is there any difference between teacher-student sex and incest if the teacher's duty of care is synonymous with that of a caring parent?" As Teresa de Lauretis (1984, 97) suggests in her psychoanalytic interpretation of semiotics in film, "all narrative cinema, in a sense, is the making good of Oedipus, the restoration of his vision by the film's representation (re-enactment) of the [Oedipal] drama." The story – on the big screen, in the newspaper, or in "real life" – must enable the boy to redeem himself for his libidinous desire for the mother. Doing so relieves his fear of paternal reprisal and brings assurance that not he but the lecherous and perverted mother – or mother-like figure (teacher) – is ultimately to blame for the incestuous infraction. The interesting distinction to be made between the sex scandals involving white female teachers and Oedipal dramas in Hollywood film that persecute the mother and express misogynist hate for her is that the boy-students implicated in the sex scandals do not overtly hate and blame the maternal presence (teacher). In most instances, the boy-students are upset with the courts and with policies governing teacher professionalism – the laws of the Father – for prohibiting their intergenerational relationships with an idealized mother figure. It is the moral majority, child protectionists, and advocates of teacher professionalism who are committed to vindicating the masculinity of the boy-student and persecuting the lascivious female teacher, coded as mother. There is, consequently, a queer permutation to the female teacher-student liaison in need of analysis.

The Female Teacher as Femme Fatale: Professional Infractions and Forbidden Love

> Film noir also presents us with racialized maternity and racialized feminine sexuality that make for the powerful and anxious origin of the dark, mysterious mood of noir. (Oliver and Trigo 2003, 25)

> Noir queers constitute a disturbance in knowledge; they unsettle the process of knowing that drives the narrative and contribute to the experience of not knowing that is such a characteristic flavour of noir. They are a gender disturbance ... they also lurk in the foundational institutions of heterosexuality, marriage ... In so far as one of the comforts of normal masculinity is to be in possession of knowledge, including and perhaps especially the knowledge of gender, queers are discomforting. (Dyer 2002, 111)

In news stories of teacher-student sex scandals like the Markson case, the female teacher bares a striking resemblance to the psychically dangerous and horrific modern white femme fatale portrayed in recent Hollywood films like *Basic Instinct, Body Heat, Single White Female,* and *The Hand that Rocks the Cradle,* to name a few. Although feminist film critics have paid much attention to dangerous women in film noir and to the way that they disrupt normative heterosexuality, less attention has been given to the racialized portrait of the female villainess (Hannsberry 1998). As Jane Caputi (2004, 51) notes in her discussion of femme noire: "Despite the linguistic commonplace, itself steeped in racism, that horror is 'dark' and femmes fatales and the films they appear in are noir ('black'), many theorists, through differing strategies, neglect to critique representations of dangerous, monstrous, and violent women of color and focus only on sexy white femmes fatales." At issue is not only that white females are the monolithic subject of study, but also that how they are imbued with racial signification, as sexual subjects, has escaped critical inquiry in most feminist film theory. As Caputi notes, a white female protagonist (or villain) becomes bad (or "noir") when her character is laced with "primitive emotions and lusts, violence, sexual aggression, masculinity, lesbian tendencies, promiscuity, duplicity, treachery, contaminating corruption, sovereignty, and so on" (52). Even when the characters in a given film (or genre) are exclusively white, their whiteness stands in as a failure to fit into an idealized fantasy of whiteness. Such whiteness depends on an imagined racial other lurking behind the scenes, which is confined to a shadowy existence yet also formidably present.

Film noir, with its anxiety about the corrupting influence of undomesticated female sexualities, hybrid racializations, and the instability of the white nuclear family, was originally a reflection of the conservative, postwar McCarthy era in the United States. The resurgence of film noir in Hollywood film production in the late 1990s and through to the twenty-first century, as feminist film critics would agree (Boozer 1999-2000; Kaplan 1998; Pidduck 1995), has been inaugurated by a return to a period of social conservativism. Such conservativism can also be seen in rhetoric about teacher accountability and professional codes of conduct and in what I describe earlier in this chapter and in Chapter 2 as an unprecedented concern about the sexual transgressions of white female teachers.

The femme fatale, the signature character of the genre, symbolizes the destruction of the white nuclear family. She is not only ambivalent about maternity but also a phallic presence that upsets the demarcations between whiteness and racialized "others." As Oliver and Trigo (2003, 5) contend, the anxiety in film noir is based on a "fear of racial ambiguity, the fear of not being able to tell the difference between blackness and whiteness." Confusion about sexual difference acts as a catalyst for a whole set of other worries about boundary dissolutions, and racial boundary dissolution is a predominant concern. Because white mothers have been responsible for policing and literally reproducing the corporeal boundaries demarcating racialized subjectivities, the maternal positioning in popular film and media culture is a particularly troubling concern to a white Canadian majority invested in white racial purity. The female heroine (or femme fatale) – whether mother, lover, teacher, babysitter, or boss – is a figure of psychic terror to adult viewers invested in white, normative, age-appropriate, reproductive heterosexualities. The maternal character signifies the decay or maintenance of traditional heterosexual family values, which include reproductivity, ideologies of white maternal passivity, binary feminine and masculine gender assignments, and protocols governing female sexual assertiveness.

The white female teacher's coupling with maternal pedagogy is therefore of great significance to understanding the symbolic threat of castration, the fear of racial hybridization, and worries about heterosexual familial forms at play in the Canadian sex-scandal stories involving teachers. To understand the literary techniques common to the media portrayals of these sex-scandal stories and modern film noir, we need only consider the class and racialized representation of a geography caught in a distant and sinister, yet strangely modern, time. For example, in an article published in the Canadian popular magazine *Elm Street* about former teacher Heather Ingram's illicit affair (discussed in detail in Chapter 5), the scandal is given an unmistakable noir-like setting. The magazine article reads like a Harlequin romance, with dashes of despair, alienation, and cynicism characteristic of film noir: "They seemed like an unlikely couple. Heather Ingram was reserved and academically inclined, Andy [a pseudonym] was a pot-smoking rebel. She lived in Gibsons, he resided in Halfmoon Bay, a 40-minute drive north on the windy, two-lane highway on British Columbia's picturesque Sunshine Coast, tucked in to the southwest corner of the province's mainland. They met between their two towns – in the sleepy community of Sechelt – and fell in love" (Schmidt 2000, 24). In this case, the seventeen-year-old seduced Ingram, who was said to be unhappy and lonely in her common-law relationship (24). Normative, adult heterosexuality seemed to bore and dissatisfy the white female protagonist, who also spoke about unhappiness and depression in her marriage (Ingram 2003).

A queer regression in time led her to fixate on a teenaged boy just shy of eighteen years of age. After a long night of being propositioned and pursued by the relentless teenager, the teacher consented to a passionate affair that inevitably cost her a career. The affair grew into a four-year relationship, and the lovers had a child. The teacher left her adult husband and spoke about an existential unhappiness that haunted her adult life as a responsible wife and teacher. The story in the *Elm Street* magazine shook the otherwise staid and sedate community of Sechelt, British Columbia.

A lingering concern about the white female teacher as underhanded seductress – as femme fatale – is evident in the shadowy black-and-white photos that accompany the *Elm Street* article. The pictures alongside the article depict fragmented female body parts, which are nearly indecipherable and strangely reminiscent of a sexually orchestrated murder crime-scene, the kind that film noir is legendary for depicting. Feminist film theorist Christine Gledhill (2000, 82) explains that the "noir heroine frequently emerges from shadows, her harsh white face, photographed without softening filters, part of the abstract lighting schemes," and this is also symptomatic of both the Heather Ingram and Annie Markson portrayals in the news media. The white face, red lipstick, and widow-like black attire (sexually alluring and provocative, yet foreboding) are basic to the femme fatale's public face and wardrobe. She is an enigma because she adopts a provocative and confident sexual charisma that undermines the passive white female's role in domestic family life, but she is also less than transparent when it comes to her desire. It is never clear (with the possible exception of the lesbian femme fatale, Violet, in the film *Bound*) what the femme fatale as temptress and/or seductress wants. She is an obscure, Sphinx-like creature who seems to incite anxieties in white male adults about normative gender roles, even in moments of intense passion, because her sexuality is enigmatic, being read as queer and perverse.

The romantic liaison between Markson and her student was similarly seen as a perversion. Teresa de Lauretis (1999, 47-48, original emphasis) astutely notes that "*perversion* means deviation from the path leading to the 'final' or 'normal' sexual aim of copulation, a deviation from the path linking the drive to the reproductive object (i.e., a person of the other sex [who is of the same peer group])." At the same time, Freud insists that the sexual drive is organized around the pursuit of pleasure (not reproduction) and that it can have multiple objects of desire. A perversion, therefore, is not a pathology and can be correctly understood only as a departure from a societal norm (de Lauretis 1999) – in this case, a normative perception about the asexuality of the relationship between female teacher and boy-student. There is also a departure from heterosexual futurity with its insistence on sexual and racial difference. The sexual transgressions of white female teachers ignite a range of panics about gender, race, class, sexual difference, childhood and adulthood, and family, all of which are key to a normative heterosexual order. A sexual transgression must not be understood as inherently pathological. Transgressions breach normative orders and thus stand in as moral barometers. There is nothing clinically perverse or pathological about the Markson professional transgression. She overstepped her boundaries as teacher *in loco parentis* and allowed herself to fall for an underage boy-student. The misdemeanour gets read as a perversion of a higher moral order because it is steeped in a culture of professionalism that depends on the repudiation of the erotic. The pedagogical power of the Markson erotic transgression is that it enables us to question our insistence on the sexual innocence of teenage students and white female teachers and our investments both in heteronormativity and in sexual and racial difference.

The Queer Pedagogy of the Femme Fatale

The femme fatale is seen as a worrisome combination of sexual aggressivity, internal neediness, and psychotic independence (Pidduck 1995). In the mainstream press, reporters often describe the white female teachers involved in the aforementioned sex scandals as similarly angst-ridden creatures. For example, Markson is described as a "30-year-old single woman who clearly didn't have enough happening in her life, either emotionally, psychologically or sexually ... It appears this relationship, this forbidden fruit was filling some emotional vacuum in [her]" (Bird 2001). The psychiatrist appointed to examine Markson aroused public fear when he revealed that he "couldn't find any deviant stuff or under-the-cover urges. She's a very straightforward woman ... [who has] been suffering from depression and insomnia since the incident ... She's certainly not a pedophile" (Nelson 2001). Not unlike actress Sharon Stone's character in the film *Basic*

Instinct – one of the most obvious examples of the contemporary femme fatale in popular culture – Markson is a psychological enigma. She passes psychological tests and examinations with ease while allegedly harbouring deviant desires and the ability to act on them. Commenting on the Sclater sex-scandal case in Canada, the writer for *Report Newsmagazine* describes the white female teacher as a "lonely spinster" and warns readers that "women are able to get close and intimate with children in a way that men can't" (Ward 2000, 46). The sex scandals involving white female teachers and the recent film noir flicks share an atmosphere of cynicism marked by moral corruption, gender ambiguity, and the return of the racialized phallic Mother.

Film and cultural critic Julianne Pidduck (1995, 66) suggests that the recent film noir movies "perform the ideological function of 'containing' the sexually transgressive, independent woman through narrative closure." I suggest that the same technique is used to contain the threat posed by the single (or married) white female teacher reluctant to curb and domesticate her desire to fit a dominant heterosexual template involving reproductive marital unions, clearly delineated gender binaries, and sexual difference.

Regardless of her interest in young boys, the lascivious white female teacher is queer because acting on her desires upsets what Judith Butler (1990b) calls the heterosexual matrix and what Lee Edelman (2004) calls reproductive futurity. She is coded as an abject subject who threatens the boundaries demarcating love objects and subjects in what Jan Jagodzinski (2002) calls the family romance in education. She refuses a maternal pedagogy dependent on a renunciation of the erotic and doesn't respect generational differences that the incest taboo is meant to uphold. The femme fatale is not a woman in any straightforward way and seems to undermine or mock feminine passivity through her outlandish display of erotic or pedagogical passion. To be queer is to be "viewed in some manner [as] dissonant, disturbing, subversive, transgressive" (Dyer 2002, 4). The teacher in this case upsets gender and heterosexual time because her misdemeanour is not in any way hospitable to reproductive futurity with its investment in marriage, paternity, and clearly delineated future generations. The lascivious white female teacher is seen to be an adolescent herself, a queer aberration or atavistic throwback. She stands in as a perversion in time and thus queers the educational milieu charged with the normative ordering of heterosexual times in the school. As Dyer observes in what he calls queer noir, queer has "something to do with not being properly masculine and feminine" (97). It also has to do with foregoing generational prohibitions on sex orchestrated by the incest taboo, as I discuss shortly.

Markson's queer sexuality, her alleged perversity, depends on a relational contrast between herself and the boy's virtuous, properly white, and maternally endowed mother. The antagonism between the good mother and the diabolic white female teacher is central to the media representations of the professional infraction. For example, the boy's mother reported that she became suspicious when she smelled Markson's perfume on her son and observed the teacher "touch her son's face in the school computer lab[. The] pair smiled into each other's eyes." Reflecting on the encounter, the mother said, "it wasn't the look of a teacher and a student" ("Mom tells" 2001). Here, the gaze of the phallic Mother is set up in contrast to the domesticated white mother and is suggestive of the former's sexual potency alongside the latter's domesticity.

The libidinous maternal gaze incites anxiety because it ignites an Oedipal desire that must be repudiated in the name of the Father and heterosexual futurity. The child cannot become an antonymous subject and enter into the Lacanian Symbolic if he (or she) remains in the purview of a desirous and doting mother. According to the psychoanalytic schemata, the infant does not have a clearly delineated sense of self independent of the mother. As he or she separates from the mother (thereby disavowing desire for the maternal presence), the child (or, later, adult) feels an acute discomfort with the maternal gaze because it is an uncanny reminder of a time when he or she was an undifferentiated subject. Maternal desire threatens childhood and teenage autonomy along with the intergenerational delineations that give rise to generational difference. Her desire, as evidenced through her devouring gaze, is racialized and marked as both regressive and atavistic. This is particularly evident in the image of the destructive Medusa figure in classical mythology and popular discourse. As de Lauretis (1999, 110) explains: "Medusa's power, her evil look, is more explicit than the Sphinx's but both achieve analogous long-term effects: they not only kill or devour, but blind as well. The legends of Perseus and Oedipus in which they are inscribed make it clear that their threat is to man's vision, and their power consists in their enigma and 'to-be-looked-at-ness' (in Mulvey's word), their luring of man's gaze into the 'dark continent,' as Freud would put it, the enigma of femininity." It is also important to note that the sexually potent maternal presence – here symbolized by the legend of Medusa – is racially coded. Female sexuality is, as Freud (1962) argues, associated with the "dark continent," all that is primitive, savage, and uncivilized. In *Imperial Leather: Race, Gender, and Sexuality in the Colonial Contest* (1995), Anne McClintock writes about anachronistic space, which she defines as "prehistoric, atavistic and irrational, inherently out of place in this historical time of modernity." In this way, Medusa is located in anachronistic space and in panoptic time characterized as a unified portrait in which "history appears static, fixed, covered in dust" (40). Panoptic time is not congruent with heterosexual time and stands in as a queer developmental or historical arrest. Undomesticated female sexuality – the horror of which is embodied in the Medusa figure – is similarly anachronistic and panoptic because there is no room for it in modernity's heterosexual time.

The future of heterosexuality in modern, Western educational cultures depends on a repudiation of the erotic in the sphere of the feminine. Licentious, queer, or in some other way coded as antifamily, the sexualities of amorous white female teachers are aligned with white racial degeneration (as I discuss in Chapter 6). Because queer desires are inconsistent with heterosexual times and their investment in white reproductive futurity, they must be contained and/or domesticated by the Father. The nuclear-family unit is the institution of containment, and the school, as a surrogate family, must also contain (prohibit, censor, or punish) the sexualities of female teachers that are incongruent with heterosexual time and place.

Heterosexual majorities fear that left to her own devices, the lascivious white female teacher would snare the boy (student) travelling along an otherwise unencumbered path to reproductive heterosexuality in a queerly feminine trap. He would then be confined to an infantile maternal world where the borders of gender, sex, race, and generation collide and intersect. In the realm of the maternal and in what Lacan calls the Semiotic, the child would cease to exist as a coherent masculine subject with a heteronormative mandate. The maternal semiotic space, as theorized by Kristeva (1982) and Lacan (Miller 1998), is prelinguistic. It does not give rise to subject- or identity-based divisions. Life is an undifferentiated mass, fluid and uncontained by language-based divisions and psychic identifications. The child is supposed to leave the mother (the semiotic) and enter into the realm of the father (the Symbolic) – what I call a normative heterosexuality with a futuristic mandate. Caught by the mother in a queer semiotic trap, the child would regress. Like the undomesticated mother, like Europe's and America's racialized "others," like homosexuals, and like all who fall outside reproductive futurity in the eyes of the white heteronormative moral majority, the student (coded as child) would be confined to a time and place characterized by that which is abject, foreign, atavistic, and uncivilized.

Building on Kristeva's (1982) theory of the abject, Oliver and Trigo (2003, xxx-xxxi) explain that it is about "separation and identification in both individuals and nations or societies ... the abject is not, as we might ordinarily think, what is grotesque or unclean; rather, it is what calls into question borders and threatens identity." As Kristeva argues, the abject is most often associated with the maternal body, and the relation between this body and the infantile body is a primary focus of horror and fascination because it is in this relation that the greatest threat to subject-based body boundaries and identifications exists. If the boy – and the worry is usually about the boy because the girl's claim to autonomy and citizenship is already questionable and tentative at best – cannot separate from the maternal semiotic realm, his gender, sexuality, white racial demarcation, and investment in the reproductive future are in question. Autonomous masculine ego formation (normative white-boy masculinity) depends on abjection not only from the actual maternal body, but also from maternal domains and spaces (like education); graduation and leaving home are futuristic musts. The incest taboo also works to ensure that sons do not hang around too long or that they don't usurp the father's place in the family. Moralistic panics about the sexual proclivities of white female teachers and the need to protect our students from their uncivilized or queer desires work the same way. Domesticating the sexualities of white female teachers and employing them in the service of the heteronormative family is a long-term cultural strategy and tradition in education.

As Freud and others have argued, the incest taboo (and anxieties about it) function to distinguish Europe (and now North America) from its colonial and now postcolonial "others." In his book *Racial Castration* (2001), David Eng contends that indigenous peoples have been associated with sexual transgressions like incest and are therefore thought to be not only sexually ravenous and hypersexual, but also savage and uncivilized in white colonial imaginations. In *Totem and Taboo* (1960), Freud wrote that "savages are even more sensitive on the subject of incest than we are. They are probably liable to a greater temptation to it" (9). As a result, racialized peoples in white European and North American fantasy formations are coupled with sexual transgressions that are thought to exert a retarding influence on civilization. There is, as Eng (2001, 9) argues, a "conflation of sexual perversions with racial difference" not only in Freudian psychoanalysis, but also in white European and other Westernized fantasy formations more generally.

It follows that the evil Medusa-like stare of the lascivious white teacher is read as an invitation to breach the incest taboo – on which modern-day, Western civilizations are thought to have been founded. The taboo, according to Freud (1960), is adhered to because the boy is threatened, symbolically, with castration by his father. Castration is an intolerable threat to the development of normative white male masculine subjectivity. The lascivious white female teacher, coded as mother, seems to invite her boy-student (son) to transgress the taboo, which in turn threatens manhood if caught by the patriarchal father. It is the father who is supposed to have exclusive access to the mother, and white male administrators are likewise charged with regulating a profession that is dominated by white women. The invitation to sexual or incestuous transgressions is worrisome not because the boys are in danger of being abused by a maternal figure like a teacher but because they are in danger of upsetting a developmental sequence on which heterosexual futurity depends. Boys would refuse to grow up. Oedipal development would be thrown off course, and normative heterosexual identifications based on traditional gender-role assignments and identifications would not be assured. Nothing is reproduced in any ordinary way. Modern-day, Western civilizations cannot tolerate such a threat to heteronormativity and its future. Even on a symbolic level, the threat to family ignited by intergenerational desire is monumental. As Lee Edelman (2004, 14, original emphasis) explains, the ultimate threat to reproductive futurity is to dislodge the "governing fantasy of achieving Symbolic closure through the marriage of identity to futurity in order to realize the social subject. Conservatives acknowledge this radical potential, which is also to say, this radical *threat* of queerness more fully than liberals, for conservativism preemptively imagines the wholesale rupturing of the social fabric." In other words, the queer or perverse threat is launched at the level of the Symbolic as opposed to the material.

Like the conduct of the other white female teachers caught up in sensational sex panics and conservative moralisms, Markson's conduct is worrisome not because she committed actual infractions but because she launched what gets read as symbolic (i.e., queer) warfare against the reproductive family and the identifications that it engenders. This is why the Markson case – perhaps the most benign of all sex scandals discussed in this book – has been raised to the level of a foundational Oedipal incestuous transgression *in the absence* of sexual touching. Markson *symbolically* breached a taboo constitutive of heterosexuality. Incest (real and imagined) is culturally abhorrent not because child welfare is at stake but because it has the capacity to upset the development of normative gender identifications and adolescent maturation cycles measurable by and giving rise to heterosexual time.

Speaking about the incest taboo in modern, Western culture, James Twitchell (1987, 43) notes: "Freud correctly pointed out that 'taboo' really meant not only 'forbidden' but also 'holy' and it is even true that 'incest' not only means 'impure sex' but also implies, through the ancillary meaning of 'cestus' or girdle (usually of Venus; by folk extension, the occluding vaginal membrane), that which should arouse passion ... This view of incest as an act denied to men but permitted to the gods is a staple of ancient mythology where the heavens are populated by precisely the kind of breeding forbidden to man. So too, the concept of horror is resolutely paradoxical." The invitation to incest is as horrific as it is tempting. It is queer in its perversity and tempting not because we want to have sex with our parents or teachers but because it throws a cog in the normative heterosexual order. We must remember that it is the relation to desire and loss, as opposed to the object, that matters and that excites the one tempted by transgression or scandal. In other words, the idea of incest has a significance and power that must be seen to have ignited the sex scandal. Incest is often represented in popular film, mythology, and religion as standing in for mortality. It negates chronological age and linear growth.

In Greek mythology, for example, incest is offered up as an incitement and passage to the heavens. Because interfamilial desire evokes a return of a repressed desire for the mother, it is also horrific. A fear of and need to expel the clandestine desire is evident in the hyperbolic insistence that Annie Markson be chastised and berated for her erotic transgressions, however benign and inconsequential to the boy's real emotional and educational well-being. The public at large is disgusted by the idea of sex between a white female teacher and a boy-student because it conjures up libidinous impulses that many of us prefer to keep repressed and unanalyzed. But we can't be altogether unhappy and disturbed given that we seek out and read about the minute details of the erotic transgressions. Many of us read much about what we distain and never ponder how it is that we come to be outraged and morally scandalized. Twitchell (1987) asks, is it a "coincidence that incest, this most unclean act, has been interpreted by psychoanalysts as representing universal desire and frustration, and by at least some anthropologists as meaning just the opposite: acts of universal dread and abhorrence?" (44).

At the heart of the Markson story is an intense public ambivalence about the incestuously coded flirtation between a white female teacher and a young boy-student. In contrast to the much-loved Hollywood maternal melodrama positioning the maternally endowed white female teacher as all-loving, queen of self-abnegation, paragon of virtue, and sacrificial martyr, the appearance of the teacher/mother as a concupiscent and libidinous femme fatale upsets the social script. Her desire hasn't been domesticated and is a queer threat. She refuses to be an asexual love object and is not invested in future-oriented heteronormativity. The femme fatale is routinely imagined to be "sadistic, hurtful, and jealous, she refuses the self-abnegating role, demanding her own life. Because of her 'evil' behaviour, this Mother often takes control of the narrative, but she is punished for her refusal to adopt the desired patriarchal ideal, the Good Mother" (Kaplan 2000c, 468). Markson is read in similar terms and, as I have argued, stands in as a queer subject inhospitable to reproductive futurity: "If the Mother reveals her desire, she is characterized as the Bad Mother (sadistic, monstrous), much as the single woman who expresses sexual desire is seen as destructive" (Kaplan 2000c, 468), queer, and perverse. At the same time, the lascivious white female teacher exposes the nebulous line between the "good" and the "bad" mother. Not only can she be one and the same, but we can never be sure which she is at a given moment because her seductions are always masked as something else.

In her discussion of contemporary film noir, Christine Gledhill (2000, 73) points out that the "twentieth century has seen an acceleration in the process of the emancipation of women and an intensification of the contradictions surrounding the sexual division of labour and reproduction, so that women perhaps more crucially than before constitute a consciously perceived social problem." It is now possible to imagine the white female teacher as an active sexual agent, independent voyeur, or lover. Her sexual subjectivity is a point of anxiety because it exists as a potential threat to conventional heteronormative masculine sensibilities and the hierarchies that they engender in school and society. The queer teacher also threatens heterosexual futurity and the gender, class, generational, and racial identifications on which it depends.

According to Gledhill, late-twentieth-century film noir, which frames the media representation of the Markson case, is a product of a white heteronormative desire to contain the threat of the sexually independent or queer feminine subject. As I have said above, the Markson story is steeped in conservative moralism, but it is also laced with pornographic representations. Because the "masculine look contains passive elements and can signify *submission to* rather than *possession of* the female" (Studlar 2000, 213, original emphasis), the visual pleasure of male heterosexuals can take on a sadistic and masochistic quality. As Christine Gledhill (2000, 77) insists, "film noir probes the secrets of female sexuality and male desire within patterns of submission and dominance. Thus the enquiries of the police or private detective come eventually to concentrate on the state of the hero's ... heart." In the Markson case, observers can never be sure whether she is an illustrious teacher with loving inclinations or a contemporary femme fatale in disguise. The illicit flirtation is a mutual engagement, notwithstanding the intergenerational factor, but it is unclear whether the white female teacher is dominant or submissive in the libidinous liaison. News reporters repeatedly attempt to construct Markson as a kind of female dominatrix, wielding her power over an underage student, but there is in the background a nagging suspicion that the boy liked the attention and sought it out.

In film noir, the "plot is dominated by questions about female sexuality, and sexual relationships involving patterns of deception, seduction and unrecognized revelations rather than by deductions of criminal activity from a web of clues" (Gledhill 2000, 79). Allegations of criminal activity on Markson's part are subordinated to the overarching concern about her sexual prowess. *Because* her undomesticated sexuality is visible in the sphere of public education, it becomes a matter of intense professional speculation and bewilderment. The story of Annie Markson is not so much a feminist acclimation of a white female teacher's independent and active sexuality as a mirror for hegemonic anxieties about heterosexuality and its future. Janey Place (1998, 47) argues that although film noir is far from progressive, it "does give us one of the few periods of film in which women are active, not static symbols, are intelligent and powerful, if destructively so, and derive power, not weakness, from their sexuality." In this way, the

Markson sex-scandal story is a contemporary, heterosexually orchestrated Oedipal myth. It is also a parable that depicts seduction by a white female teacher as perverse, queer, and debilitating to familial heterosexualities and to the binaries of race, nation, gender, time, and sexuality that they orchestrate along reproductive timelines.

For those with investments in white heteronormativity, in racial demarcations, and in gender and sexual difference, the world depicted in film noir is unstable and uncertain. For biological men (as opposed to transgendered/transitioned men) invested in hegemonic masculinities, teacher sex is either threatening because it stands in as a return of the repressed libidinous desire for the mother or exciting because it represents a symbolic opportunity to revisit and explore fantasies about the mother. Both allow boys and men to grapple with feelings of infantile helplessness. Focusing on the threat posed by the mother to normative adult masculine-identity developments, E. Ann Kaplan contends that pornographic strategies are sometimes used to divest the mother of power and simultaneously to invest the masculine subject with power. The narrative strategy, therefore, can assume a series of pornographic techniques to undermine female authority and to reveal the mother's status as a castrated subject. As Kaplan (2000b, 121) says of femmes fatales, the "sexualization and objectification of women is not simply for the purposes of eroticism; from a psychoanalytic point of view, it is designed to annihilate the threat that woman (as castrated, and possessing a sinister genital organ) poses." Audience desire to see the depraved sexuality of the femme fatale revealed and subject to punishment is the staple of film noir. The wish to restore heteronormativity is also a means to regain masculine authority and government over the white female who has come to symbolize sexual (and racial) degeneration.

Another narrative strategy employed in film noir is resistance to narrative closure. As Christine Gledhill (2000, 77) explains, the "plots of noir thrillers are frequently impossible to fit together even when the criminal secret is discovered." Not only is the inducement to crime unclear, but the moral consequences are elusive. In fact, evidence that a crime has taken place at all is the subject of debate in film noir. And this is the linchpin that binds the dissolute white female teacher and the femme fatale: evidence of crime (or abuse, in the case of the lecherous female teacher) cannot be found. As I suggest in Chapter 2, quite often the alleged boy-victims insist that they were not in any way harmed by sex with their older, female teachers, and even child psychologists and advocates struggle to show evidence of harm. The boy-student who received the lewd stare and erotic love notes from Markson claims to have invited the attention of his babysitter, who also worked as a supply teacher in his school. Similarly, in the case of Jocelyn Jaster, an Alberta teacher accused of seducing a seventeen-year-old male student (and later acquitted), close observers wondered whether the alleged crimes were of substantial import. According to one article covering the event, the alleged victim stated, "I didn't understand what I was doing at first. I didn't think I was a victim. Then I sat down and realized I was." The quotation is followed by the newspaper columnist's sarcastic response: "The poor dear" (Grace 2001, 41). The reporter, like many readers of the Canadian mainstream press, noticed that the boy saw himself as a victim *after* child protectionists, the police, and concerned parents told him that he was; the effects of the so-called abuse were not otherwise evident.

In another case involving an unnamed female teacher in British Columbia accused of sexual infractions with a number of senior boy-students on her volleyball team, the police could not complete their investigation because, in their words, "many of the fellows we have interviewed do not consider themselves to be a victim." In a public statement, the police declared that the problem is that "none of these young men are prepared to complain or state that they are a victim as a result of the actions of this teacher ... Most of them are young men now in their early 20s ... [The investigation] has all been [done] through smirks and smiles" (Humphreys 2000a, 2000b) coming from the so-called victims. The idea that the sexual conduct of a white female teacher could be inconsequential was unnerving to those who are invested in heteronormativity and intergenerational prohibitions on love, desire, and sexual activity. It is admittedly difficult to grapple with Eros in the pedagogical encounter when we are unaccustomed to talking about sexuality in school. The master narrative of sexual danger gives us licence to talk about harm, danger, and child protectionism, but as I argue in the previous chapter, it is not able to account for a pedagogical transgression based on social consent. Because we lack a means to understand the Markson transgression and others like it, we default into a moralistic narrative about declining professional standards and modern problems with teachers as sub-standard role models.

In the foregoing, I offer a queer reading of psychoanalysis to understand the fear evoked by the Markson sex scandal. I interpret the moral outrage and sardonic commentary as a symptom of the incest taboo and of Western culture's investment in heterosexual futurity. The cynical and caustic remarks made by reporters suggest that there is more at play in teacher sex than is admitted to by the master narrative of child sexual abuse. The boys cannot be in unmitigated psychic pain when their forbidden desires are met by a lustful teacher (maternal proxy) all too willing and able to satiate libidinous (although repressed) desires. The white female teacher (coded as maternal governess) demands a single displacement from what many psychoanalysts claim to be our original object of desire, the mother. It is hardly a secret that the white female teacher of elementary school children has been historically coded as loving mother figure (Grumet 1988; Klein 1989; Steedman 1985; Walkerdine 1990) in Western cultures. In fact, maternal feminists understand asexual mother love as idyllic and recommend it as an ethical self-formation for elementary school teachers (Noddings 1984). The call to maternal love is perhaps the most potent mechanism of defence called upon to renounce Eros in the pedagogical encounter.

In her discussion of the seductress and the schoolmarm, Erica McWilliam (1996, 5-6) speculates that, in *The Prime of Miss Jean Brodie,* it is the teacher's "femininity, as distinct from femaleness, which is at the heart of the issue here." Feminine powers of seduction are threatening to the professionally laden (i.e., heterosexual, phallocentric, and future-driven) power structures and identifications governing the school. Not only the seductive power of the white female teacher, but also her erotic authority in the classroom, are worrisome to the professionally educated imagination. The authoritative positioning of the white female subject as "older woman" (cougar and seductress of young men) *and* rational subject (teacher with a legitimate claim to knowledge) in the educational milieu, upsets the discourse of professionalism and the gender binaries on which the institution of education is founded. The white female teacher is not supposed to be sexy *and* smart. Markson's refusal to respect the professional code of conduct (while fulfilling her responsibilities as teacher) suggests that the white female teacher *can* possess rational capacities – required of all good teachers – *and* a sexy demeanour. It is not the kind of sexiness that is based on normative heterosexuality, nor is it sanitized femininity; the sexually dominant (and savvy) femme positioning is one of active sexual agency in the erotic pedagogical encounter. The white female teacher as femme fatale stakes a claim to intellect and sexual citizenship outside the nuclear family. Her interest in the present is based on an investment in non-normative gender and sexual identifications in the educational milieu.

What Does the Female Teacher Want: A Dream of Love Deferred?

Prior to the widely publicized stories of school sex scandals in the late twentieth century, which have continued to the present day, the desires had by white female teachers were camouflaged as something else (maternal love, selfless and altruistic investment in student educational development), so it is productive to ask the question: what does the white female teacher want?[5] In her study of cinema and fantasy formation in preservice teacher candidates, Judith Robertson (1997) wonders whether it is possible to liberate female-teacher desire from a socially sanctioned asexual dream of motherly love. In other words, she questions the form that the "want" would take and its quality. Robertson suggests that the female "teacher who commits herself with selfless devotion to the love object (working countless hours without reward and never giving it a thought) is not only subdued, but dispossessed of a vocabulary for articulating what is rightfully hers: dignity, compensation, and recognition for her efforts. Such a figure repudiates the legitimate expectation that she can be open to and deserving of the erotic potential of pedagogical relationality" (131). The erotic potential of pedagogical relationality is not about sex; it is about professional sublimation, the recognition one deserves for a job well done. It is also about a refusal to be positioned as an ascetic and asexual subject in professional and ethical codes of conduct. The dream of love in teaching demands that white female teachers renounce not only their desires for recognition, validation, promotion, and so on, but also their claims to sexual subjectivity.

In his discussion of analyst regression in the psychoanalytic encounter, Stanley Cohen (2000, 785) is troubled by the same question about the legitimacy of professional desire: "What we want from our patients has been very difficult for us analysts to talk about. We have permitted ourselves only certain very few 'unobjectionable,' 'legitimate' wishes with our analysands. It seems as if, in the analytic situation, only analysands, not analysts, have felt safe and free enough to have wishes. We allow ourselves the wish to help our analysands change and grow, so long as it remains reasonably sublimated and doesn't mushroom into more driven needs." It is foolhardy to assume that the analyst can check his or her needs, wants, and fantasies at the analytic door and step into a neutral space. The subjectivity of the analyst, like that of the analysand, is fettered by emotional engagements – much as in the pedagogical encounter. The question of what the female teacher/analyst wants from the analytic/pedagogical encounter remains a mystery, but asking the question opens the door to a more complete understanding of the maternal erotic countertransference and its associated romantic interludes.

In the current climate of professional education, "there is no way of *thinking* a proper amorous consensual teacher-student relationship" (McWilliam 1999, 35, original emphasis). Professional pedagogy demands the repudiation of the erotic. This, of course, is impossible given the sexual dimension of all encounters – notwithstanding the supposedly sanitized pedagogical encounter. At the very least, the near universal transferential engagement between teacher and student in the Western world makes this an impossible directive. The professional protocol places female teachers in a pedagogical conundrum: do you live and work in denial of the erotic *or* claim it as a necessary part of the pedagogical encounter? If the latter is chosen, what form shall Eros take in the pedagogical encounter, and how can we conceive of it within the realm of professional ethics?

Arguing against the disciplinary charges associated with participation in an amorous relation with a graduate student, Jane Gallop (1997, 57) insists that the "pedagogical relation between teacher and student is, in fact, a 'consensual amorous relation.' And if schools decide to prohibit not only sex but 'amorous relations' between teacher and student, the 'consensual amorous relation' that will be banned from our campuses might just be teaching itself." Although the professionally inclined can't imagine a place for the erotic, the teaching situation cannot exist without it. Gallop states that "our professional impulses are sublimated sex drives. The pleasure I get from working with graduate students, the intensity of my wish that certain promising graduate students will choose to work with me, and the satisfaction I get from seeing the imprint of my teaching in their work all strongly suggest a sexual analogy" (87). By declining to work with students who may be caught up in a transferential relation to her (as her administration suggested), Gallop would be refusing to "work with any student who really believed I had something important to teach her" (56).

So what is a white female teacher to do with her sexuality in the classroom? There is certainly a paucity of imagination about what a properly professional and amorous sexual relation between teacher and student might look like, but I suggest that a template lies in a French work of fiction entitled *Ces enfants de ma vie,* by Gabrielle Roy. In this story, a female teacher falls in love with a troublesome boy-student named Mederic. Bell and Iverson (1998, 630) state in their psychoanalytic review of the book: "The text also makes it clear that he falls in love with her and that she is genuinely tempted by the proposition. More than once she nearly crosses a certain line, and she tantalizes her reader with the idea of going deep into Mederic's territory. But by simultaneously observing the boundaries she is continually setting and modifying, *and* by assenting to her libidinal attraction, she brings Mederic over the line and into her own 'civilized' domain." The moral of the story is that the teacher must balance competing desires – for the student as love object and for a pedagogically sound learning environment; "It is not, however, a matter of all-out renunciation, repression, self-denial or quietism ... but one of integrating passion and desire into a sublimated order where the quest for beauty and 'work in common' are of overriding concern" (631). As I suggest in relation to queer pedagogies of desire in the Introduction and in Chapter 2, the task might also be to forge an identification with clandestine and otherwise queer desires, genders, and sexualities inhospitable to modern-day civilization and reproductive futurity. Perhaps it is the job of the queer pedagogue to incite and to foster thought about what conservative moralisms cannot tolerate in the sphere of the erotic and in the domain of education. Such thinking must be about youthful sexualities and their queer entanglements. As well, queer pedagogies must be about the ruptures to normative orders that queer desires and liaisons (consummated and not consummated) perform in the Symbolic, psychic, and sometimes material domains.

Freud (1961) tells us that modern-day civilizations in the West are founded on sexual repression, and it follows that education, as a civilizing institution, is charged with the responsibility of curbing unproductive and hence uncivilized desires. The goal of a queer planet or nation by contrast is not to act on but to forge identifications with clandestine desires, non-normative genders, and sexualities otherwise repudiated or erased in the service of white reproductive futurity. As psychoanalysis shows us, erotic perversions and queer desires in the analytic setting engender creative potentialities otherwise lost in the service of professional negations, denials, moralisms, and fear. The same can be said about the pedagogical dynamic in education. In the classroom, libidinal energy is what incites us to learn. In *Ces enfants de ma vie,* erotic energy is harnessed for the higher pursuit of education, but injustice is not done to the erotic dynamic. Bell and Iverson (1998, 632) state that the "pleasure derived from intellectual engagement with the Other can produce a form of happiness that surpasses sexual gratification." In the remaining chapters, I further excavate what a critically queer pedagogical engagement would look like and how sex scandals involving white female teachers enable us to ask new questions about such an engagement. Again, the point is not to have sex with students but to harness the erotic (which includes queer and transgender identifications, desires, and impulses) in the service of an education that doesn't reproduce a normative, heterosexual futurity.

4
Sexing the Teacher: Voyeuristic Pleasure in the Amy Gehring Sex Panic

> *I should say at the outset that Amy Gehring graduated from the Faculty of Education at the University of Western Ontario (in which I was a professor) and was a student in the Social Foundations of Education course, which I co-taught (although I didn't know her personally). On 2 January 2002 an e-mail was sent from my dean informing faculty that a teacher [then unnamed] who had graduated from our teacher-education program at Western the year before had been arrested in England. We were informed that the local and international press were hounding professors at Western for information about our former student and that the details of the case were of a "salacious nature."*
>
> *Immediately, my roommate and I rushed out to the corner store to purchase a copy of the* London Free Press. *It didn't take long to find the teacher sex scandal story because it was prominently displayed and accompanied by a large photograph. In shock and excitement, we hovered over the kitchen table reading the article until my roommate asked, with guarded skepticism and feminist bewilderment: "Do you think it is possible? I mean do you think a female teacher could sexually assault a fifteen-year-old boy?" (Cavanagh, personal methodological memoir, 2002)*

News headlines about the Amy Gehring sex panic read as follows: "Lusty lessons: Ontario teacher's fate now lies in hands of U.K. jury" (Granatstein 2002); "Boozy teacher had alley sex with two underage boys and bedded a third" (Williams and Cummins 2002); "Teacher 'too drunk' to recall having sex with boy" (Westhead 2002b); "Amy's pervy as any man" (Carroll 2002); "Sex case teacher 'in row after sex with brothers'" (Westhead 2002a); "A jury in Guildford, England, may decide today on the fate of Canada's lustiest teaching export" (2002); "Boy tells jury of drunken encounter at party: Night I lost virginity to biology mistress" (Lee 2002); "Acquitted teacher 'ashamed' of conduct" (2002); "Sex-charges teacher labeled risk by police" (2002); "Science mistress admits kissing and cuddling boy, 15" (Horsnell 2002); "Where do fallen or flagrant women turn for public rehabilitation?" (2002); "Canadian teacher cleared of sex charges" (2002); "Amy's caresses were wrong but not harmful" (Sarler 2002).

Feminist and educational theoretical frameworks demand a critique of the sensationalist media coverage surrounding twenty-six-year-old former teacher Amy Gehring and allegations that she indecently assaulted two former students in the British school by which she was recruited in 2000 from her native Canada. Like most sex scandals involving female teachers in Canada and the United States discussed in the previous chapters, the case has received a great deal of media fanfare, and the former teacher has been morally condemned by school administrators, parents, the mainstream press, child protectionists, and so on. Even though Gehring was not found guilty, she was cast as a vicious female pedophile with a penchant for submissive schoolboys. Gehring agrees that her interactions with students were unprofessional and that she breached ethical boundaries and protocols, but she explains that she did not break the law by committing acts of gross indecency. Unlike female teachers who insisted on their maternal love, their misguided innocence in matters relating to age-of-consent laws, their poor self-esteem, and so forth, Gehring was admittedly driven by her desire for the underage boys. She was physically attracted to the boys and admitted it to the courts (even though she didn't have sex with them). With the exception of her rather brief and instrumental appeal to family values and conventional moralities in court, Gehring did not shy away from her sexualized media persona but added fuel to its fire by posing with a riding crop and tightly fitted satin dress for a national tabloid.

Gehring avows what I contend to be a queer desire in the pedagogical encounter. As I explain in earlier chapters, a queer desire is not confined to homoerotic or same-sex love; it is a desire that does not accommodate itself to the narrow gender templates prescribed by what Judith Butler (1990b) calls the heterosexual matrix or by what Lee Edelman (2004) calls reproductive futurity. Queer desires are counter to the ideals of the white nuclear family committed to heteronormative futures and conventional gender assignments. Intergenerational desires that involve an older white female in a position of dominance and a younger boy-student in a position of submission are queer because they reveal a queer dynamic in what Jan Jagodzinski (2002) calls the family romance in education. Heteronormativity depends on the renunciation of intergenerational desire and joyful investments made in the future. Educational and developmental growths are key, and undomesticated or queer desires are subject to repression, disavowal, shame, sublimation, or moralistic projection. Gehring did not allow herself to be shamed, and this was a point of anxiety for conservative and heterosexual moralities. Rather than disavowing her professional transgressions with schoolboys in shame, Gehring avowed the desires that led up to the clandestine or queer flirtations, after-school meetings, parties, and kisses. Public fantasies about white female teachers' asexuality, their ascetic and heteronormative virtues, and maternal self-formations were abruptly undone.

In this chapter, I show how third-wave feminist, queer, psychoanalytic, and S/M theories allow us to see that the Gehring case is scandalous not because it involves an instance of professional misconduct (although it does) but because it taps into a fear of who the white female subject can be in sexualized power dynamics. I am interested in what these dynamics do to heterosexual bifurcations of gender in a postcolonial context, intergenerational hierarchies in the school, and Oedipal resolutions to the troubling demands of the heterosexual matrix. The sexualized power dynamics that characterized the Gehring transgression were not about the future but about the present. Hedonistic pleasure usurped the school's investment in the future, its students, and their educational advancement. It is curious that educational and professional protocols did not overtake Gehring's passion for the young men in her classes. News readers want to know what happened in the clandestine, after-school interludes, parties, and the like. This is not because they are really concerned about the welfare of teenage boy-students but because they are themselves intrigued by the desires igniting the professional infractions. Scandals are generated by the acting out of what most of us subject to repression. We get to be excited by a disavowed desire without having to account or take responsibility for it. The Gehring transgression serves such a function and offers up a queer pedagogical moment for reflection. Through it, we imagine what it might have been like if our teachers kissed and showed us physical attentions. We wonder about Eros in the pedagogical dynamic and whether it played a role in our own educational successes or failures. New questions are asked about intergenerational desire and whether it is always exploitative or harmful to educational development. If a teenaged boy is in a position to assert and negotiate his own physical boundaries and feels himself not to have been in harm's way, should we really continue to constitute him as a victim? What is at stake if we do not? Can heterosexuality and its future survive such an attack against the thesis of childhood sexual innocence and the not-so-latent presumption of heterosexuality underpinning it? Perhaps it is not the welfare of the child or teenaged boy that is at stake but normative heterosexuality and its future.

The Gehring transgression was inhospitable to the future, to the boy-student's education, growth, and advancement in the school as imagined by a heterosexual majority. The boy is supposed to want a future career, a wife, and a family of his own, not a sexy teacher uncommitted to the future. Gehring stands in not only as a distraction but as a dangerous arrest in heterosexual development. White female teachers are culturally coded as mothers, so a boy falling in lust with her is read as wanting to regress to a pre-Oedipal stage. Erotic desires enacted between teachers and students are not consistent with conventional, forward thinking about what is good for the child and for reproductive moralities governed by heterosexual ethics. Gehring was unapologetic about her desire for younger teenaged boy-students of legal age to consent. Their welfare was not foremost on her mind. Gehring did the unthinkable. She flirted with them and entered into what we might call a teenage heterosexual courting or dating ritual. Not only that, but she actively positioned herself as a desirous sexual subject and refused to be aligned with maternal pedagogies of altruistic love. Gehring seems to have also regressed as she chummed around with her teenaged school mates after school. There was nothing altruistic or adult-like in Gehring's identification as teacher, which was an acute point of panic driving the scandal.

I draw on sex-positive feminist writings about the female dominatrix to understand how Gehring's sexualized public persona and refusal to disavow or take distance from it added fuel to the scandal. The female dominatrix in British history has often choreographed schoolhouse scenes for paying customers, so it is fitting that she also be evoked to shed light on the panic ensuing around the English school where Gehring taught. Female teachers like Gehring violate Western conventions of gender associated with the prototype of the younger, presumably passive female subject and the older, allegedly more aggressive male counterpart of the normative heterosexual encounter; intergenerational prohibitions on sex, with their associated refusal of the ascetic motherly love that imbues the construction of the white female teacher's role; and the mythology of the "good-girl" attributed to the sexual subjectivity of white girls and young women in the school.

For feminists, the Gehring case begs the question of who the white female teaching subject of the feminist imagination can be and whether this vision is subject to mutation. Feminist and cultural porn historian Lisa Sigel (2002, 245) claims that "sexuality, like pottery, changes over time and across cultures, and its representation reflects broader changes in the dynamics of power and vulnerability. My job is to expose the complex interaction between erotic fantasy and political reality." Similarly, the media-induced scandal involving Gehring reveals a change in what the public is able to think about the white female subject and her sexual capacities. The case is appalling to conventional morality because it provides an instance in which the white female teacher is not a passive sexual object but allegedly an aggressive predatory object. It thus provides an affront to societal conventions and understandings of the white female pedagogue in the educational milieu.

For queer theorists, the Gehring case enables us to understand gender, sex, and power as discursively produced and how they are subject to contestation, public debate, and psychic anxiety. The normalizing function of heterosexuality, with its interest in the future, is destabilized, and queer excitations infiltrate the controls that schools place on white female teachers and their students.

The heterosexual matrix in the white postcolonial imagination is revealed to be unstable, and questions can now be asked about what a dominant white female-teacher sexual persona does to traditional, Western gender binaries governing modern organizations of heterosexuality and its future in Western nations. As in earlier chapters, I am interested in excavating a queer pedagogy of scandal that challenges the heterosexual matrix and reproductive futurity. This chapter is unique, however, in the sense that it focuses on a sexualized schoolhouse scene as a cultural fiction and fantasy in Britain. I excavate the use of the school and its rigid development and educational scripts to choreograph a sex scene based on dominant female teachers and submissive teenaged boys. I consider how the place of the school in our fantasies is used to manage regrets and compromises made in the service of heterosexuality and its future. The family romance in the school (and the home) is not all that it seems. Queer scandals involving teachers and their students expose the underside of the educational romance and its upset.

The Amy Gehring Sex Scandal

The Amy Gehring story made newspaper headlines in January 2002. It was the most controversial school sex scandal involving a Canadian-born female teacher in recent memory, even more upsetting than the Markson case discussed in the previous chapter. Gehring had been accused of indecently assaulting two boy-students aged fourteen and fifteen in Guildford, England, where she was employed as a high school supply teacher filling in for full-time teachers when needed. The case was brought to court, and testimonies were heard from complainants who told jurors that the white female teacher had seduced them. The Crown argued that Gehring was obsessed with a fifteen-year-old schoolboy and had pursued him for sex. She was also accused of having sex with the boy's younger brother to make the older one jealous. Gehring denied the charges, and her lawyer insisted that the allegations were fabrications based on "too much testosterone on the part of two schoolboys supported by a complex web of rumor, speculation and insinuation" ("Teacher 'worked'" 2002). The jury ruled that Gehring was innocent, but the voyeuristic interest in the case has yet to be understood by feminist, queer, and educational theorists concerned with the centrality of gender to sex-related moral panics.

News coverage of the Gehring case was excessively lewd and voyeuristic. For example, a Canadian journalist reported that Gehring entered the court room in "high heels, a black suit and white blouse with several buttons undone" (Granatstein 2002). In the British press, the maligned teacher was said to have arrived at court in a "tailored pinstripe number that, along with shades, marked her out as ... [a] svelte supermodel" ("Courtroom drama" 2002). Another reporter, quoting the testimony given by one boy-student, wrote: "The way she talked and moved was always very sexual. Her tops were so low she didn't have to lean down to reveal herself and she wore lots of make-up." The same journalist added: "Boy-hungry Amy Gehring dominated her impressionable pupils with her blatant sexual behaviour both in school and out" (Collins 2002).

Although Gehring was acquitted after ten hours of jury deliberation, she was placed on List 99, the British government blacklist, which prohibited her from working with children in English schools in the future. In Canada the maligned teacher was subject to review by the Ontario College of Teachers (OCT), the professional body that regulates and disciplines teachers in the province, and designated unsuitable to teach because she was believed to be a risk to children. The OCT ruled that Gehring must wait ten years and pass a series of psychological tests to ensure that she understands the boundary violation that she committed before she may apply for reinstatement. The OCT summoned her to appear before the tribunal for an official reprimand (which she did not do) and ordered her to pay $10,000 for the costs associated with the tribunal, even though Gehring agreed to have her teaching licence revoked well before the tribunal was due to meet. This is the most severe sanction applied by the OCT to discipline a teacher who has transgressed professional boundaries but has not committed an actual crime.[1]

The Gehring case is only one of a series of school-based sex scandals involving white female teachers to receive notoriety and an unduly harsh reprimand by Canadian, British, and American educational authorities in the twenty-first century. In the wake of the Gehring fiasco, for example, a twenty-three-year-old American-born female teacher described as "slim, dark-haired ... [and] highly popular with the boys at the [British] Somerset school, where blackrobed monks instill a strong religious and moral ethos," was dismissed for becoming too "friendly with one of the boys." Although there was no evidence to suggest that this teacher engaged in sexually inappropriate behaviour, she was reportedly sent home to North America because "concerns about the behaviour of female teachers are high following the recent court case involving Canadian Amy Gehring" ("All-American" 2002). In another instance, a supply teacher by the name of Carrie Rosier was "forced to leave her Bradford [England] school after appearing in a daytime TV show talking about her 'unusual sex life'" ("Focus" 2002). In addition to this, there was a scandal involving a Canadian teacher recruited to fill a position in a New York high school who was dismissed because she was believed to have used "foul language and [to have] made sexual gestures in front of her New York high school students" (Edwards 2002).

Such sex scandals are significant because they afford a means to think about the sexual subjectivity of white female teachers apart from conventional, heterosexually orchestrated gender binaries. Socially sanctioned feminine and masculine scripts are reorganized, and for a moment it is possible to imagine the female subject as someone other than the passive recipient of a heterosexual overture. In an important essay entitled "Love for Sale: Queering Heterosexuality" (1997), Eva Pendleton argues that the female sex worker offers a "performance of heterosexuality" (76) and, in doing so, queers the institution of heterosexuality. By mimicking feminine gender codes, sex workers exaggerate and render performative the conventions of passive femininity that anchor popular conceptions of who the white female subject is in the Eurocentric, adult heterosexual imaginary. Lynn Sharon Chancer (1993, 159) also contends in her discussion of the prostitute that a "rebellious woman may not be seen as femininely gendered at all (but a 'dyke,' a lesbian, off the chart of heterosexuality altogether. Or, within straight boundaries, she may be called a 'tramp,' a 'slut,' a 'whore.')" In this way, a heterosexually oriented female can be queer in the way that she may choose to refuse rigid gender binaries, the conventions of romantic love, procreative sex, monogamy, and dignified sexual propriety.

The Gehring story also queers heterosexuality by mutating conventional feminine scripts in the heterosexualized culture that governs the British school. As part of her testimony in court, twenty-six-year-old Gehring described herself (upon arriving at her teaching post in England) as a novelty with the boys, given her age. In an interview with the *Today Program* on BBC Radio Four, Gehring explained that the "boys were sexually rude towards me and the girls saw this and they were quite nasty to me" (quoted in "Acquitted teacher" 2002). As reported in one British newspaper, Gehring told the court that she had to put up with "incessant sexual innuendo [from her male students] ... [that the boys indulged in] grabbing, touching, gestures" that she "obviously didn't like" (Freely 2002). She also said that the British boys were "more forward than those she grew up with in Canada and denied she had corrupted anyone" (Freely 2002). As well, Gehring revealed that her detentions were famous: "the boys came to leer at me. In fact the boys at my second school were even more raunchy. They would pinch my backside and tell me they wanted sex. I lost count of the number of boys who scrawled their phone numbers on scraps of paper and threw them into my handbag" ("Timeplan" 2002). Her testimony reveals the extent to which she was positioned as a sexual object for heterosexual, British, schoolboy voyeuristic pleasure and the extent to which the details of her working environment can be read as emblematic of the hostile climate encountered by women in the public sphere of paid, professional employment in the school.

Of interest in the case is that Gehring does not fall prey to sexual harassment or to the prescribed gender norms governing the heterosexual ethos of the British school in any conventional way. Instead of positioning herself as an object of schoolboy voyeuristic pleasure, Gehring assumes an active sexual orientation as desirous subject. She professes to be lustful and unapologetic about her sexual preference for young boys. "I don't go around intending to pick kids up off the streets. I look young and I like young men, that's all. I realize that I am every schoolboy's fantasy – their hormones are raging and they like older women ... I was ... lonely and foolish" ("Timeplan" 2002). Insisting that she didn't act on her desire for sex with underage boys, Gehring maintains that legally sanctioned boundaries were not breached. The accused teacher claims that although her interpersonal relationships with underage students were professionally inappropriate, she never had sex with them.[2] As in the Markson case discussed in the previous chapter, we are focusing on a professional, not a criminal, violation.

What is most exasperating about Gehring's conduct to white, middle-class, conventional, heterosexual morality is that she refused to align herself with common ideals about white female teacher martyrdom in educational culture, "good-girl" sexuality, and ideologies of wholesome maternal passivity that shape the white female teacher's role. It is customary for the good-girl to feel "shame and guilt and a compulsion toward incessant people pleasing. On the other hand, the bad girl – who is often racialized as non-white, working class or vilified as whore-like – is empowered to have desires and satisfy herself" (Monet 1997, 220). Monet argues that the epistemological standpoint of the female prostitute enables her to understand how our Western culture punishes the bad girl. Through her work in the sex industry, she has come to understand how "central to feminism the liberation and the vindication of the bad girl must be" (222). Paula Webster (1984, 396) similarly contends that the female subject experiences a "mix of desires for power and powerlessness, love and revenge, submission and control, monogamy and promiscuity, sadism and masochism. Once we are able to acknowledge our own complete relationships to these feelings, we will be less likely to submit to pressures to punish our sisters who have dared to speak, act, and write about the taboos they have broken and the forbidden territories they have entered." Monet's notion of the bad girl is not confined to the prostitute but includes all female subjects who are unabashedly sexual and unapologetic about wanting, desiring, and seeking erotic pleasure in dynamics (and venues) that are anti-Oedipal.

Amy Gehring is the bad girl because her desire cannot be reconciled with the Oedipal law of the Father, which is often framed in terms of ethics, professionalism, and nationwide legalities or reproductive heterosexualities central to the nuclear family. The bad girl is bad not because she has an unacceptable desire but because she claims an identification with the desire and does not ask to be punished for it. Gehring is a bad girl in this way. She is shocking because she is unapologetic about her desire for young boys, much like the Western Canadian caricature of the "cougar" (an older, independent – usually white – woman who is unabashedly sexual and drawn to young boys for sex without strings or promises of marriage). That Gehring didn't act on her desires for young boys is a moot point because the cultural ethos of the white British and Canadian school systems depends on a psychic struggle with culturally sanctioned taboos leading to a defensive repudiation of clandestine (i.e., unfamilial and anti-Oedipal) desires. The moral majority and the sexual deviant – Gehring in this case – are begotten and spurred on by the same sexual prohibition (around intergenerational and nonreproductive desire) but have different orientations to the illicit: the moral majority refuses it (on a manifest level), while the "other" – Amy Gehring – acts on it or claims an identity in relation to it.

As Freud argued in the infamous essay "'A Child Is Being Beaten'" (1997, 13), the desire to punish (and to receive punishment) stems not only from "the forbidden genital relation [in the original, nuclear-family forum], but also [from] the regressive substitute for that relation." Those who take voyeuristic pleasure in reading about the ritualistic punishment of the estranged Canadian teacher are "good" not only because they refuse to act on clandestine desires of their own but also because they are morally outraged. The moral majority acting as proponents for normative and age-appropriate heterosexualities is excited by the punishment given to Gehring, and perversely, the punishment stands in as a substitute for the desire on which the moralistic subject cannot act and to which no allegiance can be claimed. Freud argued that the desire for punishment is a displacement enabling the subject symbolically to fulfill an illicit desire by being punished for it. The punishment is a socially sanctioned substitute for a desire on which there can be no action.

Political theorist Wendy Brown (2001, 52) contends that the Freudian analytic of the desire for punishment enables us to understand contemporary political life because there is, in the everyday, a "pleasurable fantasy in which the fantasizing subject or the subject's peers are punished by an enemy – the arbitrary, disciplining, omnipotent adult world. In thus representing at the very heart of desire a broken solidarity with oneself and/or one's compatriots, the fantasy represents a constraint on self-regard, a constraint on alliance, and a constraint on the urge for freedom represented by the pursuit or practice of desire." This broken solidarity with the self and affiliated others is at play in the repetitive fashion in which Gehring is admonished by her professional peers (as illustrated above). Brown (2001, 53) suggests that the wish for punishment to be imposed on oneself or another (professional censure in the Gehring case) might be founded on an identity shaped not only by "jealousy and disappointment [predicated on the withholding of a desired ego ideal] but also [by] persistent, yet thwarted desire."

There is a masochistic desire involved in the moralistic demand that others be punished as stand-ins for the self. Refusing to understand the desire to witness punishment as sadism uncomplicated by masochism, Freud contended that the wish for punishment is an extension of the primary masochistic yearning to satisfy a clandestine desire by submitting to punishment. Punishment can be understood more broadly, in this instance, to include the unspoken pleasure that comes from reading about the social castigation and ritualistic shunning of Gehring as licentious predator in the news press or by the OCT. "Oedipal conflict is managed by substituting punishment for love and is lived in the form of punishment as love" (Brown 2001, 51). Morality is also accomplished through a disavowal of the sexual: "Conscience and morality arose through overcoming, desexualizing, the Oedipus-complex" (Freud 1974, cited in Brown 2001, 45).

In fact, the law is the product of repressed desire (Deleuze 1991). Forgoing instinctual gratification enables the subject to develop a conscience. The strength of the Freudian superego (the moral conscience par excellence) develops on par with the extent to which instinct has been renounced. As Deleuze (1991, 85) summarizes: "The law [acting on behalf of the moral majority] cannot specify its object without self-contradiction, nor can it define itself with reference to a content without removing the repression on which it rests." It is therefore the moral majority who is most upset by the case because its need to be sexually moralistic forces it to contend with what it must disavow.

Desirous Feminists: Pornography, Sadomasochism, and the Pedagogy of the Female Dominant

> A feminism of desire would fit me, I think, like a corset. Instead of wondering why I'm corseted in the first place, and whether others have to wear a corset, or what the corset means, or how I might remove it, I could instead focus on the intensity of sensation afforded by the constraint, becoming increasingly aware of the boundaries of my own body. A feminism of desire would hold me together, prop me up, cinch me in between thick pieces of social fabric, my gross-grain ribbons pulled taut. With it, I could get a better sense of where I begin and end,

> what I am up against and what is beyond my ability to change as a single body in the world. (Lutzenberger 2002, 107)

> Women, in other words, long identified as victims rather than perpetrators of violence, have much to gain from new and different configurations of violence, terror, and fantasy. (Halberstam 2001, 251)

The Gehring story captivated news readers. People were engrossed by the details of Gehring's love life in Canada and of the melodramatic break-up with her long-term boyfriend in Otterville, Ontario; by allegations that she slept with more than fifty men, thereby demonstrating her sexual prowess outside of the marriage bed; by her flirtations with schoolboys; by her clothing; and by her positioning as whore-like temptress of boys and young men in the British school. Gehring's hometown of Otterville was also the subject of speculation and intrigue, sometimes described by reporters as a sedate horse and tobacco–farming community and, at other times, as a hotbed of witchcraft and Satanism.

Gail Rubin (1984, 278) contends that for women, "virtually all erotic behavior is considered bad unless a specific reason to exempt it has been established. The most acceptable excuses are marriage, reproduction, and love. Sometimes ... a long-term intimate relationship may serve." Such reasoning is organized to support what Edelman (2004) calls a reproductive and futuristic agenda. Therefore, it is not surprising that Gehring was compelled to assume an allegiance to a traditional, family-based narrative intelligible to a mainstream heteronormative jury in order to buttress her own defence in court. Gehring told the jury that she was a quiet homebody, swept off her feet by her Canadian boyfriend, whom she expected to marry, and then devastated when he broke her heart by ending their relationship at Christmas. On the verge of tears, Gehring said that her "dream is to be happily married with children of her own. That is all I have ever wanted and all I still want" ("Timeplan" 2002).

Andrew Thompson, Gehring's lawyer, described her as the daughter of a wealthy farmer and doting mother, saying also that she had been brought up with strict moral values. She was not permitted to wear make-up and was subject to a strict curfew until she was fourteen. She was certainly not allowed to mix with the wrong kind of boys and was definitely ill prepared to deal with the sexually assertive boy-students in her Guildford classroom. Gehring was described as a typical "girl next door," an innocent, white farmer's daughter who, through inexperience, found herself a victim of an unfortunate set of circumstances. Thompson insisted that Gehring "was not a pedophile, but an isolated and lonely young woman far from home for the first time who had been naive to befriend her students but who was innocent of the charges against her" ("Ontario teacher" 2002). Heartbroken over the ending of a long-term relationship with George Fulop (who eventually auctioned his version of the failed romance to the highest bidder), Gehring left for England to begin a new life.

Gehring's defence did not just depend on her guilt or innocence but on her capacity to present herself as a normative heterosexual and feminine subject. As queer theorist Steven Seidman (2003, 353) argues, heterosexuality with its futuristic mandates and colonizing impulses is "sustained less by social repression than by normalizing controls." In other words, heterosexuality reigns supreme not by repressing deviant sexualities such as those thought to be had by the prostitute, the homosexual, and the pedophile (although it does do this) but by making it socially, economically, and politically necessary to forge an alliance with normalcy. Writes Seidman, "Ultimately, normalization is a strategy to neutralize the critical aspects of a gay movement by rendering sexual difference a superficial aspect of a self who in every other way reproduces an ideal of a national citizen" (356). The same can be said for the prostitute or for the lascivious white female teacher who overstepped her bounds as professional *in loco parentis;* her difference is said to be superficial because all she *really* wants is a home, a family, kids, and a heterosexual futuristic dream realized. The dream, and our insistence that we aspire to it, reinscribes a normative sexual order and reduces what would otherwise be significant differences between peoples, sexualities, and genders to inconsequential superficialities.

Gehring claimed that she was not a diabolical threat and danger to male youth but a misguided young woman with an investment in heterosexual reproductivity, family, and responsible citizenship like everyone else. She presented herself in court as a traditional farmer's daughter, brokenhearted after a break-up with her long-term boyfriend, but she was repeatedly constructed by reporters as a lascivious femme fatale–like predator with a sexual predilection for young boys. For example, the British tabloids suggested that Gehring's unusual interest and predilection for young boys directly resulted from the loss of her "hunky boy-friend" and that she became sex-crazed. The loss of her former lover "changed her from a shy homebody into a man-hungry seductress as she sought to blot out the pain" ("Miss Filth" 2002).

The Gehring trial was correctly described by one reporter for the *Times,* a London newspaper, as resembling a "cross between a peepshow, a circus, an auction and an invasion" (Morrison 2002). The reporter described the court testimonies as "graphic descriptions of drunken sex in alleyways and on park benches ... [Gehring also confessed to] affixing herself to the group of fourteen and fifteen-year-old boys and girls, hanging out with them at pubs and McDonald's, buying them vodka ice coolers and Malibu rum, running up big cell-phone bills sending text messages and even sleeping at their homes on occasion" (Morrison 2002). The *Times* reporter wrote that the story had everything: "Wild stories of drunken orgies, schoolboys, saucy snaps, velvet handcuffs ... and even that heart-quickening garment without which no British sex scandal is truly complete – a see-through blouse" (Morrison 2002). Another journalist described Gehring and her student entourage as "affluent, attractive and hedonistic. They partied most nights, got riotously drunk and had lots of sex" ("Courtroom" 2002). The sensational coverage reached a peak when "pictures of the drunken supply teacher simulating oral sex on a teen at a party and giving another teen an open-mouthed kiss had been entered into evidence" (Granatstein 2002) at the trial. Gehring also allegedly felt a schoolgirl's breasts and then ran from the room saying this is just "too weird" (Churcher 2002).

After having been cleared of charges laid against her in court, Gehring overturned the good-girl persona that she and her lawyer had orchestrated to win the sympathies of jurors. She consented to an interview with the popular British newspaper the *Sunday Mirror,* and the editors printed a story from her perspective, accompanied by images of erotic domination by a white female in a sadomasochistic fantasy. In one such image, Gehring is seen in a dark evening gown, lounging across a plush sofa. In another shot, she is shown wearing tight-fitting leather gloves, wielding what some reporters described as a whip-like riding crop; some thought it to be a cane, and still others believed it to be a rod. As one columnist for the *Globe and Mail* reported: "The four-page spread includes suggestive photos of Ms. Gehring, including one where she holds a riding crop in her gloved hands. She is wearing low-slung jeans and a midriff-revealing blouse. In another pose, she is reclining on a couch, wearing a tight-fitting satin dress. The caption reads: The Scarlet Woman: Amy Gehring likes to show off her curves" ("Gehring tells" 2002). It was in this spread that she first confessed to having an affair with a sixteen-year-old boy-virgin – which was legal in England at the time of the alleged seduction – and revealed that the schoolboys compared her to Britney Spears and Xena the Warrior Princess. One British reporter described Gehring as a "slit-skirted dominatrix" ("Courtroom drama" 2002). Another British journalist wrote about one of the alleged victims: "He arrived at his biology lesson to find the busty brunette standing at the front of the classroom. [According to the boy, she] was wearing black leather boots, a short skirt and a tight jacket revealing her cleavage" ("Miss Filth" 2002).[3]

Gehring built on and attempted to take command of the image of herself as a white female dominant that had been circulating prior to her own public-relations intervention. Gehring took the media-induced, sensationalized representation of her case (which was not consensual) and managed to alter the conditions of her engagement. She sought to take control of her public persona as sexualized subject, although with varying degrees of success. In her discussion of sadomasochism, Anne McClintock (1995, 147) reminds us that "as a theatre of signs, S/M grants temporary control over social risk. By scripting and controlling the frame of representation, in other words, the control frame [in this case, the newspapers] ... the player stages the delirious loss of control within a situation as extreme control."

Feminist pornographer Marcelle Perks (1996, 66) contends that the "right to consume and create our own pornography is essential if we are to emerge as full sexual beings," and Gehring adopted a similar political tactic to deal with her lewd and predatory sexual persona in the press. She took steps to "protect herself from 'wild' media reports in the U.K." ("Exonerated teacher" 2002) and to take control of her already salacious image in the public eye and to profit from it. Gehring began by hiring a literary agent and reportedly sold her story to the tabloids for £80,000, which ensured that she would receive a monetary gain (along with the publishers that sold newspapers featuring her story without consent or financial compensation) for an image that should belong to her. The *Times* also reported that she is "expected to make 100,000 [pounds] from newspaper deals and more if she decides to sell the rights to a book or film" ("Agent for Gehring" 2002).

Because Gehring used her story for economic gain, people were skeptical of her legal innocence. People doubted that she was innocent of charges launched against her in court because she embraced her sexualized image as soon as her name was cleared. One British journalist felt that Gehring used a "prim and proper image ... [in] court" and then, via her infamous interview with the *Sunday Mirror,* "openly admitted to having had sex with a 16-year-old virgin schoolboy" ("Amy Gehring" 2002), which, for the journalist, raises questions about her credibility. "And nice girls don't pursue things like money or sex unless they have humanitarian or nurturing motives (e.g., supporting a child with money or loving a partner with sex)" (Monet 1997, 219). It has also been argued that white female propriety makes it difficult for the good-girl to negotiate desires – not just economic or sexual – with men (Goodson 1997).

In contemporary Western societies, "older dominatrices are respected for their experience and authority and are in demand for fantasy roles such as mother or headmistress" (Highleyman 1997, 150). Professional female dominants and feminist pornographers regularly report that male clients request school-based scenes involving punishment by an older, female, teacher-like figure (Au Set 2001; Highleyman 1997; Janus 2001; Lady Amber 2001; Langmuir 1996; Mackenzie 1996; Madame Tachibana 2001; Miss Prim 2001; Mistress Adelle 2001; Mistress Antoinette 2001; Mistress Chrystalle

2001; Mistress Eva 2001; Mistress R. 2001; Miss Sara Dale 2001; Mistress Shane 2001; Shamburg 2001; Turner 2001). Spankings and canings are particularly common requests in the contemporary British sex-fantasy context. Jean Grimshaw (1997) suggests that flagellation was the most typical male, heterosexual fantasy in the Victorian era. Tisdale (1994, 138) notes that in England, spanking is a dominant trope in pornographic texts. She also suggests that it is "less a kind of pain than a confrontation with the emotional baggage of childhood" (301) for the English, heterosexual, white adult male.

Gehring embraced the fantastical archetype of the sexually dominant female central to a hegemonic, British, heteronormative, masculine fantasy sequence. Because this archetype is woven into the cultural ethos of the British school, the institution of adolescent, schoolboy, heterosexual fantasy sequences involving white female teachers as dominating forces may be instructively read as indicating a desire to explore binary gender permutations, heterosexual instability, and intergenerational love, loss, and hate in Western school cultures. Sadomasochistic scenes (real or imagined) enable "symbolic re-enactments of the memory of violations to selfhood," and not coincidentally, it is most often the case that "the masochist's fantasies ... are acted out ... in fact it is the 'bottom' who is in control" (McClintock 1995, 148). Much like the masochist, it was the schoolboys in the Gehring case who shaped the representation of the sexualized scene by officiating the allegations of abuse in court and in later interviews with the media. Unlike the scene orchestrated by the professional dominatrix, the media-induced fanfare was not consensual. Because the allegations were proven to be false, Gehring stood in as a psychic marker of something else (castration anxiety, incestuous fantasies involving the mother, intergenerational or homosexual desires, unconscious memories of love, hate, and forbidden attachments in object relations, etc.) for the British schoolboys.

The dominance and submission inherent to the sadomasochistic scene (which may involve the enactment of spanking, caning, discipline, or anything else that may be associated with school culture in the mind of the once-boy, now-adult, male/masculine-identified client) necessarily involves a safe re-enactment of the original scene, image, or idea that provides the raw materials of fantasy. In other words, the boy-students involved in the sadomasochist-like portrayal of the Gehring case no longer have to be held captive either to a troubling power relation such as the one taking shape in the school culture of chastisement and punishment at the level of the psyche or to an illegitimate, Oedipal desire prohibited by the dominant, heterosexual, nuclear-family structure. "As a theatre of conversion, S/M reverses and transforms the social meanings it borrows" (McClintock 1995, 143). It also permutates institutional hierarchies, power relations between gendered subjects, and culturally sanctioned taboos in institutions like the school, the media, and the family. Sadomasochistic scenes exploit existing power relations, but they do so for pleasure as opposed to coercion. The ritualistic scenes test the limits of power, its potency, its ascendancy, its competence, and finally, its ultimate undoing.[4]

The fantasy sequence choreographed by the professional dominant is dissident: it often depends on the rupture of conventional, heterosexual, white, middle-class sexual morality with its insistence on monogamy, reproduction, binary gender positionings (with the masculine subject on top and the feminine subject on bottom), penal penetration, and formulaic erotic sequences in keeping with the missionary position. In fact, the professional dominatrix refuses to have sex with paying customers at all. Like Gehring, she takes command of a heterosexually masculine fantasy sequence that is composed of but not determined by the raw materials of a normative, masculine, heterosexual imagination and does something other than consummate it. She queers the masculine imagination and undermines normative identifications with monogamous, reproductive, and missionary-like heterosexuality.

Childhood Innocence and the Mythology of Female-Teacher Seduction

> Think of all the crazy barriers adults interpose between children and sexual experience: the breaking off of certain conversations when children appear (conspicuous enough to arouse the children's interest in the very things they were not supposed to hear); the whispering behind hands; the meaningful looks; the evasion of children's questions; the manufactured lies; the inconsistency of their alibis; the frantic attempts to hide the genitals from the little ones' eyes; the horrified embarrassment when children ask the meaning of a forbidden word; the panic when they pick up something new; the hysterical "where did you get that from?"; the punishments threatening children who discover dark continents in the mutual exploration of their bodies – all this, for the young boy, has the effect of making a monstrous secret of the opposite sex, of installing the notion of a "mystery woman," which does anything but steer his instinctual desires away from women. (Theweleit 1987, 375)

As Foucault (1978) points out, sexuality has a duplicitous history, as does the thesis of childhood sexual trauma. Reporters for the British and North American newspapers began to question the trauma thesis and the representation of the lascivious white female teacher personified by Amy Gehring as pedophile. As conservative columnist Margaret Wente (2002) of the *Globe and Mail* reported: "Despite the prosecutor's best efforts, the portrait of poor Ms. Gehring as a vicious pedophile began to fall apart when her victims took the stand," and it became clear that the boys tried to initiate the seductions only alleged to have taken place. The credibility of the schoolboys also began to wane as it was revealed that they sold their stories to the press for monetary gain and stood to make more money if they won the lawsuit launched against Gehring. As reported in the *Times,* "payments create a real risk of encouraging witnesses to exaggerate their evidence in court so as to make it more newsworthy, or to withhold relevant evidence from the court in order to give newspapers exclusive coverage later" ("Journalists" 2002). It was also suggested in the British press that if the boys were in fact traumatized by their allegedly sexual encounters with Gehring, it is curious that they so eagerly recounted the graphic details of those supposedly horrendous events for journalists.

Gehring's lawyer pointed out to the court that the "boys didn't appear traumatized when they gave their evidence via a video link from another part of the court house, remembering that they chewed gum and smiled during their testimony" ("Sex tales" 2002), seemingly enjoying the attention. In the *Guardian,* a British newspaper, one columnist referred to the Gehring case as "every boy's fondest fantasy," and the lawyer representing Gehring similarly referred to the allegations as schoolboy fantasies. The *Guardian* columnist proceeded to write that it "doesn't seem possible for a full-grown Englishman to listen to the Tale of Amy without sighing and waxing poetic about Miss Sexy who taught him in lower sixth, and who still comes back to him, all these years later, to perform unspeakable acts in his dreams" (Freely 2002). It was also written that "some reporters doubt teenage boys are capable of intercourse if the idea of it does not excite them," and remarks were made to the effect that "there was little shame attached to a schoolboy seduced by an older woman" ("Young boys" 2002).[5]

Academic Marilyn Ivy (1993, 233) asks the critical question about child abuse: "Has its discursive construction – its appearance and refinement as a category – enabled instances to become visible in ways that weren't possible before?" Might the idea of childhood sexual innocence and a flirtation (consummated or not) with an older female subject be only manifestly about the child and his or her emotional and developmental well-being? Could the anxiety reveal a latent preoccupation with the sexual subjectivity of the white adult female in the teaching (i.e., mothering) role? Underneath the obsessive condemnation of anything remotely connected to the sexuality of the white female teacher and its interest in children and teens lies a more deeply entrenched cultural taboo regarding female sexual agency and erotic (maternal) domination, as exemplified in the Gehring case.

Childhood sexuality has been a matter of public concern since the seventeenth century, and moralists have constructed the child as both innocent (although with a budding heterosexuality that should grow undisturbed, as discussed in the previous chapters)[6] and sexually ravenous and wanton at the same time (Heins 2001). The residual effects of this paradoxical construction become apparent in the Gehring case early in the twenty-first century. The boy-students were dually coded as being in need of protection and as hyperhormonal and lascivious at the same time. For example, in the closing arguments of the Gehring case, the prosecutor maintained that just because sex with a female teacher is often thought to be "every schoolboy's dream," this should not detract from the seriousness of the charges launched against Gehring. In other words, he was saying that teacher sex in the Gehring case, along with the flirtations and professional transgressions associated with it, was serious and unprofessional, even though it involved the raw materials of fantasy for many masculine, heterosexual-identified boys in the British context. The disavowed structure of fantasy is curiously instrumental to the heterosexual matrix. Without repudiated desires and criminalized sexualities, heterosexuality could not reign supreme.

Child protectionists made difficult and troubling arguments that came dangerously close to exposing the contradictions about the naturalized binary gender identifications on which the heterosexual matrix is founded. For example, they insisted that adult women were just like adult men because both could abuse and bring harm to an underage boy- or girl-student. As the argument goes, sexual acts between female teachers and boy-students were harmful, just as harmful as those between male teachers and girl-students. In making this argument, child protectionists seemed to negate the use and operation of gender in the sexual interlude. The masculinity or femininity of the teacher or student did not seem to matter or impact upon their moral assessment. Without gender, allegations of sex and abuse confuse heterosexuality. Many of us don't know how to think about relations of domination and submission without gender. So protectionists were unknowingly setting up an argument that sees and does not see binary, or "naturally" assigned, gender differences. On the one hand, gender doesn't matter (women, like men, can abuse children), and on the other hand, gender does matter (a female stood accused of sexual abuse, and because she was a female there was excessive alarm, moralism, and hysteria associated with the case). The child-protectionist argument, therefore, incited a paradox and an uncomfortable knowledge for those not wanting to think about hybrid gender formations (e.g., female masculinity) or about gender similarities (e.g., female dominance is not unlike male dominance). The gender-role reversal central to the panic was a problem for those involved in the arbitration process. It was also a problem for moralists and champions of normative heterosexuality, the reproductive family, and for advocates of childhood sexual innocence because binary gender differentiation is a tool used in the service of the heterosexual matrix. Adult femininity and masculinity were collapsed into one in ways that were – at least unconsciously – questioned by those who seemed to know intuitively that feminine and masculine positionings were relevant to the genesis of the sex panic and the criminal proceedings surrounding it.

More interesting and upsetting to the alleged boy-victims, however, were the claims made by child psychologists that cast the masculine students into infantilizing roles.[7] Insisting that the boys were children as opposed to teenagers (and preteens) and ultimately that the chronological age differences between Gehring and her students were of relevance, the protectionists refused the boys a legitimate claim to sexual subjectivity. Because reproductive futurity depends on age and generational difference, it is important to guard against the slippages to which intergenerational sex (as described in Chapters 2 and 3) gives way. Intergenerational sex, desire, and pedophilia are taboos because they do not respect generational difference, the most obvious being the boundary demarcating childhood and adulthood. Heteronuclear families depend on these boundaries, which is why grade- and age-based schooling has been set up in Britain, Canada, and the United States. However, the generational templates are troublesome to young boys and girls who wish to grow up and out of childhood. For this reason, age is contentious and troubling to the boys involved in the school sex scandals. The boys do not want to be seen as children but as teenagers or men-in-the-making. The designation "child" denies them sexual agency and a legitimate masculine subjectivity. The schoolboys cannot be children *and* sexually emancipated subjects at the same time. Nor can they be masculine if Gehring is *just like* a man (without having their heterosexual orientations subject to question). Because normative heterosexuality depends on binary gender formations (active masculine subject and passive feminine subject), the boys' legitimate claim to masculinity and to sexual citizenship was undermined by the child advocates allegedly acting in their defence.

Consequently, the boys giggled while child protectionists spoke about harm done to minors. Their sexual bravado (budding heterosexual masculinity) was not to be stunted by their alleged innocence. For the jury, reporters covering the case, news readers, and others who were following the case, the giggles raised doubt and questions about the master narrative of sexual danger and child sexual abuse – that is, about the alleged damage done to the complainants. At an unconscious level, the giggling boys troubled chronological and developmental time sequences employed by education and psychology to understand differences between adulthood and childhood. The Gehring case was queer because no one could really see the boys as victims, nor could they see the lascivious white female teacher as a pedophile. Our dependence on heterosexual time and gender stasis to narrate right and wrong began to show. Normative gender identifications used to consolidate the heterosexual matrix were at risk – not schoolboys. Perhaps what we take to be moral and immoral cannot be easily ascertained, and queer genders, desires, fantasies, and practices in the educational domain highlight these difficulties. The anxieties surrounding the Gehring case were more pressing and visible than the manifest content of the alleged infraction. Given that our moralities depend on fragile, heteronormative configurations of gender, sex, desire, and pleasure in the pedagogical – and larger social – milieu, people worried about how to maintain professional and heterosexual reproductive orders. The students in the case were not children but teenagers (with sexual knowledge and bravado). The white female pedagogue was not maternal, selfless, and innocent.

The professional transgression was not about child sexual abuse (no boy-students were shown to have been harmed) but about the heterosexual Symbolic and its investment in binary gender and generational difference. Heterosexual growth and generational boundaries demarcating child and adult were upset. The time of the school sexual infraction was not the time of the heterosexual matrix. Queer times upset reproductive futurity. As Judith Halberstam (2005, 1) explains: "If we try to think about queerness as an outcome of strange temporalities, imaginative life schedules, and eccentric economic practices, we detach queerness from sexual identity and come closer to understanding Foucault's comment in 'Friendship as a Way of Life.'" In this essay, Foucault (1997) argues that homosexuality threatens heterosexual ways of life and thus must be regarded as a threat to a normative order that can see only certain modes of affiliation, loving, and desiring. Further to this, homosexuality and queer schoolhouse practices upset gender and generational templates on which normative, reproductive, and familial heterosexualities are sketched.

In keeping with what Edelman (2004) understands as heterosexuality's futuristic pedagogy and investment in successive generations, Judith Halberstam (2005, 5) asks whether queer adolescent times and places might eclipse the "time of reproduction." In other words, might we think differently about the future, our kids, and their queer genders and sexual subjectivities if we were not so invested in biological clocks and their reproductive schedules? Might queer time tell different tales about the future and its risks to those whom we see to be children? Halberstam says that "queer time is a term for those specific models of temporality that emerge within postmodernism once one leaves the temporal frames of bourgeoisie reproduction and family, longevity, risk/safety, and inheritance" (6). Queer time, like psychic time, is not only counter to bourgeoisie order, but is also, Halberstam (2005, 11) tells us, a "perpetual present" – one that occupies the space of the perceptual as opposed to the material. To occupy a queer time and place is to forge a domain or counterpublic outside or apart from heterosexual and normative landscapes. The school is a symbolic battleground for the tug-of-war between heterosexual space, time, and temporality and their queer permutations.

Because the school is not a school without children and not a symbolic home without female teachers posing as matronly figures, generational templates and chronological ages are significant. The incest taboo orchestrates these divisions in families. Professional protocols and prohibitions on sexual touching allow the same divisions in schools. A boy-student seduced by an older female teacher, like Amy Gehring, is not really a child any longer. He has been inducted into a hall of adult masculine prowess and fame. The Oedipal taboo – the narrative and mythology through which incest is prohibited in Western cultures – not only respects, but also gives way to, generational differences that would otherwise be elusive and ill-defined. As I argue in the previous chapter, the sex scandals involving white female teachers are queer cautionary tales about the dangers of queer times and places in school cultures. "The remarkable thing about the sex taboo is that it is fully seen in transgression ... The taboo is discovered directly by a furtive and at first partial exploration of the forbidden territory" (Bataille 1957, 107). There is no incest taboo without incestuous desire, and an investigation in court and in popular tabloid journalism of the clandestine desire is what the transgression (real or imagined) in the Gehring case enables. What is remarkable about the Gehring case is that the incestuously coded infraction between female teacher and boy-student is subject to exploration along with the taboo of the white female teacher's sexuality – and its permutations in the erotic pedagogical encounter. Butler (1990b) argues that the incest taboo functions to support the heterosexual matrix and bipolar gender positionalities. The taboo compels the preadolescent child to resolve the Oedipal complex, which, for Freud (1962), is the means through which a normative, adult, heterosexual identification is accomplished. Butler (1990b, 63) contends that "because [gender] identifications substitute for object relations, and identifications are the consequence of loss, gender identification is a kind of melancholia in which the sex of the prohibited object is internalized as a prohibition. This prohibition sanctions and regulates discrete gendered identity and the law of heterosexual desire ... Gender identity appears primarily to be the internalization of a prohibition that proves to be formative of identity." The incest taboo is thus a prerequisite for heterosexuality. The rupture of the incest prohibition (real or imagined) in the Gehring case reveals the extent to which heterosexuality is predicated on a renunciation of taboo (professional or incestuous) desire.

But the rapturous entanglement between Gehring and the schoolboys also brings to light the ambiguous position of the white maternal figure in the accomplishment of heterosexuality and its future. Is the female teacher, strictly speaking, heterosexual when she defies the patriarchal law of the Father demanding the repudiation of intergenerational desire? Is she properly heterosexual when her own sexual orientation is for younger boys as opposed to older adult men eligible for marriage? Is she properly heterosexual when she is unabashedly sexual, wanton, and voracious about her sexual proclivities and uninterested in procreative sexuality? How can she be an advocate for heterosexuality and its future when she is hedonistically interested in teenaged boys and the present? As Halberstam (2005, 4) contends, heterosexual times and places are forged on a denial of the present and its queer excitements: strict bourgeoisie rules "pathologize [and render queer] modes of living that show little or no concern for longevity." As well, the "practices and structures that both oppose and sustain conventional forms of association, belonging, and identification" are threatening to heterosexuality and to "reproductive temporality" because they are not anchored by or interested in a straight and narrow life-course (ibid.).

Freud challenged the idea of childhood sexual innocence in order to expose the inner workings of the Oedipal dynamic and the requirements imposed on the child by Victorian culture, but he was less vocal about the (potentially transgressive) role of the mother in the Oedipal dyad. The Gehring story is jarring to bourgeoisie respectability because it enables the public to consider the capacity of the white female teacher, coded as white maternal figure, to upset the heterosexual matrix with its need for coherent, naturalized gender identifications bifurcated along a stable masculine and feminine grid, by entering into the realm of active – usually presumed to be masculine – desire. "To desire someone younger than oneself, with less access to power than oneself, is certainly not an abnormal desire. It is the predominant construction of masculine desire in the contemporary form of heterosexuality" (Bell 1993, 158), but it is not recognized as such. Masculine desires for subservient and youthful women do not evoke pedophilic panics. Such desires are seen not as perverse or incestuous but as staples of heterosexual romance and its seduction scenes. If gender is an attempt to mediate object-loss (as in the case of the forbidden, same-sex parent through the heterosexual injunction), as Butler (1995) argues, then the accomplishment of schoolboy masculinity (not to mention female-schoolteacher femininity) is under threat when the incest taboo is breached, even symbolically. The female teacher enters into the realm of masculine desire, and the schoolboys are, by implication, feminized by their allegiance to sexual passivity. To the unexamined heterosexual imaginary, nothing is as it seems.

Speaking about the human inclination for polymorphously perverse sexual pleasures, Tisdale (1994, 4) suggests that "to the unschooled body there are no good or bad sexual objects, no right or wrong responses. (Even the schooled body gets confused.) Sexual acts are one of the primary means by which we can act out our inarticulated lives." One has to learn to fear the Oedipal Father in order to domesticate desire. In the case of Guildford, England, something went terribly wrong. The white female teacher refused an allegiance with the asexual mother role (necessitated by the Eurocentric, reproductive heterosexual matrix proper), and the boy-students refused to displace their original desire for the mother onto a socially sanctioned, age-appropriate substitute. The female teacher was no longer a heterosexually feminine, maternal-like figure encapsulated in the persona of state-appointed teacher, and the schoolboys evidently had not resolved their Oedipal complexes in accordance with the demands of bourgeoisie British society, which would enable them to move on to an adult, unequivocally masculine, heterosexual orientation. Schoolboy desire, in the Gehring case, was anti-Oedipal and hazardous to the heterosexual matrix and its reproductivity.

Abject Whiteness and Queer Female Sexualities in School

According to Friday (1993, 1), a "fantasy is a map of desire, mastery, escape, and obscuration; the navigational path we invent to steer ourselves between the reefs and shoals of anxiety, guilt, and inhibition ... [each fantasy sequence] gives us a coherent and consistent picture of the personality – the unconscious – of the person who invented it." Schoolboy erotic fantasies about older white female teachers reveal anxieties associated with the maternal body (coded as lascivious teacher) in British (and North American) school cultures. The schoolboys both desired and feared Gehring because she was associated with the mother, and the incest taboo demands that they expunge her from their conscious fields of desire. The incest taboo produces the desire and the associated cultural demand that she be abjected in the name of normative gender identity development and heterosexuality.

The white feminine subject – be she mother, teacher, guardian, or governess – has been sexualized in the British context and, at the same time, held responsible for maintaining erotic boundaries that prohibit illicit sex in the domestic sphere. Let us not forget that the British school is culturally coded as a familial setting. As Anne McClintock (1995, 48) contends in her discussion of sexuality and colonial conquest, such women have been "tasked with the purification and maintenance of boundaries, they were especially fetishized as dangerous[,] ambiguous and contaminating." This contention is predicated on the argument made by Kristeva (1982) that social subjectivity is organized through the practice of expulsion. The need to abject the mother, which can occur through and results in fetishistic and sadomasochistic desires for authoritarian and dominating women, is crucial for the adolescent white boy who is called on to assume a normative, adult, masculine, heterosexual identification. This might help us to understand why so many men in Britain seek out a female dominatrix to choreograph sexual scenes involving women in positions of power.

The idea of the lascivious white female teacher upsets the culturally inscribed emotional (and sexual) boundary between the boy-student (coded as son) and the female teacher (coded as mother), not only because she is a maternal stand-in but also because she poses an independent threat to the Oedipal complex (as theorized by Freud) and its resolution. Speaking about the role of the Victorian nanny in the family and her alignment with working-class culture, McClintock (1995) argues that the Oedipal complex, for the white British son, is complicated by the presence of the female domestic worker. She also observes that the working woman was a spectacle of gender transgression to the Victorian cultural imagination; she appeared to lack femininity and to embody a masculine side. Consequently, the "boy has to individuate himself from two women, in very different ways. This doubling gives rise to a fragility and uncertainty of identity that is resolved, or at least deferred and managed, primarily by reference to class power" (McClintock 1995, 95) and challenges Freud's refusal to recognize the nanny in his theory of psychosexual development.

I contend that the white female teacher who is precariously positioned along the borders between the private and public is similarly implicated in the adolescent and teenage schoolboy's Oedipal resolutions. The power play is, in the case of the white boy-student and female teacher, mapped not only onto class structures (as in the case of the nanny), but also onto British and North American professional school cultures and onto the heterosexual bifurcations of gender inherent to these cultures. The boy-student overcomes his desire for domination (and possession of the mother) by submitting to a dominating maternal figure (female teacher) and uses the practice of submission to resolve the kaleidoscopically nuanced character of the Oedipal life-drama.

The incestuously coded infraction is scandalous not only because it affords an alternative means to resolve the Oedipal complex, and thereby side-step the heterosexual commandment that we domesticate our desires in the service of a futuristic agenda, but also because it exposes the precariousness of and the complications inherent in the resolution process. Many of us resolve illicit desires in queer ways. We identify with the wrong parent or gender ourselves in ways that are incoherent to the heterosexual mainstream. We desire the wrong object or want more than one object. We care more about the present than the future and refuse to grow up or out of this preference. We prefer our friends to our families and do not always grow to subordinate the latter to the former. Many of us do not respect age differences or generational and developmental prototypes that act as barriers to desire. We love across and between the lines delineating the future, and admittedly, we don't care about or respect the future in the ways that are expected of us. To summarize, queer resolutions to Oedipal life-dramas and to the heterosexual matrix with its reproductive agendas are those that "challenge conventional logics of development, maturity, adulthood, and responsibility" (Halberstam 2005, 13).

But it is not just queers who have peculiar and troubling resolutions. Everyone, regardless of our genders and sexualities, resolves heterosexual dramas and commandments in (allegedly) atypical or sometimes queer ways. Normative heterosexuality and conventional gender assignments are founded on queer repressions and psychic-identification structures that are sometimes queerer than those had by people who identify as gay, lesbian, bisexual, and so on. As well, there are numerous points at which the resolution process may be taken off course, and it is not a given that adult, monogamous, age-appropriate, reproductive heterosexuality will be the outcome. Queer pedagogies of scandal are not about an all-out renunciation of heterosexuality but about an engagement with the desires, practices, and disavowed pleasures that go into normative identification practices. A queer pedagogy of scandal allows us to excavate a queer place and time when our psychic lives were less colonized or beholden to the future: we would in this moment dispense with the future and the heteronormative mandates of the school. A queer pedagogy would be a politic, a pedagogy, and an identification with pleasures that are and have been eclipsed in heterosexuality's time-space continuum. It would not be about acts but about the recognition or remembrance of what got lost in the service of the reproductive future. This pedagogy would trouble what we take to be normal and find pleasure in what has been confined to the epistemological closet. Analyzing the voyeuristic pleasure in the Gehring case exposes the heterosexual matrix and its reproductive agendas for what they are: inventions, Western cultural logics, psychic difficulties, and (sometimes in some moments) queerly defined impossibilities.

5
Erotic Discipline: Eros, Aggression, and Maternal Pedagogies in the Heather Ingram Case

> What is going on in British Columbia? Female teachers and male students have been linked in an astonishing series of stories coming out of the province in past weeks. (Frank 2000)

> A grown man taking advantage of a young girl is one of the most horrendous acts imaginable. When a male member of the species goes bobbing in the kiddie pool, he's a sexual predator and is rightly nailed to the wall ... But when a woman – a firm, buxom blonde woman with a thing for burger flippers – makes sweet, sweet love to a young boy? That's what wet dreams (and billion-dollar entertainment franchises) are made of. (Blasengame 2005, 96)

In March 2000, the *National Post* reported that thirty-year-old Heather Ingram, a teacher at Chatelech Secondary School, had been "charged with sexual exploitation of a teenage boy who was her student" (Moote 2000). After a year of flirtation, Ingram had sex with the rebellious, self-declared bad-boy rapper Dusty Davidson five months short of his eighteenth birthday, making the clandestine interlude illegal because she was in a position of care, trust, and responsibility as his teacher. She was sentenced to house arrest and lost her certificate to teach. Starting in 2000, Davidson and Ingram were in an on-again/off-again live-in relationship for four years. They now have a child, and although at the time of writing they are no longer a couple, they are in an amicable and platonic relationship, and both love and care for their baby. The small-town community of Sechelt, British Columbia, has been scandalized by the transgression. They have, along with the media and the courts, deemed the teacher morally depraved.[1] As a columnist for the *Globe and Mail* wrote: "If she'd had to wear a scarlet A, she couldn't have been more vilified by a society that gushes over the older female 'cougar' who partakes of younger men" (Moreau 2003).

Under section 153 of the Canadian Criminal Code, it is an indictable offence to have sex with a person less than eighteen years of age when one is in a position of trust or authority. The legislation was introduced in 1985, and Heather Ingram was one of the first women to be charged under its jurisdiction. Even though Davidson pursued the relationship and considered Heather Ingram his girlfriend, the vilified teacher was sentenced to ten months of strict house arrest, one hundred hours of community service, and one year of probation. The judge referred to Ingram's actions as an affront to society. This was an unusually severe legal reprimand, harsher than punishments given to male teachers who have committed more serious sexual crimes against female students who did not offer what I call in Chapter 2 *social consent*. But questions linger about age-of-consent laws, about whether Ingram is really a sexual criminal, and about whether the case should have been in court at all. As journalist Sarah Schmidt (2000, 26) queries: "Did Ingram deserve the court proceedings, the criminal record and the humiliation?" Sharon Doyle Driedger (2003), in *Maclean's* magazine, wrote that the "idea that a woman like Ingram could sexually assault a street-smart teen would likely have been dismissed outright a decade ago. Such liaisons rarely got beyond the rumour mill, let alone into the courts."

The case received national and international publicity. For example, CTV reporter Lisa Rossington confirmed on American television that this was a "big story and it was one that we hadn't seen in British Columbia before. The details of the case obviously were very titillating. She's thirty; he's 17" (*Oprah* transcripts, 2004, 2). A feature article entitled "Sleeping with the Teacher" was printed in the popular Canadian *Elm Street* magazine with a close-up photo of Ingram's face displayed on the front cover (Schmidt 2000). *Time* magazine published a story called "Caging Birds of Prey: A Spate of Investigations of Female Teacher-Male Student Liaisons Raises the Question: Is This Abuse?" (Frank 2000). In this essay, Heather Ingram is compared to a host of other offenders who are female teachers, including the infamous Mary Kay Letourneau, discussed in Chapter 2, who had a sexual relationship with a twelve-year-old boy. In 2003, *Maclean's* magazine published an in-depth discussion about the case entitled "The Teacher's Lesson: An Affair with a Student Is Always Taboo – Even if the Teen Claims He's No Victim" (Driedger 2003). Ingram even published her own telltale memoir, *Risking It All: My Student, My Lover, My Story* (2003), which generated a host of book reviews and further public discussion of the case three years after the fact. Ingram and Davidson also appeared on *The Oprah Winfrey Show* in February 2004 to discuss what the teacher referred to as the biggest mistake of her career – not waiting until Davidson was of legal age to consent to sex – and to talk about their four-year relationship, their new baby, their commitment to parenting, and how they intended to solidify their turbulent relationship in the face of public criticism and media scorn.

The Ingram case is scandalous because it reveals an erotic dimension in the pedagogical encounter. The encounter between rule-bound white female teacher (quick to punish and correct) and boy-student renegade is laced with erotic tension, and the press exploited this tension in its coverage of the Ingram case. In fact, one of the most distinctive features of the story had to do with how Ingram was portrayed as a straitlaced, white, good-girl of rural British Columbia gone wrong in comparison to Davidson, who was described as a rebellious teen with a James Dean–like persona. In the *Elm Street* feature article, Ingram is said to be "reserved and academically inclined ... [Davidson is, by contrast,] a pot-smoking rebel" (Schmidt 2000, 24); "as Chatelech's bad boy, Andy [pseudonym for Dusty Davidson used prior to the lifting of the court-ordered ban on his name] ... skipped school, survived suspensions and flunked classes" (28). Reporters described Davidson as a bad-ass student with a dangerous temper. The former teacher didn't drink in high school, smoked pot for the first time under the influence of her student lover, and graduated from the Faculty of Education at the University of British Columbia with honours. Ingram was, by all accounts, a caring and dedicated teacher, "one of the first teachers to arrive in the morning, one of the last to leave at night" (28). She told a reporter that Davidson "teaches me how to have fun, which is not something I learned as a kid" (31).

But this is not a simple case of good-girl meets bad-boy. The media-generated scandal pinpoints an erotic charge in the relations between female teacher and obstinate schoolboy that unnerves and excites the public. As in the teacher sex scandals discussed in previous chapters, the Ingram case upsets binary gender roles and intergenerational taboos that uphold what Judith Butler (1990b) calls the heterosexual matrix. The gender-role reversal in the Ingram case – as in the other sex-scandal cases involving female teachers discussed in this book – ignites panic, and people use the caricature of the white female teacher as dangerous femme fatale–like creature preying on innocent school-aged boys to legitimate the panic. Ingram is also, as indicated above, portrayed as a good-girl, straitlaced teacher. Her dual positioning as sexual predator and as innocent adds sensational flare and intrigue to the story; she is an enigma and more dangerous because the public, the profession, and the courts are not entirely certain what to make of her or how to understand the motivational structure driving her to commit such an outlandish offence against professionalism and societal codes of decency. Much like the white female teacher as femme fatale discussed in Chapter 3, Ingram is a professional paradox, and her dual positioning as innocent and as dangerous leads the public to regard her as a Sphinx-like figure.

What is unique about this sex scandal involving a female teacher is that it makes visible an economy of discipline and power in what many presume to be altruistic maternal pedagogies. In other words, in the Ingram case, maternal pedagogies of love, care, and salvation are seen to be structured by desire and by what Michel Foucault (1977) calls disciplinary power. These power relations are eroticized through the pedagogical transgression, and the disciplinary order of the school – which is based, in part, on heteronormative formations of gender identity – is under threat. This is not to say that Ingram is or was a punishing teacher, that she was looking to have sex with her student, or that she is in any way depraved. I am, however, arguing that "good" teachers – like Ingram – are imposed on to inculcate maternal pedagogies based on an ethic of care, selflessness, and altruism seemingly at odds with power, discipline, and overt displays of heterosexual activity.

The pedagogical seduction in the Ingram case reveals an erotic engagement between a mutinous teenaged rebel and an orderly, scholastically inclined, self-declared "good-girl." The Ingram case portrays the white female teacher's pedagogical investment in student care, salvation, and rescue as sexual and thus self-interested. Ingram is seen as an ascetic and morally pure agent of care who acts as a missionary in the domain of the school. Her life narrative fits into a heteronormative script based on what Lee Edelman (2004) calls reproductive futurity: she marries her college sweetheart and sublimates her energies into the teaching and care of troubled youth. People were shocked to learn that Ingram was unhappy in her socially legitimate marriage and that she would dare to take on a student lover. I argue that the Ingram case is upsetting because it reveals the pedagogical encounter between a white female teacher and a bad-ass male student, racialized through his investment in street culture and rap music, to involve an erotic charge laden with power. The rebellious student who misbehaves to get attention is not looking for academic tutelage but for an anti-Oedipal engagement with a white mother-substitute, and the teacher, as a paragon of virtue, is vulnerable to seduction.

The caring function is not without carnal excess, and as I argue below, there is a disciplinary component to this pedagogical function that gets played out in teacher-student relations. It is, after all, the bad-boy student renegade (not the scholastically inclined "good-boy") who entices and then snares the teacher. The turbulence between the teacher in pursuit of order, discipline, and scholastic success and the pot-smoking rebel uninterested in grades ignites not only a desire for discipline and punishment on the part of the student or teacher, or both – depending on how we look at it – but also an erotic engagement between both parties. It is important to note that this engagement envelops both the student and the teacher. This chapter is concerned with what it is about the bad-boy that so enchants the teacher and why the bad-boy cares so very much about a maternally endowed teacher in charge of discipline. What does this enchantment do to heteronormative school cultures based on an allegiance to what Jan Jagodzinski (2002) calls the family romance in education? Does teacher seduction queer the pedagogical encounter, or is it best characterized as a lapse in good judgment on the part of the teacher – a professional failing?

Using psychoanalysis as a methodology, I analyze the erotic tension in the story and media fanfare about Ingram and her student lover. I argue that it is laced with anxieties about gender, heteronormativity, and reproductive futurity. As I note in Chapter 3, Eros is not quantifiable, and psychoanalytic theories are increasingly used to interpret and understand school cultures and the transferential dynamics central to those cultures. Freudian and Lacanian approaches to psychoanalysis allow us to theorize about the ambivalent and oxymoronic components of the pedagogical incitement to care in teaching. Love and hate, for example, are not mutually exclusive. Together, they constitute a pedagogical impulse that might appear to be an unencumbered expression of maternal care in the pedagogical encounter. Through my use of psychoanalysis, especially Freud's writing on aggression, love, and desire in his now-famous essay "A Child Is Being Beaten," I contend that pedagogies of salvation are enigmatic and conceal teachers' contradictory feelings toward the students subject to their care. Using the Freudian analytic of A Child Is Being Beaten, I will show how the teacher sex scandal is related to the wish for punishment (and the desire to give it); to the romance between female teacher and boy-student masked as pedagogical incitements to care, love, and rescue; and to the will to violate heteronormativity, gender, and generational differences central to reproductive futurity. I argue that the matrixes through which normative genders, desires, and identifications are structured seem to be at risk in the Ingram sex scandal and that these perceived risks are the stuff about which the scandal is made.

Child welfare, professionalism, and popular discourses about ethics are not what they seem. By appealing to the child, to professionalism, and to moralistic discourse, people are able to establish or call for a normative heterosexual order without appearing to do so or having to acknowledge what they are doing. The child – like the Freudian cigar – is never just a child but a stand-in for another more pressing set of worries and anxieties, which I suggest are really about heteronormativity in the Ingram case. Freud wrote about condensation and displacement in *The Interpretation of Dreams* (1900), which are psychic techniques through which an individual – or society – expresses a wish or desire for something without explicitly recognizing the thing wished for or sought out. Through condensation, an appeal to "the child" becomes an open signifier and does not signify a child per se. Appeals to child welfare – in the Ingram case, for example – represent a whole set of concerns about heteronormativity, the future, the status of binary gender, and sexual and generational difference. Displacement is the technique through which we redirect and mask our energies and investments in a given idea, relation, image, or process by pretending that they are about something else. "Freud describes displacement as the operation by which an idea's or desire's intensity is detached from it and attached to other ideas or images that otherwise were of little intensity but are related to the repressed idea by some sort of association" (Oliver and Trigo 2003, xvii). I suggest that the energy attached to child welfare and professional ethics in the Ingram case is displaced. There is no child at risk in the Ingram case. As Davidson and others maintain, he was not harmed by teacher sex and was a developmentally mature *teenager*. In this chapter, I argue that the energy driving appeals to teacher morality, professionalism, and master narratives of child sexual abuse in the Ingram case come from an unacknowledged fear, anxiety, and ambivalence about the inability or ineffectuality of the white female teacher, and of the school more generally, in the reproduction of heteronormativity.

Queer and feminist theorists have used the Freudian analytic of A Child Is Being Beaten to conceptualize gender and its subversion (Brown 2001), shame and guilt in the classroom (Litvak 1995), and sadism and masochism (Deleuze 1998), along with the psychic difficulties associated with compulsory heterosexuality in patriarchal culture more generally. Educational theorists have also begun to apply psychoanalytic theories to the educational context (Britzman 1998, 2003, 2006; Gallop 1995; Jagodzinski 2002; Sykes 2003, 2004). In order to theorize about the teacher sex scandal and the vicissitudes of gender, generational, and sexual differences at stake in the case, I draw on the components of the beating fantasy related to gender, sexuality, masochism, and desire. It should be noted that beating fantasies recounted by psychoanalytic patients in Britain and North America tend to be tied to the culture of the school, so it is essential that the contemporary manifestation of the Freudian analytic of punishment be examined in the educational context. The apparition was so deeply entwined in the life of the school and tied to the headmaster and mistress that Freud's patients "were at first tempted to trace back their beating-phantasies exclusively to these impressions of school life" (Freud 1997, 3). However, it is clear to Freud that the fantasies originated in a much earlier, infantile stage in the development process. Nevertheless, it is frequently the teacher who stands in for the parent (or if we adopt a devoutly Freudian reading, the father), who remains obscure. Teachers often say that an obstinate boy is "just looking for attention." The mantra masks a deeper, more primal, and libidinous desire central to a student's psychic life. School culture is also associated with the trauma of separation (kids leave their parents to attend school) and with rage (for having been left), so it is not surprising that the beating fantasy assumes the stage (or scene) of the school.[2]

Freud argues that gender is partially established through an engagement with beating fantasies, and this is central to the resolution of the Oedipal complex. He also claims that beatings (lived or fantastical) are erotically charged and central to the accomplishment of heterosexuality. I argue that the Ingram scandal provides an instance in which the beating fantasy is transformed into a desire for an alternative to heterosexuality and reproductive futurity and to the normative gender binaries that they sanction. Davidson and Ingram seem to want another resolution to the classic Oedipal tale. They seem to upset the prohibitions on generational and sexual difference in their pursuit of a clandestine and intergenerational affair. Ingram and Davidson do have a toddler and what has been called an on-again/off-again relationship, but as I will argue, the path that their relationship took is structured by ambivalences and hesitancies about normative heterosexuality, gender, and reproductive futurity. This is not to say that Ingram and/or Davidson are uninvested in heterosexuality or normative bifurcations of gender but that their transgressions are viewed as queer and at odds with these normalizing regimes. The pedagogical seduction gets cast by media personnel as abnormal (and thus criminal, immoral, and unprofessional), and then, as soon as the villain (the teacher) is punished and brought into line with conventional feminine morality, professionalism, and other normalizing regimes, heterosexuality recoups itself. The relationship is recoded (after Ingram's criminal sentence) as a wholesome, budding romance based on a normative white heterosexuality that was wrongly subject to persecution by the courts, the teaching profession, and a prying public.

Freud and his psychoanalytic followers theorized the beating fantasy from the perspective of the child, but they didn't theorize the desire on the part of the parent – or teacher as parent-substitute – to punish, love, and desire the child subject to punishment. Because of this oversight, the pre-Oedipal child has been seen to embrace a desire to overthrow the Oedipal laws of the Father, while the Mother – who, according to Freud, is also less committed to patriarchal structures – is not seen to have an orientation toward desire in the administration of discipline. Questions about what the disciplinary (or erotically charged) relationship between the maternally endowed teacher and defiant schoolboy does to the female psyche have not been adequately explored. I contend that the Ingram affair must be understood within a long history of impassioned relations between troublesome boy-pupils and female-teacher disciplinarians about which we have not adequately theorized in terms of the Freudian analytic of punishment.[3]

Erotic Discipline and the Female Teacher in Education

> Ingram doesn't find it that odd that she would end up with Andy [pseudonym]. She always had an affinity for "problem" students who didn't quite fit in. Andy became familiar with the legal system as a juvenile: "assault, nothing super serious," he explains. (Schmidt 2000)

Heather Ingram, like many female teachers portrayed in popular film culture and resurrected in educational history, was excited by bad-boys. The Warner Brothers film *Up the Down Staircase* (1967), based on the novel by Bel Kaufman, offers director Tad Mosel's portrait of a single white female teacher who has an unusual interest in an insurgent boy-student, who eventually threatens her at knife point. In a *New York Times* film review, Bosley Crowther (1967) writes that "the new teacher's heedless interest in one of her more arrogant, sullen pupils ... pays off powerfully and plausibly in a crucial scene wherein the lad, misunderstanding her interest, presumes to make advances to her ... the teacher's being frightened by this encounter [led to her] ... resigning." But did the student *really* misunderstand her interest, and can we be sure that the desire was not reciprocated by the teacher? In the Hollywood remake of the film, *Dangerous Minds* (1996), starring Michelle Pfeiffer, reviewer Lizzie Francke (1996, 37) pays particular attention to the troublesome boy-student named Emilio, describing him as a "dangerously good-looking toughie gang member ... who attempts to put a machismo spell on his teacher." Commenting on the portrayal of teachers in the movies, Dale Bauer (1998, 306) writes that Pfeiffer's character engages in a "drama of erotic desire and discipline." Emilio, as the renegade student outlaw, says to the good-girl teacher dressed in a conservative white blouse and respectable skirt: "the last teacher was too ugly, but I will 'eat' *you*" (original emphasis). "At once, the rather asexual newly divorced teacher finds herself in an eroticized zone, supercharged with violence, disrespect for authority, and moral chaos" (307). She loves Emilio, and her desire for him is no longer disguised as platonic, even as she endeavours to rescue and protect him. This erotic tension is implicit – and central to the plot – but never acted on or acknowledged by the teacher.

In educational historiography, female-teacher disciplinarians are similarly thought to be beguiled and enchanted by the disobedient, older boy. For example, early-twentieth-century sociologist Willard Waller (1932, 144) noticed a unique sexual attraction between the unmarried white female teacher and the troublesome senior boy: "There is the common case of the spinster lady whose affections are attached to one of her larger boys, and who thereupon proceeds to use the machinery of discipline to impress her personality upon him ... Her interest in disciplining this one youngster amounts almost to an obsession ... She confides to a friend that she just can't stand that boy, the while she arranges her life and his so that they spend many hours together in an association that is at once hostile and very personal." Early-twentieth-century psychoanalysts adhering to Freud's investigations into sadism argued that spinster teachers sometimes sexualized aggression in their rituals of male student punishment (Cavanagh 2005a, 2006b). In some instances, the act of administering corporal punishment for the female disciplinarian was thought to be accompanied by a perverse pleasure. The sadistic impulse was believed to exist in the female teacher who "frequently administered ... disciplinary whippings ... [and] ... displayed an odd pleasure in the process" (Basset 1931, 46). Whether these psychoanalytic accounts are sexist or sensational, pathologizing or misogynist, accurate or the troubling projections of analysts lacking sympathy for the independent, lesbian, or unmarried female career-teacher, there is – regardless of our response to what many would quite rightly call disparaging images of female teachers in educational historiography – a recognition that school-based discipline might involve Eros, power, and intemperance on the part of female teachers, not just male teachers.

Contemporary educational theorist Erica McWilliam (1999, 80) concedes that the pleasure to be had by physically disciplining or shaming students in earlier decades is difficult to accept today, and the idea that such acts involved "caring and/or understanding is generally unthinkable for most ethical citizens." It is even less admissible to claim that the teacher experiences erotic gratification in the enactment of a disciplinary regime. Today, techniques of class management call for a disciplinary structure that regulates without appearing to do so; for a "less Sadean, more sanitized, demeanor" (98); and for a pedagogy of salvation (otherwise known as the caring function) dependent on interpersonal growth, student transformation, and ethical self-stylization. Although the techniques have changed, I contend that the excitement accompanying the will to discipline, to take charge, or to impose the self on the student has not disappeared but merely been channelled into the pedagogy of salvation, which, in the Ingram case, is shown to have an erotic charge.

I contend that the shock and moral outrage accompanying the Heather Ingram scandal in the present day is a reaction to the modern incarnation of the impassioned pedagogical encounter. As Foucault (1977) teaches us, discipline in modern, Western, advanced capitalist societies is no longer so much about punishment as about pastoral care, professional guidance, and loving intervention. It is not that Ingram wants to physically discipline or punish Davidson – or any other student, for that matter – but that pedagogies of love (which sometimes slip into the terrain of the erotic) are techniques of power involving intervention and concern about students' ethical and educational development. A teacher's love and care are no more platonic than they are innocent and unencumbered by structures of discipline that characterize other institutions and relationships in modern-day, Western societies. In light of Foucault's analysis of what he calls disciplinary power (1977) and pastoral guidance (1978), it is more difficult to see white female teachers' dreams of rescue and salvation as unencumbered by power and Eros. As I argue in earlier chapters, there is aggressivity in the pedagogical caring function that warrants analysis.

While I don't believe that Ingram has in any way harmed her teenage student lover, her erotic investment in him – as demonstrated and consummated through her transgression – reveals the caring function on the part of all teachers to be less than innocent and benign. This doesn't mean that teachers ultimately want to seduce or beat their students. It does, however, mean that our investments in students are not exclusively altruistic and magnanimous but egocentric and sometimes intemperate. I am in agreement with Jagodzinski (2002), who argues that teachers can and should displace erotic feelings onto the subject matter or onto the art of teaching itself. Eros can be well used and harnessed in the pedagogical encounter; many teachers are skilled at sublimation in precisely these ways. My argument is that the reigning discourses of maternal love, care, and salvation in the teaching profession do not acknowledge desire, egocentricity, and narcissism on the part of the female teacher. These discourses mask power and desire on the part of the pedagogue, thereby enabling teachers to use students in their own personal dramas while claiming allegiance to the pupil. Appeals to student care are perversely employed by the teacher to enact fantasy formations that are not always pedagogically sound and/or "good" for the student. The Ingram case prompts the profession to grapple with the erotic, the intemperate, and the narcissism that informs child-centred pedagogies, maternal love and care, and desires for salvation in modern-day pedagogies.

The Ingram sex scandal should not be read as a model or recipe for "how to reach" troubled students. I am certainly in agreement with those who view her transgression as unprofessional. The scandal does, however, queer pedagogies of care, love, and salvation employed by white female schoolteachers who disavow and refuse to lay claim to egocentric investments in students. Postcolonial scholars and First Nations people in North America, for example, have long observed the aggressivity and colonizing function of the missionary or philanthropic encounter between white, moralistic Christian teacher do-gooders and previously colonized and indigenous peoples now working toward independence and sovereignty (Stoler 1997, 2000). Less work has been done to trouble the normalizing and disciplinary function of pedagogies of care by queer and critical pedagogues. I contend that the Ingram scandal performs a queer pedagogical function: it outs the egoistic and sanctimonious content of the claim to care. By insisting on an ascetic and sanitized version of care, white female teachers and others who have been charged with the management of children – their educational development, growth, and future reproductivities as heterosexual citizens – have performed not only a civilizing, but also a heterosexually specific, function. Agents of care domesticate gender and sexuality in the name of heterosexuality and white reproductive futurity. Without an appeal to care, teachers cannot guide children toward a salvation marked by heteronormativity, reproductive citizenship, and futurity. Without care, a pedagogue could legitimately focus only on scholastics. To be clear, I am not suggesting that teachers *should* confine their time and attention to official curriculums and subject-matter. However, I am suggesting that there is ethical work being done in the name of care that sometimes operates to instil heteronormative values and conventional gender identifications to which teachers must hold themselves accountable. In other moments, the ethical work or pedagogy of care is about undoing those very same structures of desire and heteronormative identifications within which we find ourselves centred. This is not just a hidden curriculum: the pedagogy of care is about an irrational and sometimes ambivalent position in which the white female teacher finds herself and that she may sometimes wish to reverse, subvert, or disavow. By acknowledging that there is more at stake in pedagogies of care than the welfare of the student, we are able to consider how the teacher negotiates heteronormative power relations and psychic investments in a reproductive future. It would be a mistake to read pedagogies of care as being exclusively about the student. Pedagogies of care are very much about teachers and how they are positioned and elected to act in the service of the reproductive future, heteronomativity with its investment in binary and intelligible gender identifications, sexual citizenship, and heterosexual time. The teacher's will to punish, seduce, or care for students must not be seen as selfless. It would be a mistake to say that teachers' commitments to students are exclusively about educational priorities, democratic citizenship, or even professionalism. Of course, they are invested in these things, but this investment is never the end of the story.

Through an exposé of the Ingram affair, I wish to highlight what I take to be queer and less than professionally devout in pedagogies of love, salvation, and maternal care. The Ingram case must be situated in the rescue and punishment fantasies central to the culture of education because it provides an example of erotic discipline taken to extremes. This is not to say that Ingram wished to discipline and punish Davidson. I see both love and hate as structured by a use and investment in its object. Nor do I wish to cast Ingram and Davidson in a moralizing and pathologizing light. I am most concerned with how the case incites public and professional anxieties that are not really about the clandestine lovers. I wonder why the courts, the public, and the teaching profession are compelled to criminalize Ingram for what is best characterized as a professional infraction. I mean to read the Ingram case as a narrative, a story, and a cautionary tale. My reading is not intended to produce a truth about Ingram and Davidson but to tell us – as teachers – something about how maternal pedagogies of care might compel us toward the allure of the bad-boy. For teachers who have ethical self-stylizations based on images of saints, missionaries, self-abnegation, and altruistic motivational structures, there is much to be learned through a psychoanalytic reading of the Ingram sex panic.

I contend that pedagogies of care manifest themselves differently in different historical epochs, in different teachers and cultural contexts. In the early to mid-twentieth century, a female teacher sentenced bad-boys to detentions and corporal punishments and sat him near her desk so that she could keep a watchful eye on him. Today, there is room to befriend (or seduce) a student through enactments of maternal pedagogies based on love, care, intervention, and physical proximity. Ethical and intemperate engagements based on discipline in earlier times are now supplanted by the caring function. Pedagogies of care are able to mask desires that are less than prudent and innocent. They also mask desires that defy heteronormativity and reproductive futurity. Pedagogical masks conceal a mixed bag of queer and heteronormative identities and identifications, desires and objects worthy of analysis and individual self-reflexivity. I am not arguing that all maternal pedagogues wish to have sex with students or that nothing good can come of ethics of care. Rather, I am suggesting that teachers – like everyone else – are not altruistic beings and that there is an erotic and aggressive dimension to all interpersonal encounters. The Ingram case reveals an unacknowledged desire in the pedagogy of salvation that is, as educational theorist and historian Carolyn Steedman (1985) argued more than twenty years ago, the primary structure of maternal thought through which white women learned to identify as teachers.

The Heather Ingram Story

In *Risking It All: My Student, My Lover, My Story* (2003), Ingram writes: "When teachers talk about the need for alternative education, they are talking about students like Troy [pseudonym for Davidson] ... he does not recognize formal authority except as an inconvenience or obstacle" (49). In a tender moment captured by Ingram in her book, Davidson reveals his rage at his father for having abandoned his mother when he was six months old. The teacher gives voice to her desire to rescue Davidson from his pain, and this desire is not unencumbered by carnal desire: "I don't know if I can help, but I do know that he will do school work for me as for no other teacher. Maybe I can use this flirtation to give him something of value – or at least someone to talk to. And yet my intentions are not pure. I feel myself falling into the seductive illusion of being needed, of being important enough to make a difference in someone's life" (56). Not unlike the seduction attempts portrayed in *Up the Down Staircase* and *Dangerous Minds,* Ingram recounts the moment that Davidson crossed the line between innocent flirtation and intent to seduce: "Troy raises his fingers to his lips and blows a kiss through the glass from the other [class] room. It hits me like a real kiss. He has never been this overt, this directly sexual with me before. All of a sudden I feel scared. I have let this go too far: my job could be in danger. At the same time I feel a shot of happiness – like I imagine heroin would feel – that I know will last for the rest of the day ... I feel joyful, as if he is a regular guy who likes me, and I am a regular girl who is hoping to get asked out" (47). Not long after, Ingram allowed herself to be seduced by the student whom she longed to save. Experiencing difficulty keeping the affair secret, Ingram confided in a colleague, who threatened to report the affair. Consequently, Ingram resigned and later learned that criminal charges would be filed against her (she was unaware that the affair was illegal under the Canadian Criminal Code because this was a relatively new change to the law governing teachers and other social-service workers). The persecuted teacher was shocked: "A criminal? How could that word apply to me? In high school, I would have been voted most likely to succeed, not most likely to get a criminal record" (144). Even though Ingram said that she would resign, the superintendent, Clifford Smith, suspended her from teaching and wrote that she was "considered a danger to all of my students ... and notes that the district and the police are launching separate investigations" (145).

When the story broke, reporters condemned Ingram for her actions. As a result, she was publicly humiliated. She describes her first encounter with the media as the moment in which she saw her school yearbook photo superimposed onto a much larger image of her hometown community with the "words in inch-high block letters, 'Student Sex Scandal'" (Ingram 2003, 149-50) on the cover page of the *Vancouver Province* newspaper. Noting that her case generated more publicity than other cases involving male teachers and female students, Ingram felt keenly the injustice of the sexist and sensational press. The now-infamous teacher was called a sexual predator, a child molester, and an affront to community morals. "The moral outrage is strong; it comes through in letters from parents, raging against me. A mother of a sixteen-year-old boy rants, 'I know karate and I'm not afraid to use it'" (152-53). The female judge similarly called Ingram an "affront to society" (173) in court and issued her an unusually harsh sentence when compared to male teacher sexual offenders.

The teacher was mesmerized (and later enraged) by the banality and the extraordinary aspects of her case. Knowing that she had put her career in jeopardy by having sex with a student, Ingram (2003, 69) recalls

> rumors of male teachers who slept with young students when I was in high school. I think about my seminar at UBC, where the guest speaker asked us who knew of a student-teacher affair when they were at high school and almost every hand immediately went up. I am thinking about what Robin, my sponsor teacher during my practicum, said about the BC College of Teachers newsletter: that the only thing worth reading was who got fired for having sex with a student. I think about my high school art

> teacher, whom I loved and who loved me in ways that may or may not have been appropriate.

Educational culture is chock full of teacher-student affairs, but Ingram's seduction is unique because she is a *woman* in a position of trust. She has "gone from hiding [the affair] to national fame in a two-week period" (155-56). Media personnel are similarly focused on what they see to be a double standard. But the double standard is read as operating in favor of the female (as opposed to the male) teacher. For example, Oprah Winfrey said, "I swear to you that if this were a guy, a male teacher, and a female student, you all would ... not be laughing about it" (*Oprah* transcripts, 2004, 8). Sara Schmidt (2000, 26) of *Elm Street* magazine wrote that it is "easy to condemn a more typical case of sexual exploitation involving a middle-aged male teacher who seduces a starry-eyed teenage girl. He usually showers her with attention before he deflowers her, with no pretence of love."

But Ingram was in love, and so was the student. As Davidson describes it, he "felt a really strong attraction for her and it just escalated from there to a – a lust at first and then into a love – [a] loving relationship for sure" (*Oprah* transcripts 2004, 7). Even Davidson's mother approved of their intimate relationship. Donna Davidson told the court that she "welcomes Ingram into her family as 'my adult son's choice of partner in their consensual relationship'" ("Teacher guilty" 2000). Claiming that her son is independent and strong-willed, the mother denied that Davidson was a victim or subject to coercion by the teacher. In a mock re-enactment of the court case, an editorial pokes fun at the judge for punishing Ingram as a sexual criminal: "Your Honour ... the paper says you may send my client to jail. I beg of you not to do that. For what she stands charged and now convicted of, by pleading guilty, is really being in love with the wrong person, at the wrong place, at the wrong time. She is not convicted of taking advantage of anyone let alone any sort of sexual aggression" (CKNW editorial 2000). Unlike cases in which a teacher's sexual advances are unwelcome and the student sees him- or herself to be a victim, the Ingram case is based on social consent and thus in need of an alternative explanatory paradigm. The lawyer representing the accused teacher told the court that this was the "only case he has seen in which the victim refused to give a victim impact statement to the police" (Ingram 2003, 173).[4]

The Freudian Theory of A Child Is Being Beaten

> Oedipal conflict is managed by substituting punishment for love and is lived in the form of punishment *as* love. (Brown 2001, 51, original emphasis)

> What if such a fantasy is not at all a muted scene of punishment/love of the girl by her father, but is rather an angry retort by the humiliated feminine psyche to the privileged place of the male, whether brother, father, or ... schoolmates or teachers? If such a reading of this "sex change" is viable, might the scene produce a certain release from the relatively closed economy of guilt and punishment that Freud schematizes? (Brown 2001, 60-61)

To understand the legal and moral uproar surrounding the Ingram transgression, I suggest that we turn to Freud's analytic of A Child Is Being Beaten. Ingram is a danger because she exposes the underside of the beating fantasy had by the bad-boy student rebel and the maternally invested teacher. Of course, beating fantasies should not be used to justify childhood sexual abuse or to argue that a given teenager (or anyone else for that matter) wishes to be abused or subject to corporal punishment. As fantasies, they allow us to negotiate relationships with those in positions of power over us. Freud argued that punishments stand in for forbidden love. I suggest that this love is not only about a given object – parent or teacher – but also about an identificatory relation to heteronormativity with its investment in gender binaries, intergenerational taboos, and reproductive imperatives. Anna Freud (who was Freud's daughter/patient and the subject through whom he developed his insights about childhood beating fantasies) claimed that punishment fantasies were substitutes for incestuous longing. The "desire to be punished is distributed onto others such that it does not appear as one's own desire but rather as the inevitable fate of the punished ... [the] love of the object itself is almost completely disguised as the object is rendered mercilessly punitive" (Brown 2001, 59-60). The beating fantasy is a psychic defence used to negotiate having a desire that one is not permitted to avow or act upon in the heteronormative family unit. By making the aggressor mercenary, the subject is able to have what cannot be overtly acknowledged because it is imposed on him: my father (or mother) beats me because he (or she) loves me. The incestuous longing is displaced onto a corporal punishment. Some who repudiate homoerotic desire, for example, insist that gay men are out to recruit them. The homoerotic desire is in the fantasy sequence about the aggressor, not in the subject, and is thus a safe re-enactment of a taboo desire or identification. Psychoanalytically inclined queer theorists like Judith Butler (1995) have argued that incest and homosexuality are the taboos on which heterosexuality is founded. Therefore, it is not surprising that beating fantasies, as observed by Sigmund and Anna Freud, are used to negotiate and grapple with incestuous desire. A spanking stands in for the sexual love of a parent. The prohibited love object (usually a same-sex parent) is retained in the unconscious of the child through a beating-fantasy formation. My father beats my bottom in a show of love, and this beating is initiated by him, not me. This is a psychic strategy used to grapple with having desires inhospitable to heteronormativity and reproductive futurity. If the child continues to love his mother, he will not seek out an age-appropriate partner for marriage and paternity. Similarly, the girl-child must forgo her love for her mother and a masculine identification with the father in the service of a heteronormative reproductive future. Non-normative gender identifications, homosexuality, and incestuous desires must be disavowed in the service of normative heterosexuality (Butler 1995). The punishment in the beating fantasy stands in for the love that the child cannot have or forge an identification with. The beating fantasy is not *"only the punishment for the forbidden genital relation, but also the regressive substitute for that relation"* (Freud 1997, 13). In other words, the punishment stands in for a forbidden wish or prohibited object.

In lay terms, the wish (or fantasy) for punishment stands in for a forbidden desire intolerable to the psyche. Heteronormativity and reproductive futurity instil very particular taboos around queer gender identifications and sexualities. Such taboos are repressive and injurious not only to those who identify as gay, lesbian, bisexual, transgender, and so on, but also to the heterosexual or conventionally gendered subject. In other words, the moral majority, the professional, the child advocate, the concerned parent, and so on, all manage disavowed (often queer) desires inhospitable to heteronormativity. The beating fantasy – as it is narrated through the Ingram sex scandal – allows the moral majority to have a prohibited love object, relation, or non-normative idea by identifying with Davidson (the student at risk): *My teacher (maternal stand-in) desires me and I am not compelled to relinquish her love in the service of normative masculinity. I protest her seduction but she forces it upon me; I thus have what I must forgo in the theatre of the real.*

Here, the analytic of punishment is used to argue that the scandal accompanying the Ingram transgression is only manifestly about a teenaged boy being beaten or victimized by his teacher as understood through dominant discourses about childhood sexual abuse. Child advocates, developmental psychologists, and the like insist that Davidson has been harmed and reject the idea that the student really did desire and, in this case, want to have sex with the maternally endowed teacher. The beating fantasy in the Ingram case is not only utilized by an individual teenaged boy. The fantasy structure is used by a moralistic society and professional body at large to guard against difficult knowledge about Eros and queer desires in the pedagogical encounter. The professional beating fantasy goes like this: *The boy is hurt by the teacher. This is sexual abuse, and he had no agency because he is a child (we agree to forget that he is almost eighteen years of age). The boy is innocent. Ingram is a dangerous pedophile. Our pedagogies of maternal love, care, and salvation are not erotic or aggressive but altruistic. Ingram is the criminal, our pedagogies of love and professionalism are above reproach.* The fantasy structure employed by the teaching profession, the courts, and the public at large secures the mythology of childhood sexual innocence and the fantasy of white female teachers' altruism in the pedagogical encounter. Good teachers – those who do not have sex with their students – need not acknowledge the underside of the beating fantasy or the libidinous impulses driving their impulse to care. *There is no sex or aggression in our maternal pedagogies, so it must reside exclusively with the teacher accused of child sexual abuse.* The queer composition of the societal fantasy remains underground and confined to the public and professional unconscious.

Clinically oriented psychoanalysis might pose questions of individual students with self-declared bad-boy reputations such as: What does the ungovernable student want from a maternal pedagogue? What precisely is being asked for and elicited when one breaks the rules, pursues the teacher, and quits school? In what ways are normative gender templates and heterosexual timelines interrupted? Is the bad-boy rapper macho and heterosexual or negotiating a feminine instinctual composition with homoerotic desires undeclared? According to Butler (1995), we all negotiate a range of gender and sexual identifications based on melancholic loss, Oedipal life-narratives and taboos, and normative social protocols. Of course, there are no absolute or transparent answers to these questions and individual analysis is best left to the clinical setting. More helpful and relevant to the project at hand is a socially oriented psychoanalytic theory focusing on a societal and professional fantasy-formation insistent upon a child being beaten. The insistent reading of Davidson as a child being beaten is not only unwarranted but queerly perverse. I suggest that there is something disavowed through an obsessive insistence upon a child being beaten in the Ingram case that must be brought to professional consciousness. Through my analysis of the societal-based insistence on childhood sexual abuse, I argue that the public fantasy formation reveals societal misgivings, equivocations, and troubles with heteronormativity and with what gets to constitute gender normativity.

The character of the mutinous bad-boy rebel is shaped by contradictions, disavowals, and ambivalences in the fantasy-formation choreographed by a concerned public and professional body. Moralists, child protectionists, guidance counsellors, reporters, school administrators, lawyers, and others who want to make Davidson into a child at risk turn a blind eye to his defiance, his difficulties with authority, his chronological age, and sexual bravado. This posturing renders attempts to see him as a sexually innocent child preposterous even as they are given legitimacy in court. Davidson is not really a child at risk, and the scandal is spurred on by a public and profession struggling to deal with this knowledge. He is a matter of concern because he seems to have survived teacher seduction unscathed and flaunts the taboos on which heterosexual time, reproductive futurity, binary gender roles, and identifications with innocence are forged. Davidson is a character who does not remain true to childhood developmental sequences, as imagined by child protectionists, or to professional education's morality plays.

It is important to note that Freud's curiosity about childhood beating fantasies was mainly about gender. In the modern-day societal fantasy involving Ingram and Davidson, I contend that the matrixes through which heteronormativity constitutes itself – gender being one such matrix – are at stake in the public and professional imaginary. In his analysis of beating fantasies, Freud sought to clearly establish the gender of the parent doing the beating. As Ethel Spector Person (1997, xix) writes in her introduction to an edited collection of the Freudian theory of A Child Is Being Beaten, "Freud would have said that on an unconscious level the figure of the father lurked behind that of the mother." More contemporary psychoanalytic theorists suggest that the "wish to be beaten by the father is not the only and probably not the major determinant of this paradigmatic fantasy" (Modell 1997, 73); it can take many and distinct forms both in the individual and in the social. I contend that the question about which parent is doing the beating (mom or dad) is less critical than the fact that the gender of the parent administering the beating is indecipherable. Even if – as Freud says – the father may be the main actor in the beating fantasy, the psychic anxiety surrounding the fantasy (as it is expressed in the Ingram case) has to do with the interchangeability of the gender of the adult giving the punishment. In the fantasy scenario, the disciplinarian can be mother or father, and frequently, the gender assigned to the one administering the spanking is either reversible or indeterminate.

The child receiving the punishment is similarly ambiguous. As Freud (1997, 8-9) observes: "The child being beaten is never the one producing the phantasy, but is invariably another child, most often a brother or a sister if there is any. Since this other child may be a boy or a girl, there is no constant relation between the sex of the child producing the phantasy and that of the child being beaten." Because the child oscillates between being beaten and observing the punishment (and because the gender of the one being punished is interchangeable), he or she can imagine him/herself to be a boy- or girl-child being beaten. In the beating scenario, "Freud views girls as wanting to be boys and the boys as wanting to be girls" (Shengold 1997, 89). Therefore, it is reasonable to speculate that the beating fantasy is, to a large degree, about a desire to cross gender and intergenerational borders that act as barriers to love. The beating fantasy (dominance and submission in sadomasochistic play by contemporary standards) is, in essence, a denial of or will to refuse socially sanctioned gender assignments – necessary underpinnings to normative heterosexuality – and generational difference, the latter of which is the claim on which the incest taboo is predicated in Western cultures. Perversely, the beating fantasy represents a transgressive desire *and* a means to manage the desire. As Freud (1997, 199) contends in regard to the homosexual wish: "The boy evades his homosexuality by repressing and remodeling his unconscious phantasy: and the remarkable thing about his later conscious phantasy is that it has for its content a feminine attitude without a homosexual object-choice."

To apply the theory to the case at hand, it is important to examine the role of Davidson's machismo, his bravado, and his insistence that he is not a victim (a child being beaten) but an initiator of the real-life seduction in the media and professional fanfare. Not only did Davidson not see himself as a victim, but he boasted about his powers of seduction and sought to wield his notoriety for profit. Frustrated by the publication ban on his name, Davidson successfully appealed to the courts to end the censorship that prevented him from being identified as the student involved in the sex scandal. He then told reporters about his gangsta rap CD entitled *Teacher Scandal,* in which he sings: "Sunshine Coast / Teacher scandal / Nothing in the world I can't handle" (Driedger 2003). Davidson also boasted about his teacher seduction to reporters interested in his side of the story. As reported by Rod Mickleburgh (2003) of the *Globe and Mail:* "Mr. Davidson is clearly enjoying his 15 minutes of fame. He poses willing for television cameras and struts cockily through the streets of Sechelt ... He is not shy about his success with Ms. Ingram." Mickleburgh also notes that the student outlaw described teacher seduction as the ultimate challenge. By all accounts, the affair worked to boost his self-esteem and public persona as Sechelt's bad-boy rapper.

Not only did Davidson outwardly manage what Freudian analysts would call a feminine instinctual composition associated with the masochistic desire to be punished, latent homosexuality, and the age difference that justifies protection from the courts, but he also reaffirmed his identification with heterosexuality and masculine bravado. Davidson insisted that he was neither a child nor a child being beaten, as moralists, lawyers, child advocates, and teacher professionals wished him to be. He assumed a hypermasculine identification, matched by sexual sophistication and experience with women. But Freud (1997, 200-1) argued that we should not see gender identity and the identifications on which it is based as straightforward or unambiguous: "The dominant sex of the person, that which is the more strongly developed, has repressed the mental representation of the subordinated sex into the unconscious." The point of the Freudian analysis is not to speculate about Davidson's gender and sexual identifications so much as it is to better understand *societal* and *professional* worries and fascinations with male teenage gender and sexuality. Davidson's hypermasculine and heterosexual persona were harnessed in articulations of the sex scandal in the media, and so I am interested in how they functioned in the professional and public fantasy formation. I want to pinpoint how our interest and upset as well as our denials and blind spots about Davidson's gender and sexuality – whatever they may be – reflect ambiguities and contingencies that we all face, and continue to face, in navigating gender and sexual subjectivities. This is not to say that Davidson is or is not *really* a heterosexual (or homosexual) or a gender-normative subject but that he refuses the developmental sequences and timelines that school guidance counsellors, child psychologists, and other professionals utilize to measure developmental templates and reproductive futures. Davidson did not grow up straight. He entered into the terrain of queer time when he seduced his teacher. Davidson's outwardly expressed hypermasculinity and sexual bravado are an outcome of a queer developmental route that is neither sanctioned nor advised by experts giving testimony in court. Davidson has become a heterosexual and reproductive citizen but not in a conventional or normative way.

It is important to notice how our appeal to protectionism, along with our willful ignorance about his life, enables us to use Davidson as a pawn in the reproductive and heteronormative future. For example, to protect Davidson from Ingram, to refuse to lift the court-enforced ban on his name, and to lay charges against his "girlfriend" for sexual exploitation is to endanger or, at the very least, upset the repressed sexual character on which his masculine heterosexuality is based. To seduce (or to be punished by) the teacher is to say that she loves only me. She stands in for either the mother or father yet, at the same time, is not the mother or father. In other words, an incestuous longing is fulfilled through the fantasy sequence (or in this case, through the student-teacher affair), but the incest taboo proper is ruptured because Davidson refuses to be identified as an innocent child. Paradoxically, the insistence on childhood sexual innocence and the ignorant refusal to recognize his relationship as valid, chosen, and real upsets his entry into masculinity along with the heterosexuality on which the entry depends. The social fantasy – Davidson is being beaten – is ambivalent and enigmatic. The fantasy goes like this: *Davidson is a child, and he must be protected so that he can become a normative, reproductive citizen. Davidson isn't a hypermasculine and heterosexual subject because he is a child, and children are innocent (without sexual subjectivity, desire, and agency).* Thus Davidson is to be and not to be a child.

Time plays a queer trick. Davidson is to become what he claims to be already. The courts, school administrators, developmental psychologists, and concerned parents cannot see him for what he says he is – sexually sophisticated, macho, and adult-like – because for them he has yet to become these things. Teenage sexuality, like childhood sexuality, is queerly out of place and time in the adult, heterosexual imaginary. As Davidson's case illustrates, even when the subject is heterosexual and properly masculine, the developmental interruption is condensed into a problem of queer, or otherwise non-normative, identificatory relations. Ingram cannot be anything but culpable, and Davidson cannot be anything other than an innocent child (victim) in the heteronormative and professional fantasy formation. But the social and professional fantasy is in trouble because the teenaged boy-student renegade escapes a childlike (or masochistic) designation in the press through his self-presentation as a street-wise, irreverent bad-boy. Davidson also reaffirms his masculine dominance despite his alleged wish for sex with an older, more mature woman in a position of power. *He* seduced *her;* he did not ask to be punished.

The great irony in the case is that Davidson upsets the master narrative of childhood sexual innocence and in so doing renders the pedagogical encounter between maternally endowed teacher and boy-student (coded as son) sexual – and symbolically incestuous. At the same time, he staunchly affirms his heterosexuality even as his developmental sequence follows a queer or non-normative timeline. Because his father left his mother, he is read as never a child but a man. Davidson's insistence on his maturity (and eventually the public's willingness to read him as an adult) coincides with the constitution of Ingram as childlike, feminine, immature, and so on. Ingram is said to lack self-esteem, to have emotional problems, and to be in need of psychiatric guidance and support after the court verdict. As in the aforementioned female-teacher sex scandals, in the first instance, the female pedagogue is depicted as a dangerous predator – aligned either with a dangerous masculinity or with a ravenous, female, sexual or racialized subjectivity. In the second instance, she is realigned with a passive configuration of white femininity. As people learned about Ingram's criminal sentence and (real-life) punishment, they began to see her as feminine, emotionally unstable, and in need of sympathy. Reporters began to construct Ingram as a passive victim of low self-esteem and feminine frailty. The guilt-ridden teacher writes: "I believe it was low self-esteem that enabled me to cross the teacher-student line and betray my professional responsibility as I did" (Ingram 2003, 224). As a journalist for the *Globe and Mail* wrote: "It's difficult to read *Risking It All: My Student, My Lover, My Story* and realize that Ingram was not so much a predator as a paper-thin deck of cards waiting to collapse, and that she, unfortunately, did so in the arms of a boy cleverly disguised as a 6'3 Adonis" (Moreau 2003). Sharon Doyle Driedger (2003), in *Maclean's* magazine, contends that "psychological profiles of female teachers who indulge in sexual misconduct with students show they're typically socially immature rather than sexually deviant." In her book, Ingram (2003, 33) tells us that Davidson was the "kind of guy I would have swooned over in high school but who would never have given me a second look."

That the boy-student (Davidson) assumes an active, predatory orientation in the clandestine relationship, while the female teacher (Ingram) assumes a passive and immature role, suggests an important reversal in the beating fantasies observed by Freud in his patients. It is no longer Ingram who is thought to have administered the beating, but the courts or, perhaps, Davidson who allegedly choreographed the teacher seduction. Much like Freud's patients, the one administering the beating transmogrifies into someone else. This metamorphosis is not only essential to understand the duplicitous relationship between the masochist and the sadist at the level of fantasy, but the reversibility of gender in the domain of fantasy. Once again, I am not speaking about actual sexual abuse or physical assault, but about the mechanism through which the individual and the larger, societal fantasy formation may be invested in gender reversibility. For example, Giovannetti argued in relation to the Freudian analytic of A Child Is Being Beaten that it is, ultimately, gender that is at stake in the beating fantasy. "What is it that distinguishes males and females if there is only one libido" (Giovannetti 1997, 98) and this libido is polymorphously perverse (meaning that its sexual object and aim are unstable and subject to reversal at the level of fantasy)? In short, the enigmatic character of the fantasy sequence suggests there is not only an individual but also a social ambivalence about binary gender regiments sustaining the heterosexual matrix.

It is unclear in the contemporary case whether Ingram is the girl being beaten or the adult wishing to administer a beating/seduction. In the Freudian analytic, the adult administering the punishment assumes the dominant and masculine role. (Freud did not recognize, let alone validate, the feminine subject's capacity to dominate). And so professional publics are, likewise, unable to understand how the maternally endowed white female teacher can be coded as both an aggressor and a feminine subject. The role of the white female teacher (incorrectly assumed to be passive and selfless in the service of altruistic love) in the beating (i.e., sexual though legally coded as sexual abuse) fantasy is plagued by uncertainty. We do not know whether she assumes a masochistic or sadistic role in the teacher-student sexual transgression, which, again, is central to the genesis of the scandal. The beating fantasy is paradoxical and upsets the certainty through which we invest subjects with either a normative masculine or feminine persona. But, more importantly, it upsets the logic through which we designate teachers sexual criminals. If Ingram is a victim of the law and of a street-wise boy, mature beyond his years, she cannot also be a dangerous pedophile in the theatre of the real. Legal and professional discourses (based on logic and linearity) do not recognize queer or cryptic desires, genders, and duplicities in crime (particularly when they involve those designated underage). Within legal, professional, and public discourses about the boy-student being beaten, the younger party cannot be active and passive, masculine and feminine. The teacher cannot be loving and disciplinary. Subjectivity is self-evident and not laced with regret, loss, ambivalence, and melancholia (Butler 1995) in the dominant discursive fantasy formation.

The master narrative of child sexual abuse cannot sustain itself in the face of a sexually savvy male student who actively refuses the position of a "child being beaten." Davidson assumes an active sexual orientation (and masculinity) in relation to a mature, older woman (motherly teacher) by reversing the dominant parental order of the school. The teacher (as mother) is no longer in charge and the student (as son) is not only sexually potent (not a child being beaten) but the one in charge of seduction. Why does the rebellious bad-boy student assume an active orientation in relation to a more mature woman unless the beating fantasy (including the modern-day incarnation) is a cover for a latent desire for gender-role indeterminacy and an alternative to the heteronormative reproductive future? If the wish to reverse the more prototypical dreamwork is about the necessity not only to accommodate ourselves to societal demands (relating to gender identification, desire, and generational prohibitions) but also to undermine – through fantasy – those very same scriptures, it is imperative that we contemplate what the modern-day reincarnation of the beating fantasy (consummated in the Ingram case through love, sex, and a common-law relationship) does to professional school cultures and their heteronormative investments.

I contend that the modern-day genesis of the beating/lovemaking fantasy is crucial to understanding the vicissitudes of knowledge in the erotic charge between female teacher and bad-boy student renegade. As Freud argued, the original scene of beating (represented in fantasy) is mystified by ignorance (itself an orientation to knowledge, as Deborah Britzman [1998] and Shoshana Felman [1987] contend). He observed that his patients frequently did not know the sex of the person beaten (or administering the beating) in the dreamwork (or claimed that it didn't matter). According to Freudian theorist Mario De F. Giovannetti (1997, 104), the child is devastated by the knowledge that he or she must abandon a primary sexual object in order to abide by the injunction against homosexuality, incest, and gender ambiguity. The beating apparition refuses and, at the same time, assimilates the troubling knowledge. The adult disciplinarian – Heather Ingram – refuses to abide by the injunction against intergenerational love, age-appropriate heterosexuality, and conventional femininity (aligned with passivity). Instead of entering into a fantasy formation through which she can make amends with modern social conventions governing sex, gender, and desire, she acts on a primary wish in the everyday (she has sex with her teenage boy-student). Ingram does not submit to the primary law of the patriarchal Father and sidesteps the need to invent an imaginary scene from which a more conventional heterosexually appropriate gender identification can be attained.

Freud claimed that the girl renounces her desire to be a boy (to enter into the realm of the masculine) by assuming the role of the boy being beaten: If I cannot be a boy in the real, I will be one in my reverie. It is sometimes argued that a girl or feminine child desires to be the husband of her mother (Quinodoz 1997, 120) and that the beating fantasy obscures (and drives underground) the homosexual predilection. It is also written that the girl-child experiences her mother as a "harsh judge, forbidding the girl's incestuous desire for her father and threatening her with loss of her female genital organs" (122). Although it is difficult to ascertain the original point of desire (and its vicissitudes are always more interesting and provocative), it is important to the contemporary Ingram case to note that Freud claimed there to be a hostile and accusatory response on the part of the client to the analyst resembling the punishing maternal superego. The masochistic position, as he concludes, takes the form of chastisement. The maternal superego surfaces in and through discussions of the beating apparition. The patient, assuming the role of the mother, enforces and acts on behalf of the Oedipal law of the Father. In essence, the mirage of beating enables the girl to become her mother in service of the primal Father.

The parallel to be drawn between the maternal superego bent on persecution, prohibition, and denial of primal gratification and the punishing female teacher in educational folklore and history is not to go unnoticed. Educational historians note that the single female teacher designated spinster (allegedly asexual and bent on persecution) was mocked and ridiculed in the public eye. She was seen to be sexually frigid (latent homosexual), unfeminine (masculine), and unnerved by talk (let alone expressions) of sexuality (Blount 1996, 2000). Feminist educational historians have pointed out that a female teacher's capacity to wield the strap in the early twentieth century called into question her femininity and, by implication, her sexual orientation (Cavanagh 2005a, 2006b). The female teacher confronted the problem of how to administer a beating without entering into the masculine realm (dominance being associated with male masculinity in the public imagination). The early-twentieth-century female teacher could not easily assume a feminine sacrificial (martyr-like) pedagogy (equipped with a wish to rescue troublesome boys) because she was responsible for corporal discipline. Her capacity to punish stands in for masculine desire, so her Oedipal resolution is undone or, at the very least, troubled in the social imaginary. She reverses a claim to heterosexuality by assuming what Freud calls the masculine (sadistic) role in the beating fantasy (because she is beating or assuming an active sexual position in relation to a male student), and as a result violates the heteronormative order of the school.

Unlike the early-twentieth-century spinster-teacher, Ingram does not punish but falls in love with the older, refractory boy-pupil. Anna Freud had beating fantasies that metamorphosed into what Lacanian theorist Darian Leader (2000, 117) called "nice stories" about rescue and salvation built on legendary kingdoms in classic literary tales. Similarly, Ingram wrote a memoir (within the genre of a Harlequin romance) about her tragic life story, foregrounding her fall for a younger male student, not so cleverly disguised as a Greek god named Troy. She explains: "I thought that once people understood that we both loved each other very much that somehow there would be an understanding. I certainly didn't anticipate this incredibly negative response that I would be a child molester" (*Oprah* transcripts 2004, 2). Ingram tried to undo the social-fantasy formation and investment in child sexual abuse by writing a "nice story," one that would affirm heteronormativity and its hegemonic gender bifurcations. It is because Ingram wrote her book about how she is a victim (a child being beaten) that the media, the public, and the teaching profession now cast her in a more favourable light: she was immature and unhappy, not a child predator. She claims to have been unhappy in her family home and then, again, in her adult, common-law relationship with its domestic and conventional entanglements. As she writes about her relationship with her spouse in her much-talked-about memoir:

> We have fed our relationship with mortgages and RRSPs and approval from our parents. It has become so heavy that it is crushing us. We are supposed to be doing this, it is how to create a life, and all our well-educated professional friends are creating these structures too. We have been taught that jobs are scarce, that a university degree is essential, that buying a home and having other couples over for dinner is the way to achieve adult happiness ... I am a failure, living for a future that I don't even know if I want, and I am starting to doubt that we will ever achieve happiness. We can't give each other what we need; our only expertise lies in wounding each other. (Ingram 2003, 45)

She recounts a difficult childhood with emotionally absent parents, a distant spouse who was unloving and inattentive, and a chronic loneliness. Ingram confesses to having been unhappy in her adult life and to having longed for rescue by a more loving and attentive suitor. "With Troy I felt sexual and desirable. I got to experience freedom to try things I'd never tried before, and permission to explore being a teenager, which I found irresistible" (224-25). Ingram said that she "wanted to be special. I wanted to be picked" (*Oprah* transcripts 2004, 9). The female teacher's desire to rescue was turned in on itself: I do not want to rescue but to be rescued by my student.

The "nice stories" are – according to Freud – feminine defences designed to guard against the threat of punishment while, at the same time, enabling the one fantasizing (or acting in pursuit of the forbidden love object) to take pleasure in the not-to-be-had, or forbidden, object. Attending to the logic of the fantasy sequence, Lacanian theorist Darian Leader (2000, 109) wonders: "If the girl relates to a paternal [knight in shining armour?] and the boy a mother substitute, is there a difference in status between a representative and a substitute?" Does it matter to the public whether the teacher actually has sex with the student if, in the fantasy sequence, she is punished for the forbidden wish? In short, the punishment makes the wish real. I suggest that the public and the profession are less concerned with an actual sexual transgression and professional violation than they are with the fantasy made real. If there is an erotic charge associated with punishment, is the threat of persecution (real or imposed), strictly speaking, punishing? In other words, the punishment itself legitimates and recognizes the prohibited wish (in this case to seduce or be seduced by a student), which is, as Freud contends, really about a difficulty with normative gender identity, heterosexuality, and its disavowals. As Leader, (2000, 119) deduces: "If the beating fantasies represented a return of the repressed incestuous wish, the nice stories form their sublimation, the tender emotional tie which is the result of an effective repression." I am not suggesting that Ingram wanted or sought out criminal proceedings, community service, and house arrest as a punishment. Rather, I am arguing that the beating fantasy, including the "nice stories" softening it, are themselves attempts to illicit the thing (object of desire, interest, or identification) that the subject cannot have. In other words, the altruistic (and sometimes masochistic) tales that teachers tell of their work with and commitment to a troubled or "needy" child can also be about what they, as teachers, want from the child, which they cannot acknowledge within the confines of professional discourse. As I contend, there is a perversion in the martyr-like appeal to the child and his or her best interests and to the self-abnegating position staked out by maternal pedagogies preaching love, care, and salvation. It is not the child whom the teacher longs to save but her own immersion in professional discourses and practices predicated upon a denial of the erotic.

I contend that Ingram's "nice stories" are not only attempts to ward off public and professional persecution, but also reflections of love, loss, and melancholia that accompany heteronormative and reproductive futures. Ingram does not administer punishment in the tradition of the spinster but engages in a quest to have sex with a teenaged boy-student, who, in educational folklore, is coded as son. Can her narrative of love (and familial tragedy) not be read as a defence against persecution *and* a desire to consummate – in the jurisdiction of the Real – an alternative to the nuclear family with its normative mandates? Might the professional transgression upset the heterosexual matrix and the developmental timelines on which it is mapped? Could the reproductive future with its investment in childhood sexual innocence, generational difference, and heteronormative bifurcations of gender be troubled by alternative (intergenerational and incestually coded) roots into the institutions of heterosexuality?

"A Teacher Is Being Beaten" and the Paradox of Gender

> For Lacan, sexual difference is not a firm set of "static" symbolic oppositions and inclusions or exclusions (heterosexual normativity that relegates homosexuality and other "perversions" to some secondary role), but the name of a deadlock, of a trauma, or an open question, of something that *resists* every attempt at its symbolization ... a deadlock inherent to the symbolic order ... "formulas for sexuation" provide the logical matrix of this deadlock. (Salecl 2000, 2)

> There is a violence in the disruption and modification of the imaginary by the symbolic register, a violence which we see quite clearly in the beating scenarios. (Leader 2000, 112)

Anxiety surrounding teachers' professional protocol, discussion about Canadian age-of-consent laws, and the difficult question about whether Davidson was harmed by the so-called lascivious teacher are all spurred on by the gendering of the teacher as female and the student as male. People are fixated on the gender of the alleged sexual perpetrator. In a curious way, gender matters more than the professional infraction itself, and the infraction is understood through popular discourses about gender. For example, University of Saskatchewan professor of education John Lyons is quoted as saying that a "grade eleven boy who is hit upon by his female teacher typically does not complain. I doubt very much that you would find young women who would feel that way" (Driedger 2003). Speaking about another British Columbia case in which a female volleyball coach was said to have had sex with up to fifteen boy-students in the same year that the Ingram scandal hit the newspapers, University of New Brunswick professor of psychology Sandra Byers told reporters that the boys tend to "feel lucky or they enjoyed [the encounter, but some boys will] ... be damaged by a sexual relationship with an adult woman" (Frank 2000). An unnamed Queen's University psychology professor states: "You wonder what social harm is being done if people aren't complaining and the participants don't seem to be perturbed." Another expert is quoted as saying that "men generally aren't at risk of being violently abused by women when the male is fully grown or almost so. Men are more interested in sex than women and they have less to lose" (Humphreys 2000a).

University of Toronto sociologist Walter Podilchak, by contrast, contends that we need to ignore gender: "Sexual abuse is intolerable in any care giving institution. It is sexual assault – it doesn't matter if it is a male or female. It is just more prevalent with men" (Humphreys 2000a). Larry Nisan, director of the Psychotherapy Institute in Toronto, was quoted as saying that while "women abuse at a lower rate than men, the motivations are similar ... power and sex" (Frank 2000). University of Guelph professor Serge Desmarais challenges the idea that it is "worse for girls to be exploited by adults than it is for boys." Miriam Kaufman, a Toronto psychotherapist commenting on the case, insists that there was an abuse of power and that there is a "big difference between the way [an underage boy involved with an adult woman] ... presents [himself] and the actual effect" (Galloway 2001). Others believe that consent is notoriously difficult to define and that "even older teens may not have the emotional maturity to know if they are being exploited." It also goes against the "macho grain to complain of sexual assault, especially when the predator is a woman" (Driedger 2003).

Confusion about the status of sexual crimes involving women in positions of power over boys and young men, age-of-consent laws, and gendered power relations in the seduction scene can be read in terms of the Freudian analytic of A Child Is Being Beaten. At present, we are uncertain about what the seduction/punishment scene between an older female and younger male student means to Oedipal developments and to the vicissitudes of gender, desire, and reproductive futurity they manage and reproduce. Freud contends that there is a desire – in the beating scenario – to distinguish between the subject administering the punishment and the child receiving the punishment in the latter stages of the fantasy. This can be read as a psychic need to be clear about gender, power, and pleasure (all of which underpin adult heterosexuality) given the demands of reproductive futurity. The Ingram school sex scandal incites public debate about when childhood ends and adulthood begins, whether intergenerational sex is necessarily exploitative, and the wisdom behind the educational reprimand (not to mention the criminal charges) launched against Ingram. People are uncertain and anxious about the gender-role reversal and wonder what it is about heterosexuality that is at stake.

In a controversial essay entitled "The Collapse of the Function of the Father and Its Effect on Gender Roles" (2000), Paul Verhaeghe argues that we are now living in a time when the primal Father of Freud's *Totem and Taboo* has been killed and when, as a result, reactionary forces are calling for a "return to the authoritarian father" (132). In other words, people fear that the law is lax, moral codes are sliding, children are taking over the school, and queer sexual forms (including intergenerational) are now the norm. *There is no discipline! Children are out of control! Teachers are sleeping with their students! The future is at stake! Where is the Father to lay down rule, law, and order? If the Father is dead, who will protect the child (always coded as male) from the mother, who, as Freud claimed, has less of a stake in modern-day civilization and morality? How will reproductive futures be consolidated and given form when queer timelines upset the prohibitions on love, desire, gender, and their identifications?* Given that the law of the Father is supposed to enforce binary gender identifications and age-appropriate heterosexualities, his downfall (or symbolic death) ignites anxieties about more than the loss of child sexual innocence. The sex scandals involving female teachers stand in as markers for the assumed death of the Father; his professional protocols and investments in a heteronormative future no longer seem to apply. The paranoid fantasy formation sees only gender-role reversals, intergenerational prohibitions breached, and queer entries into the heterosexual matrix. The Ingram sex scandal crystallizes these fantasy formations and triangulates them into one overarching fear of gender and sexual indeterminacy.

The quest for law, order, and the accountability of female teachers is suggestive of a perceived shift not only in the beating fantasy, but also in social (and symbolic) rule more generally. This is not to say that the dominant heterosexual Symbolic is shifting so much as it is to suggest that it is perceived to be shifting and that normative gender identities are seen to be at risk. The courts and the profession took a hard line against the Ingram teacher-student affair because it is read as a symbolic threat to binary gender formations and heteronormativity. As reiterated by then superintendent Clifford Smith, "I had no alternative but to suspend Miss Ingram from the classroom. The reasons were plain: violation of the law, violation of school board policy and violation of the fundamental principle of trust between teacher and student" (*Oprah* transcripts 2004, 2). Doug Wilson of the Ontario College of Teachers made what journalist Sharon Doyle Driedger (2003), in *Maclean's* magazine, called an "unprecedented tour of fifteen communities, briefing teachers to avoid even the appearance of impropriety. They urge teachers to avoid sending e-mails to individual students and ask them to watch colleagues for signs of a sexual enticement." Names and details of teachers dismissed are now published in the notorious Blue Pages of the Ontario College of Teachers' magazine, *Professionally Speaking,* and in British Columbia by the provincial federation. Aiming to eradicate cases of (and speculation about) child sexual abuse perpetrated by teachers, teachers' professional associations across the country are taking stiff measures to identify and reprimand those found or appearing to have crossed professional boundaries. Even the staunchest of "child advocates say teachers may be singled out unfairly," and in some instances – the Ingram case being one example – teachers are unfairly prosecuted. "Criticized for past cover-ups, the College [of Teachers in Ontario] now holds disciplinary hearings in public and posts names on the Internet". (Driedger 2003).

Agents of the law, the profession, and child advocates all insist on treating Ingram as a male sexual criminal: *no double standard shall be admissible in the court of law, in professional protocols, or in police arrest.* At the same time, agents of authority cannot forget that the so-called child molester is a woman, so an unusually harsh sentence is given by the court judge to remind everyone, once again, that gender doesn't (or shouldn't) matter. Ingram (like the child beaten in the real) explains in her memoir that she was treated as a dangerous male or masculine sex offender, pedophile, and general menace to society. Because authorities could not (or would not) distinguish her from male or masculine sexual criminals, Ingram was given psychological tests designed for male rapists, pedophiles, and repeat offenders that had little (if anything) to do with her professional infraction.

Freud shows us that the person (likewise the agent or institution) administering the beating does not know that he or she is reproducing a parental relationship (a beating fantasy) marked by socially sanctioned restraints on desire, gender, and love. According to Berenstein (1997, 152), "beating comes about as an attempt to turn the child into something similar to the beater himself, just as the father becomes similar to his own father." For this reason, I suggest that Ingram and Davidson have been turned into conventionally gendered (and heterosexual) subjects because of, not despite, their clandestine desire staged in the theatre of the real (no longer fantastical). By treating Ingram as a man and then not as a man, the courts and the profession were endeavouring to reproduce the paradox of the beating fantasy. The fantasy allows for the maintenance of socially sanctioned binary gender categories by enabling the child to pretend – through a dream-like hallucination – that he or she is not restricted to them.

Psychoanalytic inquiry mediated by feminist and queer theories leads us to question the judicial (and professional) management of the Ingram case. She is not a sexual predator akin to the more prototypical male or masculine teacher who in some instances (although not all) harms his students. Hyperbolic child-protectionist discourse is also malapropos in this instance. Experts who insist that teenage students are sexual victims in need of protection from adult teachers (despite their chronological age, gender, and sexual maturity) are now deemed out of touch with modern youth and their sexual capacities by critical commentaries in both the academic (Heins 2001; Kincaid 1998; Levine 2002) and the public spheres. One teacher was quoted in *Maclean's* magazine as saying that "kids know more about sex than we ever did." Another teacher spoke about a female colleague who had to "fend off the advances of a junior high student who was so aggressive he was eventually suspended for his behaviour" (Driedger 2003). Speaking about the series of sex scandals involving female teachers reported in the North American media, Bart Blasengame (2005, 96), in *Details* magazine, wrote of the allegedly abused male students: "What about the children? Are you kidding? Right now, any one of those little Miss Crabtree-bagging twerps is probably being carried atop the shoulders of his classmates like some conquering hero."

Conclusion

The key to understanding the Ingram case is again to focus on the gender-role reversal permitted in the disciplinary (i.e., sexual) schoolhouse scene. In the first stage of the public fantasy, Ingram is a sexual predator, and the public demands that she be treated like a man who has committed a comparable sexual crime, but then she is recast in the role of feminine victim, incapable of abusing a sexually savvy boy like Davidson. Although I am of the belief that Ingram is not a sexual criminal (but unprofessional, as she acknowledges), it is curious that popular opinion – if media reports are any indication – shifts at the very moment that Ingram is punished by the courts. Following the stiff sentence given to Ingram by the female judge, the media come to be more sympathetic and interested in the nuances and specificities of the case as told from her perspective. As Ingram (2003, 174) writes in her book: "The *[Vancouver] Province* reporter ... the one who wrote the most damaging and insinuating stories, spends almost fifteen minutes trying to convince me to give an interview. [The reporter is quoted by Ingram as saying:] ... I've changed my mind about you."

The attempt to realign Ingram with conventional femininity (marked by passivity, martyr-like heterosexuality, and inexperience) is spurred on by the psychic need to repudiate the threat posed by the lascivious female teacher (i.e., mother) to the institution of normative heterosexuality with its dependence on gender binaries, sexual and generational difference. The Oedipal sequence, as Freud shows us, is supposed to result in an adult heterosexuality that is both gender- and age-appropriate. The sex scandals involving female teachers seem to lay claims to desires and melancholic formations at odds with reproductive futurity – that is, until the teachers are recast as agents in the service of professional protocols and heterosexual futures. After the sensation had reached a peak, Ingram and Davidson were no longer constituted as gender and sexual outlaws. They came to be represented as conventionally gendered and committed to familial protocols. Ingram was aligned with passive femininity and cast as a good-girl and maternal agent of care who had overstepped her role but who was now on the right track to her own redemption and salvation. And Davidson's masculinity was now validated because he had reached the age (eighteen) when heterosexual timelines tell us that he is an adult. The queer times that he had experienced were forgotten, and the story was retold in such a way that heterosexuality, and the binary gender identifications on which it depends, appeared to organically reassert itself. As I have argued, the scandal's genesis is in need of queer scholarly analysis because reproductive futures, heterosexualities, genders, desires, and relations to loss are at stake in the maternal pedagogical encounter. Both the altruistic teacher and the renegade bad-boy student are involved in a pedagogical exchange that is both sexual and laden with disciplinary power. This exchange has not been well-theorized in educational theory and has been disavowed in professional discourses.

The pedagogy of maternal care, selfless love, and altruism is a ruse, a cover, a mask for an anxiety about the white female teacher's role in the cultivation of gender indeterminacy, intergenerational desire, and sexualities that seem to defy reproductive futurity. The Ingram case is a queer tale that embodies the vicissitudes and troubles with gender, sexuality, and reproductive futurity to be found in school cultures.

6

Sex in the Lesbian Teacher's Closet: The Hybrid Proliferation of Queers in the Jean Robertson Scandal

> Nothing, it would seem, is more difficult than to conceive, to elaborate, and to put into practice "new ways of being together." Foucault used this expression to define what he thought of as our most urgent ethical project, one in which gays, according to him, were destined to play a privileged role ... what disturbs people about homosexuality is not "the sexual act itself," but rather "the homosexual mode of life," which Foucault associated with "the formation of new alliances and the tying together of unforeseen lines of force." (Bersani 2001, 351)

> The lesbian just might be the harbinger of a different order threatening the Name-of-the-Father with a new name. (Roof 2001, 248)

> Lesbianism interrogates ethically the very terms of sexual structure. (Lukes 2001, 258)

In 1993 six news reports relayed the story about a female teacher, Jean Robertson, who had been convicted of sexually abusing a former student, Brenda Johima, when the complainant was in ninth grade.[1] As the Vancouver news reports explained, the alleged victim, thirty-one at the time of the media release, claimed that her year-long relationship with Robertson, who was twenty-seven at the time of the alleged abuse, began in a school bathroom near the physical education office, where the lesbian teacher kissed her. The teacher would allegedly lure her victim into the office to have private talks with Johima. In this office, at New Westminster Secondary School, Johima alleged that her coach would "kiss ... and fondle her breasts." The former student also testified that Robertson would "fondle her during rides home from school ... give her a full body massage while she was naked and digitally penetrate her" (Hall 1993a). Allegations were also heard that the teacher took Johima on a camping trip to Shawnigan Lake, took a sauna with the preteen, gave her pornography and liquor, and lay naked on top of her.

A key eyewitness in the trial, Victoria Harris (also a former student), told the provincial court that she "saw Robertson in a sleeping bag, kissing Johima passionately, during a party for the volleyball team at another teacher's house in 1976" (Hall 1993b). What made matters worse was that Harris also had a sexual relationship with a female teacher at New Westminster High School at the same time as the alleged affair involving Johima. Harris, now a prison psychiatrist, claimed that she told Heather Cranston, the school vice principal, about the affair between Johima and Robertson but that the female administrator did nothing: she "shrugged and walked away," apparently having chosen not to look into the report at the time of the clandestine affair. Provincial court judge Ross Tweedle said that Cranston "gave the appearance of a witness with something to hide ... she is covering up something serious" (Hall 1993d). Robertson, now forty-five, was sentenced to four months in prison while maintaining, throughout the court proceedings, that the allegations were false.

Harris later pressed charges of her own against school counsellor Murline Beltain (then known as Merle Bottaro) for gross indecency because she could "no longer keep her feelings [about the abuse] bottled up." The prison psychiatrist said that she was ashamed of her relationship with Beltain during her final four years of high school. The complainant recalled that the teacher used her "troubled family history to coerce her into an illicit relationship. She said the incidents included being forced to have sex with Beltain in front of another teacher while on a field trip to a volleyball championship in Courtenay." Despite allegations of coercion, Harris admitted to the court that at the time of the affair she moved into Beltain's condominium and gave her a copy of *The Joy of Lesbian Sex*. The former student explained that the book was a "peace offering because she [Beltain] was so angry at me for not being aroused" (Lee 1995).

The public is led to conclude that there was something sinister going on at New Westminster Secondary School, something diabolical, queer, and endemic to the homosocial underworld. The two sex scandals involving lesbian teachers are entwined and seen to be dangerously duplicitous. In this chapter, I use queer and postcolonial theories to identify a problem with the status of knowledge about white teacher lesbianism in legal, professional, and rationalist discourse. I contend that the panic about child protectionism in the Robertson and Beltain cases is a guise for a more deeply entrenched worry about what I call postmodern eugenics and about the proliferation of queer subjectivities in the school. Using Lee Edelman's (2004) conceptualization of reproductive futurity, Judith Butler's (1990b) formulation of the heterosexual matrix, and Judith Halberstam's (2005) investigation of queer time and space, I underscore societal-based upset about lesbianism in the high school. I argue that the sex scandals involving Canadian[2] and American lesbian teachers are less about an investment in child welfare than about queer school cultures, queer timelines, and identifications inhospitable to heteronormative futures. In the final section of the chapter, I theorize a relationship between whiteness, lesbianism, and death in the imaginary of the heterosexual mainstream and how this impending doom gets read as an end to reproductive futurity.

Concern about the proliferation of queers in high school cultures can be seen as an example of what I call a postmodern eugenic angst about sexual contagion, infection, and contamination. I understand postmodern eugenics to be a contemporary concern and panic about white reproductive futurity in the face of homosociality. In other words, postmodern eugenic angst is directed toward those who do not reproduce and who seem to be indifferent to the purity of the "white race" and its heteronormative future. White lesbian teachers, with their powers of seduction, are threatening and seen to be a source of contamination that infiltrates schools and the lives of otherwise heteronormative and reproductive girls. Worry about the survival of heterosexuality – which is often subsumed into the domain of whiteness – is akin to the panic about "interracial" breeding in late-nineteenth- and early-twentieth-century eugenic discourses and practices. In this chapter, I examine sex panics involving white lesbian teachers as one example of a societal investment in a racially specific (white) heterosexuality and its proliferation. The school, as a microcosm of society, reproduces the social and Symbolic order. The white lesbian teacher does not reproduce the heterosexual Symbolic, as does the heterosexual teacher, coded as sacrificial white mother, but introduces what Foucault calls a "new way of being together" (1997). "Foucault seems to have thought of cultural subversion and renewal [what I later refer to as the desire for an alternative to the colonizing heterosexual Symbolic] as inherent in homosexuality" (Bersani 2001, 351). Homosexuality is not so much a sexual orientation as a desire for an alternative relation to the white, futuristic, heterosexual Symbolic, a desire that is yet to be rendered intelligible outside the lesbian teacher's locker-room closet.

All sex panics are structured by secrets, suspicions, disavowals, and projections that have little to do with the event that acts as a catalyst for the upset. The sex scandals involving lesbian teachers are structured by the problem of knowledge, by the paradox of knowing and not knowing, by the "relations of the known and the unknown, the explicit and the inexplicit around homo/heterosexual definition" (Sedgwick 1990, 3) central to the epistemology of the closet. The female teachers act on lesbian desire while maintaining an official silence, which Eve Sedgwick characterizes as living in a glass closet, noting that "coming out is a matter of crystallizing intuitions or convictions that had been in the air for a while already and had already established their own power-circuits of silent contempt, silent blackmail, silent glamorization, silent complicity" (79-80). As Beltain explained: "It was not okay to be a lesbian teacher then or to be a lesbian teacher now," suggesting that she lived a secret, an open secret that was shielded by the pretence of ignorance on the part of colleagues and students alike. When Beltain was questioned about why she hadn't told administrators that Jean Robertson was having a sexual relationship with Brenda Johima, the persecuted teacher insisted that she "didn't have anything specific to report" (Bellett 1995b). The trouble with knowledge is thus exacerbated by queer time zones. In the time of the affair, the teacher and student were in love, and there was nothing sinister to report. In the 1990s, the affair is remembered as an instance of abuse and punishable by law. The relationship and the recollection of it are out of sync and produce a psychic schism. Teacher-student lesbian sex based on love, trust, and social consent is illegible in contemporary legal rationalist and professional discourse. It does not translate into professional time and cannot be remembered as anything but abuse. The lesbian teacher who fondly remembers and offers joyful reminiscences about the intergenerational relationship is seen to be an atavistic throwback to a queerly primordial time. She is also cast as a predatory lesbian, a danger and threat to children. In effect, the lesbian teacher is caught in a problem of educational time: how to tell of a queer moment when the teacher-student relationship was not coded as, or felt to be, predatory or abusive. I argue that the transgression against the teenage female student was not in the time of the relationship but in the time of the present. The story the lesbian teacher of the 1970s has to tell the courts today about female teacher-student love, adoration, and sex does not translate into contemporary professional ethics. Professional discourses and practices of the late twentieth and early twenty-first centuries are predicated on a disavowal of Eros in the pedagogical encounter. Lesbian desire in the educational milieu is even harder to validate, let alone comprehend (given its non-normative status in North American educational cultures), and so it is subsumed into a unifying narrative of child sexual abuse. Parents, school administrators, developmental psychologists, child advocates, and so forth are confronted with the temporality of their insistence upon child sexual abuse as they listen to Robertson and Beltain's queer enunciations and remembrances of love. As I demonstrate in what follows, the public and those invested in professionalism and child advocacy are troubled by how the idea of child sexual abuse did not register with the teenage girls in the time of the clandestine affairs. Despite the temporal rupture (child sexual abuse discourses, policies, and interventions are relatively new), the listeners are unable to historicize the lesbian teacher sex scandals. There is, as we shall see, a resistance to questioning an overarching and ahistorical narrative "truth" about child sexual abuse by those who have a stake in professionalism, the repudiation of the Erotic in modern pedagogies, and the longevity of the child sexual innocence thesis.

Through an in-depth examination of the lesbian sex scandals involving Jean Robertson and Murline Beltain, I demonstrate what Sedgwick (1990) calls a problem of disavowal, secrecy, and willful ignorance. I also draw on three separate lesbian-teacher sex scandals in the United States and several others in Canada to provide context and to illustrate the operation of social consent and how the sexuality of white teenaged girls is channelled into the domain of heterosexual time and reproductivity. It should be noted that the lesbian teachers' sexual infractions received conspicuously less media attention than did the scandals involving boy-students. Although the legal penalties and professional reprimands were equally severe, less has been written about the lesbian teachers' seductions in the mainstream press. Given the subterfuge surrounding lesbian teachers in Canadian contexts (Khayatt 1992), it is perhaps not surprising that lesbian teachers' seductions receive less media time. However, the scandals involving lesbian teachers do garner public upset and professional consternation that warrant critical commentary and queer scholarly analysis.

The methodological problem of lesbian secrecy is not particular to education; in popular Hollywood film, for example, there is a long history of covert and conspiratorial liaisons involving lesbian teachers. Film theorists of queer culture concern themselves with homosexual desire "where you wouldn't expect to find it, where it's been diverted or repressed or else obliquely expressed or unknowingly sublimated" (Dyer 2002, 4). In this chapter, therefore, I propose a methodology used by film theorists that depends on popular, cultural readings of Hollywood films that exploit the secret of lesbianism as a plot device. Constructions of lesbianism as the odious crime whose name cannot be spoken, as the libellous offence against white womanhood and motherhood that is so deeply singed with public shame that it cannot be seen, except under the most extreme and unusual circumstances, are central both to Hollywood film *and* to media news reports of the contemporary scandals involving lesbian teachers.

Reproductive futures and heterosexual timelines depend on eclipsing queer and nonreproductive times, spaces, and cultures of pleasure in high school. I am curious about time-space distanciation in the lesbian-teacher seductions in film and in the mainstream media. In particular, I wonder how secrets and disavowals circulate to coordinate heterosexual timelines while also functioning to expose the relativity and temporality of heterosexual futurity. In other words, how does knowledge of lesbian-teacher seduction – what we might call queer time in the classroom – upset reproductive futures, binary gender assignments, and mythologies about the sexually innocent child?

Lesbians in Film: The Problem of Representation, Knowledge, and Illicit Love

As a comparison case through which to explore the interlocking nature of sexual panic and postcolonial anxieties about genetic breeding, I draw on Lillian Hellman's play *The Children's Hour* (1934) and on its Hollywood film adaptation in 1962, a play based on an actual nineteenth-century Scottish court case involving allegations of lesbianism between two teachers running a school for girls. The similarity between contemporary scandals involving lesbian teachers and *The Children's Hour* – not to mention a host of other films, including *Diabolique, Oleanna, Maedchen in Uniform, Therese and Isabelle, Picnic at Hanging Rock, Heavenly Creatures,* and *Notes On a Scandal* – is striking when we consider that both grapple with the problem of sexual knowledge in the postcolonial context. Speaking about *Oleanna* and *The Children's Hour,* Sauer (2000, 421) claims that "both problematize the possibility of making objective judgments and thereby question the very foundation of the realistic conventions that they seem to espouse," both grapple with belated discoveries of lesbianism, and both underscore the panic that is endemic to the generation of queer subjectivities and timelines in the school.

In her discussion of the play and the later film adaptation, Mikko Tuhkanen identifies an overlapping anxiety about dissident sexuality, white-race suicide, and eugenics in the lesbian-teacher sex scandal. On the one hand, white female homosexuals were not considered a threat by eugenicists because they didn't biologically reproduce themselves (unlike the "darker races"). From a eugenic standpoint, the homosexual *was* a congenital defect, but this defect was well contained by the biological injunction against same-sex reproduction; the homosexual could not reproduce her (or his) own kind. On the other hand, there was, as noted by Tuhkanen (2002, 1002), a parallel concern with biologically nonprocreative coupling and eugenic worries about "race and lineage, purity and hybridity." Lesbians are culturally read as women who do not reproduce. Their investments in heterosexual futurity are weak at best. Of course, many lesbians do have children, but their investment in reproduction is presumed to be secondary to the pleasure of homosexuality and the lifestyle it is assumed to engender. Those invested in heteronormativity wonder about the kind of parents lesbians (or gay men, for that matter) make and whether or not they may be giving birth to a new generation of gender mutants or sexually hybrid and otherwise non-normative children. Lesbian teachers, therefore, stand in to mark a triadic panic about non-reproductivity (the white race will die out), non-normative reproductivity (the children of gays, lesbians, bisexuals, transgendered peoples, etc., will not be normal), and symbolic reproductivity (lesbians will make the nation's otherwise normal girl students into lesbians).

Lesbian teachers do not always reproduce biologically, and when they do, their families tend not to be seen as normative. Regardless of the extent to which a particular lesbian mother may wish to enter into a normative time-space continuum structured by heterosexual appeals to the future, the good citizen, the nation, and the like, her familial composition is often read as an aberration. The monstrosity of lesbianism is difficult to recoup into the terrain and time of reproductive futurity. A postmodern eugenic concern about heterosexual futurity maps itself onto the body of the white lesbian teacher. But this eugenic panic is not of the same ilk as those that flourished in the late nineteenth and early twentieth centuries. The contemporary eugenic panic is concerned not only with biological but also with symbolic reproduction. Queer lessons learned in class and formations of new gender and sexual subjectivities are subjects of concern on the postmodern eugenicist's radar. The proliferation of queer subjectivities in school is not so much a problem of breeding (or congenital defect) as a problem of teaching. Queer pedagogies, erotic countertransferences, and sex educations (official and not) are seen as dangerous and threatening to reproductive futures bent on heteronormativity because they are about desire in the present. Queer identifications are not congenital but products of erotic educations that do not respect the future or the heterosexual mandates central to it.

The contemporary sex panics involving lesbian teachers are laced with secrecy and disavowal because it is symbolic contagion that is of paramount concern to heterosexualities based on ignorance. One cannot be what one says he or she is not, yet queer pedagogies ironically circulate through an unspeakable vacuum. As Robert Young argues in *Colonial Desire* (1995), homosexual generation – "recruiting," as the contemporary homophobe would call it – is "silent, covert and unmarked"; the contagion, which is a fear of knowledge itself, travels amid those vulnerable to exposure in a surreptitious and oracular manner. People are infected by knowledge, and the pretence of innocence (usually the child's) is both a shield and a defensive refusal to acknowledge an already complicated relation to desire and adult sexual subjectivities in colonial and now postcolonial landscapes. The white female teacher is also caught in a problem of knowledge demanding disavowal. She is supposed to be sexually pure and innocent even as she is a sexual subject invested with a diasporic and colonizing mandate (see Chapter 2). Her whiteness depends on a defensive legacy of purity, morality, and innocence. White femininity is structured on a negation of the horrors and colonizing initiatives actualized through recourse to the caring function, which we can now read as laced with aggressivity, nationalism, heteronormativity, and futuristic mandates. The white woman is positioned as mother, teacher, and guardian of the white race, as an agent of love, care, and devotion supposedly unsullied by desire and carnal knowledge. The lesbian teacher seems to flaunt this positioning and shows the public and profession how it is riddled with desires and identifications, on the part of individual teachers and publics, that are neither virtuous nor benign.

Tuhkanen (2002, 1003) argues, in relation to *The Children's Hour,* that the concern about breeding – where "racial otherness infects white femininity with illicit sexual knowledge – [is connected] to 'reading' [or acquiring knowledge of, a devious order and that] the danger of ... contamination of the adolescent female mind" is key to unpacking the scandal of lesbianism in the Scottish school. Those who receive and can understand deviant sexual knowledge become vulnerable to homosexual contagion, an infection caught through the spread of illicit knowledge. The sex scandals involving lesbian teachers are a blow to postmodern eugenics because they seem to achieve a symbolic victory over reproductive futurity. White female teachers know about nonprocreative lesbian sex and are seen to actively recruit. There is a distain for the reproductive future, the white race, and its investment in citizenship, nationality, and nuclear-family forms. Conservatives do not so much panic about child welfare as get upset about what Tuhkanen calls the "hybrid proliferation of queers" (1003). Tuhkanen explains that "homosexuality is at once completely barren *and* intensely fecund; it signals the dying out of the race *and* a generation of unforeseen hybridities" (1002, original emphasis). The white race does not so much die out as undergo a permutation, a hybrid transmutation inaugurated by queer circuits of knowledge, desire, and timelines spread in the school.

In her discussion of lesbian sexuality, Judith Roof (2001, 246) argues that the social worry is that "as teachers, lesbians might proselytize; as athletes, they might recruit; as military personnel, they create disorder; and as feminists, they threaten patriarchal order." The theme of contagion is again evident in the discourse of reproduction. Lesbian teachers infect the school (coded as symbolic family) by upsetting heterosexual futurity as well as the binary and compulsory gender identifications that coordinate the heterosexual matrix. The panic about lesbian-teacher seduction must be contextualized within an overarching fear of sexual and racial contamination. "Thus lesbians are an aberration, a sickness, not unto themselves but unto the system by which they are defined as aberrant in the first place. They are the out-of-laws" (246); that is, they are out of time and of an earlier primordial developmental stage, when our sexualities were unbounded by colonizing ideas about heteronormativity, its future, and binary gender imperatives.

Sexual Contagion, Foreign "Others," and the Problem of Knowledge

> Homosexual desire is the ungenerating-ungenerated terror of
> the family, because it produces itself without producing.
> (Guy Hocquenghem, quoted in Tuhkanen 2002, 1001)

As in the contemporary Jean Robertson case, the conviction in the nineteenth-century Scottish verdict depended, in part, on statements given by a female student, Jane Cummings, who was said to possess intimate knowledge of a devious order. In the Scottish verdict, so well documented by Lillian Faderman (1983), the child witness, having been born in India by a South Asian mother, was thought to have come into contact with deviant sexual knowledge that a Scottish-born child would supposedly not be able to comprehend, so her court testimony, which was based on "half-heard whispers and faint, indescribable noises" (Tuhkanen 2002, 1007), was not only admissible but also instrumental to the conviction. The child could understand the noises in the teacher's bedroom suite as indicative of a deviant act because her genetic breeding, her "Indian-ness," and its association with foreign eroticism, fetishistic sexuality, and carnal knowledge enabled a kind of recognition that was allegedly incomprehensible to the white British-born children in the school. The foreignness of the child leaves her vulnerable to contagious knowledge about deviant – in this case, lesbian – sexuality.[3]

As observed by Mikko Tuhkanen (2002, 1007), in the original case on which the *The Children's Hour* was based, there continued to be epistemological uncertainty following testimony given by Cummings: "The bewildering disparity between Jane Cummings's seeming innocence and her graphic accusations, repeatedly stated in the transcripts, suggests a concomitant anxiety that the East elicited in confounding such easy legibility of content from form." Tuhkanen draws on Victorian stereotypes about Eastern women documented by Simeran Man Singh Gell to conclude that there was a binary between "British middle-class women who were supposedly readable" (1007) and Eastern women – characterized by the Indian student – who were secretive, deceptive in that they could split their inner worlds and outer self-presentation with apparent ease, and privy to knowledge that escaped white visual scrutiny.

The evidence given by Cummings, based on sounds heard in the night, confounded the demand for visual evidence, proof that could be uncontested. "The clues from which Jane Cummings had drawn her conclusions were based on things not seen: the room had always been dark, the women covered with bedding, or, when she had slept in a separate bed, a curtain had been hung between the beds" (Tuhkanen 2002, 1007). The difficulty lay in the fact that the illicit sex could not be ascertained by the British onlooker; it required a special, transgressive, foreign, or queer knowledge circuit that seemed to be lost to the white heteronormative subject. Deviant sexuality was not visible or subject to disciplinary power and surveillance in the way that race was in this historical moment. Interestingly, Cummings was well integrated into the culture of the Scottish school despite her South Asian background. This fuelled related anxieties about the difficulty in detecting foreign "others."

According to Tuhkanen, deceptive traits – powers of knowledge acquisition that were foreign, wanton, and illicit – were also to be found in lesbian or closely knit same-sex female friendships in the school. Thus it should not be surprising that in the contemporary case, former student Victoria Harris was also a reliable witness in the suit against Jean Robertson because she had experiential access to lesbian sexuality; her affair with Beltain enabled her to stand as an educated eyewitness. Harris observed an illicit kiss between Robertson and Johima. As Jim McDowell (1995) wrote in the *BC Report:* "She knew what the kiss implied because she was having a lesbian affair with her counsellor-volleyball coach, Murline Beltain, then thirty-six." Harris worried that "her lesbian relationship might be brought up and damage her credibility as a witness. So she disclosed the affair to the court" (ibid.). To her surprise, her proximity to lesbianism enhanced her credibility and ensured that she would be positioned as someone in the know. Her credibility was further buttressed by the fact that she was a prison psychiatrist at King County Prison for Women who worked with prisoners who had been sexually abused as children. Harris believed that if she "was to help her clients she had to resolve her own conflicts first" (ibid.).

To recognize homosexuality where it can't be seen by the heterosexual mainstream is to admit that one is also a homosexual or, at the very least, to reveal a fluency in the language of queer culture. The capacity to read lesbianism where it cannot be seen by the heterosexual majority is to have learned the signs and symbols of the closet, an epistemology that depends on heterosexual ignorance. As Sedgwick (1990) explains: "Insofar as ignorance is ignorance *of* a knowledge – a knowledge that may itself, it goes without saying, be seen as either true or false under some other regime of truth – these ignorances, far from being pieces of the originary dark, are produced by and correspond to particular knowledges and circulate as part of particular regimes of truth" (8, original emphasis). To be ignorant of homosexuality (as the dominant heterosexual mainstream claims to be) is to be entrenched within a regime of truth that cannot tolerate homosexual knowledge without injury. "The double-edged potential for injury in the scene of gay coming out ... results partly from the fact that the erotic identity of the person who receives the disclosure is apt also to be implicated in, and hence perturbed by it" (81).

Victoria Harris – as an eyewitness – is caught within a difficulty of knowledge. She cannot know about the Jean Robertson affair without herself having participated in a similarly licentious relationship, and she cannot escape persecution for having once loved another woman without disavowing her lesbian past. The disavowal was accomplished primarily by remembering the four-year live-in relationship as abuse and admitting to shameful feelings for having had such a relationship. Harris told police that in 1977 the accused teacher "lured her into a sexual relationship which, sixteen years later, she finally realized was a case of sexual abuse" (McDowell 1995).

The remembrance is questionable when heard alongside the confession given by Beltain. With tears in her eyes, the accused teacher told the court that Harris "came to her apartment in March 1977 and talked about being upset by her attraction to an older person." Shortly thereafter Beltain realized that the student was speaking about her. The teacher and student admitted their love, and Beltain told the court that they "fondled each other" (McDowell 1995). Recalling the beginning of the affair in 1977, the teacher said that it was a "joyous day ... exciting to be in love, a buoyant, exuberant time – standing here saying this – it just sounds tawdry" (Bellett 1995a).[4]

It would be foolhardy to suggest that there aren't ethical or professional questions to be asked about teacher-student sex in this case. Eros does, as I argue in Chapter 3, permeate the pedagogical encounter, and we must consider its impact on students, teachers, and the learning environment. I do not mean to argue that Harris' recollections and testimonies are fabrications or lies. I am, however, suggesting that the truth as Harris understands it might be constrained by the master narrative of child sexual abuse, which cannot comprehend an intergenerational lesbian-teacher affair based on social consent. If we lived in another time and place where sexuality was subject to another ruling regime – one not so upset by intergenerational lesbian sex – might Harris have a different story to tell? Given that she enjoyed and sought out a sexual relationship with Beltain in her teenage years, lived with the accused teacher, and saw herself as a dominant party in the formation of the relationship, might the discourse of abuse in the present be playing a queer trick? There seems to be a queer lapse in time, memory, and narrative that cannot be substantiated in the evidence of abuse brought to court by Harris. In fact, there was no evidence of abuse, except for the difference in age, which, for the courts, is evidence of abuse in and of itself.

Beltain openly acknowledged the intergenerational affair and was consequently found guilty of gross indecency involving a minor. The teacher insisted that she and Harris were in love and that the relationship, at the time of the affair, was not understood to be abusive, as it is now in professional and child-protectionist discourse. Beltain tried to explain that what is seen as gross indecency today was not seen as abusive in the 1970s. Beltain testified that there were "differences in attitude between the 1970s and the 1990s concerning student-teacher relationships ... [and that] terms like sexual abuse, boundary violations, these are common in our language" today, but they were not talked about at the time of the relationship (Bellett 1995b). The convicted teacher also testified that at the time of the affair, she was in love, but today she grieves and seeks forgiveness because of how the relationship is understood in the discourse of abuse, the regime of truth intelligible to the courts.

Johima is also caught in a similar problem of knowledge demanding disavowal. The former student confessed to going along with the affair with Robertson because she was in love and kept the liaison secret because her "dad would have [had] a fit." The complainant explained that she "knew it was something she had to keep secret." Paradoxically, Johima said to the court: "Then I thought I was in love with her. I was a kid and thought that's what love was ... I didn't define it as I see it now – as sexual abuse." Because of the affair, Johima told the judge that she had difficulty trusting people and that she had intimacy-related struggles in her adult life. To further demonstrate the lasting trauma associated with the lesbian affair, the former student testified that "she feels ill every time she hears a Karen Carpenter song, Close to You, because it brings back memories of her former high school volleyball coach sexually abusing her"; the teacher used to sing the song to her. Upon hearing the tune, the alleged victim reports, "I feel like vomiting" (Hall 1993a).

Getting sick is, in itself, an act of expulsion. Johima speaks about illness and nausea upon remembrance. In the film *The Children's Hour,* the lesbian protagonist responds to her aunt's innuendos about her niece's unnatural proclivities by saying: "You are making me sick" (Tuhkanen 2002, 1014). The knowledge of lesbianism, in both the historical and contemporary cases, is nauseating. But this sickness is a hysterical reaction to contagious knowledge about female homosexuality: it cannot be about me, and if you say that it is, I will throw up. There is much about the contemporary sex scandals involving lesbian teachers that is repulsive to the media-reading public. Heterosexual mainstreams are upset by the knowledge that maybe, just maybe, the teenage girls involved in the lesbian-teacher sexual improprieties were less than innocent and naive. Perhaps Harris remembers her year-long, live-in relationship with Beltain as sickening and abusive even though the original incarnation was based on love and social consent. Lesbian-teacher sex might be abusive only in retrospect. The relationships seem to be more traumatic for the adults remembering the intergenerational affairs than for the teenagers who had the affairs. I suggest that the sex scandals involving lesbian teachers might be products of *adult* identificatory trauma. Memory, as opposed to seduction, is the source of difficulty. "To the degree that the remembered child is the child who liked the sexual contact, the child is killed off; the narrative brought to define him is one of fear, power, abuse, and shame" (Bruhm and Hurley 2004, xxix).

Contrary to the master narrative of abuse, one of the defining features of childhood and teenage years is that it is a time of sexual openness, a time when our sexualities have not yet been fully colonized by heteronormativity, gender binaries, and futuristic agendas. The sexual openness of children and teens is, for some, incongruent with a more stable adult heterosexuality, so recollections of intergenerational and queer seductions can be traumatic because they render our adult sexual identifications less than coherent. Recollections of adolescent and teenage lesbian sexualities are anachronistic. They queer the developmental timelines that heterosexually identified adults often use to consolidate their relation to adulthood. In an effort to manage anxious heterosexual identifications shadowed by memories of queer desire, polyamorous pleasures, and engagements with adolescent bodies not yet developed into clearly demarcated gendered and sexual subjects, the adult condenses the otherwise nuanced character of an intergenerational lesbian teacher affair into an instance of abuse.

I contend that many of the sexual relationships between lesbian teachers and students reported in the North American and British news might not have been traumatic at the time of the affair. They are, however, sometimes traumatic for the adult who lacks a conceptual template to process lesbian-teacher love outside the master narrative of child sexual abuse. Time and the insistent rhetoric of abuse play a queer trick on all parties involved in the arbitration of lesbian teachers' sexual improprieties, perverting love into abuse, teenagers into children, and teachers into sexual predators. Our culture imagines any sex between an adult and a younger person to be traumatic and debilitating because we are beholden to the master narrative of child sexual abuse. Like all master narratives, it sets the parameters for what can be thought and legitimately said in court and in school. If the teenager speaks about love, she (or he) has been manipulated into mistaking abuse for love; if the teenager seeks out teacher sex, she (or he) is said to be emotionally unstable – probably abused in the family home – and in need of guidance and psychological counselling; if the teenager moves in with her (or his) teacher, it must be under duress, and the relationship cannot be in any way good for the younger party. In all cases, the teacher should know better, and the teenager (imagined to be a vulnerable child) is said to be harmed. Of course, any of these things *could* be sexually harmful and detrimental to teenage emotional and academic development but the point is that they are not necessarily so. By failing to consider the politics of social consent and teenage sexual agency we criminalize those who may have only been unprofessional (as measured by present-day standards). Gender, sexuality, and context are typically not taken into consideration, and the older person is almost always constituted as a predatory pedophile in legal and professional discourses. The master narrative forecloses on alternative explanations and experiences that would otherwise trouble the absolutism now confounding discussions about intergenerational and homoerotic desires in high school cultures.

Adult time perverts knowledge, and what cannot be digested is expelled. People cannot know about lesbianism because it is reminiscent of disavowed homoerotic desire and other taboos on which heterosexuality is founded (Butler 1995). Equally troubling is the idea that the alleged victim(s) may have initiated the courting sequence. The problem of knowledge, in the contemporary cases, is riddled with a hysterical ignorance. The question of how to remember and enunciate an intergenerational relationship between a lesbian teacher and her female student is comparable to the question of how to comprehend and give voice to a desire that – until the moment of exposure – has been confined to a shadowy underground existence: call it the proverbial closet or the willful unconscious. I contend that the teenaged students are hurt not so much by teacher sex (although individual students might be) as by the master narrative of child sexual abuse that refuses to recognize teenager homoerotic cultures, their capacities to act as legitimate sexual agents, and their understandings of intergenerational sex.

It is noteworthy that in most sex scandals involving female teachers, the alleged "victims" are not so much hurt by the teachers as upset by the media, the courts, school administrators, and parents, who either sensationalize the relationship and bring it to an abrupt halt or criminalize the teacher. Teenagers and adolescents are often silenced in professional investigations and criminal investigations. Unless they draw on a discourse of sexual abuse, their stories lack credibility. When they talk about love and/or social consent, they are seen to be caught up in or reliving trauma. There is no legitimate alternative explanation, and attempts to narrate another story are subsumed within an abusive rhetoric or seen to be evidence of abuse. For example, in the United States, four sex scandals involving lesbian teachers have been reported in the new millennium, and in none of these cases has the narrative testimony brought forth by the teenager been validated by the courts, school professionals, parents, or psychologists. In all these cases, the students insisted that the relationships were loving and consensual. For example, in January 2006, Amy Lilley, a thirty-six-year-old Florida teacher at Citrus County High School, was charged with "lewd and lascivious battery on a child" stemming from her eighteen-month relationship with a female student. Lilley was said to have special access to students because she coached the girls' basketball and softball teams. The teenager did not view the relationship as harmful or coercive; she insisted that the two were in love and was heartbroken to learn that Lilley – in the early stages of the investigation – denied that they had a sexual relationship: "The girl was 'very distraught' when investigators told her that Lilley had initially denied having any sexual contact with her. The two loved each other, the girl told investigators" (Ramirez and Reiss 2005). Lilley later pleaded no contest, admitting to the sexual relationship with a minor. The judge sentenced Lilley to house arrest and eight years of probation and banned her from seeing the student in question.

According to media reports, the alleged victim asked the judge, with tears streaming down her cheeks, to remove the stipulation that Lilley cease contact with her as part of her sentence. The judge refused.

Only two days later, another Florida teacher, Jaymee Lane Wallace, was alleged to have had an eighteen-month relationship with a female student on her softball team. She had been put on administrative leave until the sheriff's investigation could be completed. The alleged victim was sixteen years old at the time of the relationship, and the teacher was twenty-seven years old. Wallace is charged with "lewd and lascivious behaviour," which carries a maximum sentence of fifteen years in prison. The teacher and student exchanged love letters, kissed in the teacher's car, stroked each other's genitals, and had oral sex. The student offered what I call social consent and wrote in her police statement that she initiated both the sex and the relationship with Wallace. The pupil destroyed love letters so that they couldn't be used as evidence against Wallace in court. According to media reports, the relationship proceeded according to the teenager's interests and desires – the teen asked for lesbian sex (not the teacher) – and the teen saw herself as an active and consenting participant.

Perhaps the most sensational case, of late, involves a thirty-six-year-old American teacher at South Haven's Baseline Middle School, Elizabeth Miklosovic, who was accused of sexually assaulting a fourteen-year-old girl and marrying her in a deep-woods, pagan ritual. Both Miklosovic and the student professed their mutual love, and the student told the judge that Miklosovic was a wonderful woman and that she, as a student, was neither manipulated nor taken advantage of in her relationship with the accused teacher. Even police agreed that both parties understood the relationship to be consensual. The judge disagreed. He insisted that consent was impossible, and the lesbian teacher was sentenced to serve from five to twenty-five years in prison. Even pagan communities, which hold more liberal ideas about sexuality, shunned Miklosovic and went to great lengths to condemn her while disassociating themselves from the sensational press, which saw her as a lesbian pedophile. Both the teacher and the teenaged student felt that many people, themselves included, had been hurt by the homophobic and sensational coverage of their case. The student was said in the news media to have gone to great lengths to protect the teacher and their relationship and to wrestle her interpretation of events from the courts, which appealed exclusively to the discourses of abuse and child sexual innocence (despite the actual age of the student involved).

Common to all these cases is that the relationships developed in pace and time with teenage desires as opposed to teacher or adult wishes and inclinations. But the courts and the profession could not acknowledge this fact. In the vast majority of cases, it is the criminalization of the relationships (and the teachers) that causes anxiety, distress, and emotional upset to the youth involved in the teacher sex scandals. It is only children who have their legitimate claims to sexuality denied through recourse to their own best interest in court. As I demonstrate in the following section, this denial is intimately related to the epistemology of the closet and to the problem of knowledge, disavowal, and ignorance that surrounds the lesbian teacher in court. The irony is lost to those who adopt a defensive insistence on abuse and turn a blind eye to queer and intergenerational desires in high school cultures.

Can the Lesbian Teacher Speak? Knowledge, Confession, and Disavowal in the Lesbian Teacher's Closet

The problem of lesbian secrecy, structured by what Eve Sedgwick (1990) calls the epistemology of the closet, makes it difficult to enunciate lesbian desires without disavowal, shame, ignorance, and fits and starts. For example, the teacher rumoured to have "un-natural" affections for her female teaching colleague in *The Children's Hour* is struck by the absurdity of knowledge and ignorance. In her climactic confession, Martha Dobie says to her best friend and teaching colleague:

> It's funny ... it's all mixed up. There's something in you, and you don't know it and you don't do anything about it. Suddenly a child gets bored and lies – and there you are, seeing it for the first time. I don't know. It all seems to come back to me. In some way I've ruined your life. I've ruined my own. I didn't even know ... I love you that way – maybe the way they said I love you. I don't know ... There's always been something wrong ... But I never knew it until all this happened ... You've got to know it ... It's there. I don't know how, I don't know why ... maybe it's been there ever since I first knew you ... I never knew why before. (Tuhkanen 2002, 1013-14)

As in the contemporary sex scandals involving lesbian teachers Beltain and Robertson, the crisis of knowledge around lesbianism is precipitated by the court of law.[5] But the confessions given by Martha Dobie in the *The Children's Hour* and by Beltain in the contemporary case are laced with uncertainty and disavowal. It is unclear whether the confessions are coming-out stories or indicative of a larger problem, that "of the realist's inability to convey lesbianism in language, to express something that can only be represented by suppression ... At issue is the whole concept of realistic form and its inability to deal with issues that cannot be simply and directly articulated" (Sauer 2000, 424). Following a teacher's confession, the audience or jury is imposed upon to know a truth about lesbianism, but they are left wondering whether the confessions were induced by the courts (lies and fabrications) or delayed discoveries dependent on hindsight (a reordering of self-knowledge) and time. "The conventions of realism require the enigma to be revealed at the end so that the reader [or jury] feels the power of knowing all as outside observer and judge" (424). The confession of lesbianism confounds the court because it cannot be verified and is time-dependent. Such confessions are threatening to legal rationality, which is the modus operandi of the court, and the temporality of the knowledge is upsetting to heterosexual time, with its need for coherence and linearity. Identities and identifications are unstable. As Foucault tells us, our sexuality does not reveal an inner truth, and our deliberations about what did or did not happen in any given lesbian-teacher encounter are more about confronting problems of knowledge, power, and discourse than about facticity.

In the court cases occasioned by lesbian-teacher sex scandals, lesbian confessions – as closeted speech acts – expose an analytic of knowing/not knowing peculiar to the symbolic law of the Father; he cannot know about the proliferation of queer subjectivities in the school because they do not fit into the postcolonial and heteronormative familial ensemble. For example, in the Scottish verdict (on which *The Children's Hour* was based), the judge (Father stand-in) could not comprehend lesbianism. "The counsel for the accused women argued that since no dildo, or as he put it, no 'artificial object designed to resemble the male instrument of procreation' was alleged, no venereal congress can be assumed" (Martin 2001, 403). In an absurd pronouncement of guilt, the judge convicted the teacher of performing an act that he could not comprehend. In short, the Scottish verdict depended on an idea – lesbianism – that in the minds of the court did not exist.

The insistence on not knowing is a deliberate act of refusal that also manifests itself in the contemporary sex scandal involving lesbian teacher Darlene Smart, who was accused of having two lesbian affairs with students in British Columbia in the late 1980s. Judge Stephen Harding of the British Columbia Supreme Court said that he saw no "reason why a female offender should be treated any differently than a male offender" ("Lesbian teacher" 1992). The judge refused to see the difference that a lesbian intergenerational love affair makes to the logic on which the discourse of child protectionism is based.[6] The students were fifteen and sixteen, while the teacher was twenty-seven. In essence, the judge could not see the particular threat posed by the lesbian to the heterosexual Symbolic, yet he condemned her for precisely this infraction. The lascivious lesbian teacher is equivalent to the male-teacher predator, yet she is not a man. The judge insists on seeing the lesbian as a man. As Roof (2001, 246) contends in her discussion of lesbian representation in the law, the "system thereby rids itself of sameness, which is represented by the lesbian's incomprehensible, undifferentiated feminine ground. This conceals the operations of a coexistent but different logic of difference. And this logic is based not on the binaries of sexual (or even racial or age) differences, but on a logic of separation premised on castration – the Law lesbians in their guise as fake men appear to deny." Paradoxically, the judge maintains binary sexual and gender categories by insisting that the lesbian is the same as a heterosexual male predator. The difference that lesbianism makes cannot be overtly acknowledged in court unless it is couched in the discourse of pathology to neutralize the threat. In short, the lesbian is and is not a man, as she is and is not a threat. The paradox enables the court to persecute her while denying, and thus neutralizing, her upset to heterosexual futurity and to heteronormative gender binaries.

That the judge is willfully blind to the threat posed by the lesbian teacher is understandable when one considers that ignorance is the last defence. Because the lesbian teacher does not seem to balk at the threat of legal punishment (she acknowledges a love affair while knowing that she will be persecuted for it), she is worrisome. She seems to mystify the point of difference between the penis and the phallus (Roof 2001, 244-45) central to the Father's heteronormative house rules. She does not have a penis yet acts as though she possesses the phallus. The lesbian teacher seduces young girls as a man and does not seem to fear or cower in the face of persecution by the courts. When castration is seen to be inconsequential, it is "possible to posit an imaginary female world whose existence and communal relations are impossible without a sense of castration – without the law" (245). Regardless of the law, the lesbian can wield the phallus even though she lacks the penis. Through her very existence, psychoanalytic theorists maintain that she sublimates the question of gender (Lukes 2001, 252) by denying the reality of castration (Buccino 2001), upsets the law of the patriarchal Father (Roof 2001), and seeks to enact revenge on the symbolic structure (Lukes 2001, 251) with its need for intelligible familial subject positions and heteronormativities.

The threat posed by the lesbian teacher as seductress and sexual predator is not tolerable to heteronormative orders. She represents a threat to law and order and to the heteronormative and reproductive future. The judge attempts to mitigate her threat by insisting that the lesbian is emotionally infantile, criminal, or pathological.[7] It should not go without notice that Johima, the student in the contemporary case involving Robertson, was also said to be "delusional." In his final submission, the legal defence for the accused, Donald Muldoon, said that Johima "had a history of emotional and psychiatric problems ... We know there is a lack of emotional stability in this woman." The lawyer for the defence was suggesting that Johima invented the allegations against Robertson and that she has "explored the idea that she had been sexually abused by her mother, although there was no evidence to support that notion" (Hall 1993c).

The defence lawyer attempted to shift the taint of lesbian psychosis from the teacher to the student, but with little success. The judge sentenced Robertson to jail time. Roof (2001, 246) contends: "The representational existence of the outlaw lesbian is, of course, necessary for maintaining the system of binary, heterosexual logic ... The lesbian, more than the male homosexual, is the point of failure certifying that the rest of the system – the complementary opposites, heterosexuality – continues to work." Roof argues that lesbian sexuality refuses "acquiescence to social norms (in this instance, patriarchy)" (245), so the lesbian must be equated with psychosis. In other words, her existence signals a challenge to the rule of the heterosexual Father and his investment in reproductive futurity: "While this pathologized lesbian and her inherent contagion underwrites a fearful imaginary in most media representations of lesbians, she also evokes a more dangerous and substantial challenge to the logic of the system itself" (245-46). The law must, over and over again, designate the lesbian a monstrous threat while simultaneously denying her existence as a threat.

The courts deny the specificity of the teacher-student lesbian relationship while constructing the lesbian teacher as a particular menace to the sexual innocence of white schoolgirls without noticing the contradiction. The lesbian teacher is not a maternal lover of children but a professional monstrosity, a child abuser and evil, predatory viper, and the teenaged girl is her prey. Knowing that the teenage girls could have been active initiators as opposed to passive victims does not sit well with the court, and the tensions associated with this difficult knowledge are palpable. "Again, the paradox of innocence for women is that it certifies her claim to victimization and denies her moral agency and human complexity" (Hart 2001, 298). But the question of innocence is not transparent, and the pretence of innocence holds at bay a knowledge that can not only upset but also undermine the foundations of heterosexual futurity with its investment in binary gender and sexual difference. Stories of incest – when liberated from the bonds of erotic innocence – can "tell us what cannot enter into the symbolic order of representation and interpretation and therefore, in their omissions, silences, and obliqueness, evoke how the incest taboo is being transformed from an unspeakable, impossible act into a prescriptively representable prohibition" (296).

Whiteness as Death and the Proliferation of Queers in the School

> Eroticizing exists in symbiotic relation with sanitizing, and the veiling and the exposing exist in an encircling doublespeak.
> (Kincaid 1998, 102)

As argued by James Kincaid in his book *Erotic Innocence: The Culture of Child Molesting* (1998), our culture loves stories of childhood innocence, which is particularly true in discourses about pedophilia. The great irony in child-protectionist discourse is that the insistence on "childhood innocence" is productive; it produces the child as a queerly erotic entity – a sexual object for adult, voyeuristic pleasure. This is the same process of sexualization that child protectionists attempt to prohibit when they persecute child pornographers. The child is alluring precisely because she (or he) is proscribed to be out of bounds. The moral majority, according to Kincaid, is revealed through this paradox to have a fetishistic investment in childhood asexuality and is excited by the danger of pedophilia because it is an incitement to talk about innocence betrayed.[8] The fetish operates as a distraction; the morally predisposed express disgust (at pedophilic acts) so that they may refuse to acknowledge a more deep-seated cultural investment in childhood sexual innocence, a queerly erotic designation in and of itself.

Kincaid (1998, 20-21) writes that we are "instructed by our cultural heritage to crave that which is forbidden, a crisis we face by not facing it, by writing self-righteous doublespeak that demands both lavish public spectacle and constant guilt-denying projections onto scapegoats." This is not to say that children are not in need of protection but that the insistence on childhood innocence produces an erotic intrigue with the child. To see the child as pure, chaste, and unencumbered by lascivious thoughts is to animate an alluring and sexualized portrait of the child. The prohibition incumbent on the pretence of child sexual innocence (another form of ignorance) incites the erotic appeal that the moral majority cannot stomach. Kincaid writes: "If we posit openly that children are activated by sexual energy, the evasive screens necessary for eroticizing them disappear; that is, it is necessary that they be 'innocent and pure' if they are to be alluring and also give adults the sentimental stories of denial and projection we find indispensable" (16). The moral majority finds this idea repugnant because it is invested in an ignorance about youth sexualities.

Kincaid (1998) argues that "'the child' is a product of ways of perceiving, not something that is *there*" (19, original emphasis). In the sex scandals involving lesbian teachers, there is a curious temporal slippage; teenaged girls (alleged victims) are *seen* to be children. Even though Victoria Harris was sixteen when the affair began and was said to have initiated the affair by kissing the teacher on the lips following a counselling session, her case was seen to be synonymous with *child* sexual abuse. Justice William Selbie sentenced the teacher to jail time so that the conviction would be a "deterrent to other teachers, counsellors or professionals entrusted with *children*" ("Ex-counsellor" 1995, emphasis added). Johima was also said to be a "vulnerable *kid*" (Hall 1993b, emphasis added) even though she was a teenager. Negating her earlier feelings of love for the accused, Johima similarly positioned herself as a "kid" who confused abuse with love. Referring to the Mary Baxter sex scandal in the United States, which involved an adult female teacher and a seventeen-year-old boy-student, Kincaid (1998, 31) documents how in the court proceedings a "smart and active older adolescent is shrunk into a child, a generic 'essence-of-child,' by this cultural story [of pedophilia], remolded as passive, innocent, and guileless. His actual age, activities, particularities are melted away to fit our needs" so that we can see the teenager as a child.

But it is not only age differentials that are rendered inconsequential to the discourse of pedophilia, but child and teenage sexualities as well. It is not possible to theorize child and teen sexualities without evoking the phantom of the pedophile, not coincidentally rendered queer in homophobic discourses. While many believe that the pedophile exploits child sex, it is our cultural insistence on childhood sexual innocence that both creates the pedophile and utilizes the child to serve an adult political and psychic end. Because childhood innocence is used to evoke heterosexuality without appearing to do so, the institution of heterosexuality is buttressed without having to explain how child sexual innocence is its natural incarnation – we are left to imagine and infer a relationship between the underage child and heterosexuality that is in need of protection. The child is read as the anti-queer (Edelman 2004, 25).

The fantasmatic equation is upset when childhood sexuality manifests itself explicitly and can no longer be camouflaged by a pretence of innocence as in the case of the lesbian-teacher sex scandals involving sexually savvy and all-too-willing teenaged girls. It is most upset, however, when an adolescent or, more often than not, a developmentally mature older teen initiates relations with or is seduced by an adult in a position of professional care and trust. Any vision of adolescent or teen sexuality seems to be at odds with child protectionism. Those designated underage are seen to be sexually innocent and naive, as she or he is a budding heterosexual; this is the contradictory doublespeak that reveals itself in the sex scandals involving lesbian teachers. This is a problem of knowledge that gets contained through disavowal and polemics of knowing and not knowing. Our culture imagines that any "sex between a child and an adult, regardless of the gender of either party, is inevitably traumatic and debilitating for the child" (Bruhm and Hurley 2004, xxii). That many queer children have their "initial sexual experiences with older men or women, experiences they will probably not define as traumatic or exploitative as they reflect on them later" (xxvi) is an enigma that North American and British cultures tend to ignore.

But what if the queer child or teen enjoyed the allegedly abusive encounter of concern to the courts and the teaching profession even though the adult remembering the incident reconstitutes it as a professional boundary violation? This is certainly the case in the Robertson fiasco, where the complainant required the better part of two decades to recall as abusive a four-year, live-in relationship based on social consent and love. Because adults lack a normative template to understand intergenerational affairs, it is sometimes the case that they default into an abuse narrative. "The adult narrator overlays his own remembered experience with another narrative, one that renders him victim. Significantly, that victim narrative is the only one available to him – and to us, in our culture. We lack the possibility to narrate a pedophilia that will have been benign (let alone benevolent, in the Greek way)" (Bruhm and Hurley 2004, xxix). The memory as opposed to the seduction is the source of trauma: "To the degree that the remembered child is the child who liked the sexual contact, the child is killed off; the narrative brought to define him is one of fear, power abuse, and shame" (xxix).

Kevin Ohi (2004, 82) makes the same point in his discussion of the queer child. He writes: "Panics about childhood sexuality concern above all the adult's fears about his or her own desire, the threat posed by the sexual child to the serenity of adult self-understandings ... To say that children aren't queer is a way of asserting that we know what children are and that we therefore know what adults are." Adult-refused identifications with the queerness of youth are accomplished through the hyperbolic insistence on childhood sexual innocence: the child or teen cannot be seen as queer because the adult does not see her or himself as queer, so anything queer about the child must not be about the adult but about a predatory queer-like pedophile. The refusal to avow the queerness of our younger selves produces the child/teen as a future heteronormative citizen and discounts his or her own legitimate claim to queer and nonprocreative sexualities. By refusing to avow the queerness of our younger selves we ward off memories at odds with heteronormativity. By refusing queer remembrances we lay claim to an officially sanctioned developmental sequence that might not have been our own, one that leads organically to heterosexual citizenship. In so doing we discount the complexities of our own sexualities and those of school-age youth who are queer and in other ways non-normative.

The defensive insistence on childhood sexual innocence produces a domesticated heteronormativity that is itself the rationale upon which the child and teen are protected. As Bruhm and Hurley (2004) note in their edited book about the queerness of children, the thesis of child innocence is paradoxical: the child is to be innocent (devoid of desire and intentionality) *and* heterosexual at the same time. We don't need to look far to see images of budding, preadolescent heterosexuality in film, television, and popular culture, but pairing this sexuality with innocence is not only incongruous, but also absurd. Children cannot be innocent and heterosexual at the same time. If anything, children and teenagers are queer and non-normative. They do not have domesticated desires and sexualities but profoundly ambiguous and polymorphously perverse sexualities. "If there is anything 'natural' about children it is their curiosity about bodies and pleasure, their desire to make stories that are not the colonizing narratives of heteronormativity" (xxi). Childhood and teen sexualities defy developmental templates issued by psychologists, heteronormalities structuring everyday life, and gender polarities while refusing to abide by coherent identifications central to adult sexual codes. But the variegated sexualities of children are branded innocent, so the radical potentialities of these orientations are contained. "Childhood sexuality is exploited so that it can be dismissed, sacrificed on the altar of secular gender normativity" (xvii), heterosexuality, and marital domesticity.

Ideas about child sexual innocence are used by members of the profession, the public, and the media to legitimate their own upset about the queer composition of the family romance in education. The moralists, the child advocates, and the profession harm and use school-age youth in the service of heterosexuality, the future, and their own investments in adult time. Child protectionists, educational administrators, legal experts, and teacher professionals alike condemn teacher-student sex in one fell swoop as de facto abuse. I suggest that we cannot accurately predict or determine the impact of intergenerational and/or queer teacher sex on students, particularly when the sex is based on social consent and when the student is in his or her teenage years. Some cases might fit the template of child sexual abuse, but others may not. We might agree that teacher-student sex is unprofessional but not, as I contend, criminal. It is the defensive insistence on *abuse* that is symptomatic of another more deep-seated anxiety about the position of those designated underage in the reproductive and heteronormative future. In short, the sex panic is not really about child or teen welfare but about heterosexual futurity and the adult. The idea of the child is here exploited as a narrative device to secure heteronormativity. But it is not only the reproduction of heterosexuality that is secured through the mythology of the sexually innocent child; postcolonial power structures are stabilized as well. Alternative sexualities bring about different ways of being together, as Foucault (1997) claims, but they also enable new sexual cultures to proliferate in postcolonial contexts. For example, Kincaid (1998, 17) shows us how our cultural investment in erotic innocence is mapped onto the child's body, and without overtly acknowledging it, he shows us how the use of whiteness, as a racialized technique of representation, is central to the presentation of an ideal of childhood virginal purity: "Baby-smooth skin is capable of inciting desire; unsmooth, or contoured skin is not: is this because flatness is innately more titillating than texture, or because flatness signifies nothing at all and thus doesn't interfere with our projections? In the same way, desirable faces must be blank, drained of color; big eyes round and expressionless; hair blond or colorless; waists, hips, feet, and minds small." The images employed to construct a fantasy of innocence (so nicely captured by Kincaid in this description) depend heavily on whiteness as a visual trope. There is something invisible or perhaps ultravisible and thus unspeakable about whiteness. As Richard Dyer (1997, 13) observes in his book on whiteness in popular film culture that white heterosexuality structures desire as dark, so I wish to claim that the mythology of childhood sexual innocence is also tinged with a postmodern eugenic concern about the proliferation of sexual appetites that are not conducive to white heterosexual breeding. There is "something at stake in looking at, or continuing to ignore, white racial imagery" (1) that is intimately connected to the proliferation of queerly hybrid subjectivities in the school.

As Sander Gilman (1985) notes in his study of race and sexuality, the technique of displacement was harnessed by whites to disavow their illicit sexual desires; darker races were seen to be hypersexual. Using the same technique of displacement, heterosexuals saw the lesbian (or homosexual body) as hypersexual. I do not wish to claim that racist and homophobic visual techniques are one and the same, although I do contend that there is, in the case of the sex scandals involving lesbian teachers, a related anxiety about the propagation of the species as white and heteronormativity. Devoid of colour, just as she or he is devoid of sexuality, the white child is innocent. The spectacle of childhood sexual innocence is white, and as Dyer (1997) writes, there is a curious association between whiteness and death in popular film culture. This death is intimately related to postmodern eugenic worries about the end of reproductive futurity.

In his discussion of whiteness, Dyer (1997) interrogates how the colour (or absence of colour) is laced with anxieties about death. He carefully demonstrates how whiteness signifies all that is chaste, modest, delicate, pure, clean, untouched, and – most of all – transcendent in Hollywood film. Noticing also that Western Christianity reserves a special place for the Virgin Mary, the crucifixion of Jesus Christ, martyrs, and saints, Dyer provides an example of the dual fascination with death and transcendence. Because the ideal of whiteness is an impossibility (no mortal is ever pure and untouched by carnal knowledge), the spectacle of whiteness is always "haunted by misgiving, even anxiety." Dyer contends that "whiteness as absence [is] impossible ... To relinquish dirt and stains, corporeality and thingness, is also to relinquish both the pleasures of the flesh and the reproduction upon which whiteness as a technique of racialized power depends. To be nothing is to be dead" (81). There is also the actual threat of death carried by white Europeans during the Age of Exploration to non-European and indigenous peoples around the world. Dyer notes that the "idea of whites as both themselves dead and as bringers of death is commonly hinted at in horror literature and film" (210).[9]

The exhibition of whiteness is terrifying because it is envisioned as both threatening and under threat. Seeing whiteness triggers anxieties, and associated disavowals, about heterosexual procreation, racial hybridization, and the continuation of the species. Dyer (1997, 216) contends that "it is a specifically white, aghast perception of the unstoppable breeding of non-whites, that deep-seated suspicion that non-whites are better at sex and reproduction than are whites, that, indeed, to be truly white and reproductively efficient are mutually incompatible and that, as a result, whites are going to be swamped and engulfed by the non-white multitudes." But displaying whiteness and, in particular, child vulnerability *as* white signals an angst about queer breeding. The spectacle of the innocent white child in the sex scandals involving lesbian teachers symbolizes white-race suicide. The vulnerable white child represents foreboding; he or she is accompanied by a misgiving about the white female teacher and her failure to biologically reproduce. Let us not forget that for most of the twentieth century, the prohibition against marriage was imposed on female teachers and that social historians, such as Lillian Faderman (1991) and Martha Vicinus (1985), have shown how girls' boarding schools – with a uniformly female teaching staff – have been hotbeds for lesbianism. Interestingly, the failure to reproduce was associated with the problem of educated women, who "would be rendered barren and unable to populate the nation with the right breed of citizens. Well into the twentieth century, many commentators saw in women's education an incipient 'race suicide'" (Tuhkanen 2002, 1021).[10]

It is also important to note that death plagues the queer child as a symbol of nonproductivity. For example, parents who learn that their child is gay or transgender often go through processes of bereavement and feel like their little girl or little boy has been taken away from them. As Terry Sanderson (1996, 8) explains, the bereavement effect leads the heteronormative parent to feel that the "previously beloved son or daughter suddenly seems to disappear from life and is replaced by a sinister version of the same person. Parents ... grieve for what they have lost." The beloved child becomes a stranger and is associated with a racialized shadow haunting the white, heteronormative family. Gay kids are also thought to suffer from a developmental arrest. The homosexual influence of gay, lesbian, or otherwise queer teachers and/or students is contagious, and in the homophobic imagination, gay influences can lead to declining birth rates, AIDS and HIV, adultery, queer family forms, divorce, and sexual voraciousness – all of which are associated with the "gay lifestyle" – a synonym for death and an end to reproductive futurity.

Female whiteness gestures to an important intersection between race and sexuality that bears on the lesbian teacher sex scandals. Dyer (1997, 29) writes that "there are special anxieties surrounding the whiteness of white women vis-à-vis sexuality. As the literal bearers of children, and because they are held primarily responsible for their initial raising, women are the indispensable means by which the group – the race – is in every sense reproduced." Forever compared to the Virgin Mary, the white woman is trapped within a uniquely Christian paradox. She must biologically reproduce without losing her virginal status, give birth without bleeding or tarnishing the sheets, and locate herself within heterosexual futurity. The white woman is the guardian of the white, patriarchal, heterosexual family but, enigmatically, is forbidden to enjoy or seek out the sexual union that she is key to consummate.

In the Western imagination, the white female teacher carries with her a heterosexual civilizing mission compatible with eugenic desires for racial purity; she was responsible for curtailing homosociality between men (Dyer 1997, 186); for redirecting heterosexual, white male attentions away from non-European women and toward the white lady of refined social graces (186); and for introducing "expectations of affect, obligation and mutuality in heterosexual arrangements" (186). White female heterosexuality was key to the fantasy of racial purity and to the reproduction of the white race. Women's role is to guard against infidelity in marriage, to ensure racial purity in breeding, and to cleanse the nation of immorality, degeneracy, and sexual turpitude. In short, the white female teacher (coded as mother) is responsible for policing identity borders (racial, sexual, gender, and otherwise), such that the patriarchal rule of the Father can propagate and that he can recognize his brood.

Kelly Oliver and Benigno Trigo (2003, xix) suggest that the fear of maternal sexuality can be displaced onto or condensed into the threat of racial difference." It follows, therefore, that the solicitude around the sexual transgressions of white female teachers (coded as maternal sexuality gone wrong) gestures to a more profound anxiety about queer contagion and the proliferation of queer breeding practices in the school. It is as though the darker races have infected whiteness through the intermediary channels and pedagogies of queer culture. Infection (the inevitable outcome of racial contagion) is carried out through a virulent strain of queer antibodies. Queer infestation is accomplished by lesbian seductions, by reproductive practices that confound normative heterosexual coupling, and by the quintessential lesbian refusal to respect binary gender designations, which depend on the mythology of castration and the Oedipal narrative as well as on the language and logic of heterosexual futurity.

In their study of film noir, Oliver and Trigo (2003, xiv) comment on how a "primal anxiety over borders and boundaries ... that manifests itself in specific fears and phobias of race, sex, maternity, and national origin" is central to the genre. In other words, the audience is drawn to film noir because it enables them to visualize what would otherwise be an unconscious angst about border crossings – racial, sexual, and otherwise. The sexuality of the femme fatale disguised as maternal teacher (Sharon Stone's role as matronly teacher in *Diabolique* is a good example) is not only enigmatic but also tinged with a nervous apprehension about white-race degeneration, death, and dying. Oliver and Trigo note that often the "most telling elements of noir threaten from the margins and are associated with maternity, mothers or an absent mother. Significantly, many of these threatening mothers are inflected with race" (26). The racialization of the monstrous mother as non-European points to a nervous apprehension about the relationship between heterosexual and racial reproduction in popular visual culture.

The desire for boundary maintenance is not only formulaic to film noir, but also central to the contemporary lesbian-teacher sex scandals. For example, the lesbian seduction involving Robertson and Johima was said to have taken place in the "washroom adjoining the gym office" (Hall 1993d); in yet another article, the clandestine affair was said to have begun in the "gym office ... the teacher would close the door ... [and also in the] first-aid room at the school" (Hall 1993a); Harris testified that the teacher and student kissed in a sleeping bag during a school trip. The Jaymee Lane Wallace affair occurred in a car. The Elizabeth Miklosovic transgression took place in the woods. In each report, the teacher's transgression was seen to have taken place at the margins. Danger lies in the margins, in the intermediary spaces where ambiguity lies and where the messiness of identity formation is revealed. "In-betweeness and ambiguity are repressed to form proper stable, if always precarious, identity" (Oliver and Trigo 2003, xxxii). Identities are, for Oliver and Trigo, defensive operations that are easily seen to be artificial, arbitrary, and most important, subject to mutation, and it is this capacity to incite a metamorphosis that is endemic to the school.

The lesbian teacher reproduces queer subjectivities among the student body by inciting desire (erotic seduction) and by achieving a fluency in the epistemology of the closet. The domain of the closet, the interior space that serves as a network for troubling knowledge about queers, is leaky. The contagious knowledge seeps into the heterosexual culture of the school: it undermines the mythology of sexual innocence; the promise of white, heterosexual, racial purity; and binary gender positionalities, on which patriarchy is based. The pedagogy of the lesbian teacher depends on the reproduction of new desires and identifications with queer cultures. Her brood is born of knowledge (not white virginal innocence) and is intent on the fantasy of seduction that cannot speak its name in the white heteronormative Father's schoolhouse. But queers do proliferate and live alongside heterosexual mainstreams. Queer developmental times cannot be read through the logic of heterosexual futurity, the courts, or master narratives of child sexual abuse. Queer time does not respect chronological age and generational differences that organize thought about children and adults, abuse, and legal consent. The age and temporal violations of the present stop heterosexual time and its futuristic agendas.

Conclusion

Queer subjectivities seem to be flourishing in the school, and the role of the white lesbian teacher in the proliferation of new hybrid sexualities is subject to nervous speculation. The white teenaged girl-student, coded as child, transmutes into an indeterminate subject (or object) of lesbian desire – a quintessentially queer subject. She is infected by a queer contagion akin to the racial contagion of the nineteenth and early twentieth centuries. As Oliver and Trigo (2003, 236) conclude in their discussion of spatial politics, unstable borders, and dark corridors in film noir, there is an opportunity to remake or to undo the closures of stable identifications in intermediary zones: "Occupying analogous in-between spaces can be a means to escape the logic of identity that binds and kills the subjects of noir." The washroom adjoining the gym office, the door, the car, the woods, and the first-aid room can all be seen as thresholds that provide opportunities for non-normative gender identifications, anti-Oedipal desires (i.e., homosexual and intergenerational), and clandestine liaisons – new ways of being together as hypothesized by Foucault (1997). Queer reproductive practices disturb heteronormativity because they depend on a desire for an alternative Symbolic. The proliferation of queerly hybrid subjects (i.e., bastard children in the eyes of the white patriarchal Father) confirms that there *is* something productive that is engendered and procreative in and about the lesbian teacher's closet.

7
Conclusion: Troubling Methodological Memoirs and Queer Pedagogies of Pederasty

> Yet the act of telling the story of deviance blurs with the deviant acts themselves. (Sigel 2002, 243)

> Perhaps we can write ourselves into the plot directly, give up our immunity ... But none of this is going to happen without a fuss, without a most distressing and ignominious set of scandals – which is where you come in. (Kincaid 2004, 15)

> The challenge of radical pedagogues is to re-examine the assumption underlying the perversity of pederasty concept. (Sears 1998, 99)

Writing this book has not been easy. There is a curious way in which the topic of sex scandals implicates me as a researcher. I have been caught in the troubles that I subject to critical and queer inquiry in this book. By this, I mean to suggest that I have had my share of raised eyebrows when I tell colleagues what I am writing about. People wonder why I am writing a book on teacher sex scandals and what this could possibly say about my own pedagogical practice or my ethics as a scholar. After all, who does research on sex, particularly in the educational milieu, without moralizing or condemning what many people take to be obvious sexual transgressions and improprieties? There is Jane Gallop (1997), but she wrote about the colonizing aspects of sexual harassment *after* she was accused by her graduate students. James Kincaid (2004), who critically examines narratives and panics about pedophilia, has been branded a danger to British and American society. He is said to violate childhood sexual innocence, to be grossly misinformed (despite his exhaustive and brilliant critique of the master pedophilic narrative), to support the Paedophile Information Exchange, and to advocate child sexual abuse. Kincaid writes: "I became a scandal myself, but it was a comic miniscandal ... my book tapped, predictably, a small feeder line of outrage and caused hardly more than a belch" (14-15). Similarly, Judith Levine, who wrote *Harmful to Minors: The Perils of Protecting Children from Sex* (2002), was accused by the media and Christian right of condoning pedophilia. Even though only a portion of her book dealt with sex between adults and children, it became known as "'the pedophilia book'" (229). She faced threats of censorship, death threats, and slanderous accusations, and she was given the dubious honour of publishing what some called the "'most controversial book of the year'" (230).

While the publicity might have increased sales in the above-mentioned cases and while there might, as I argue in Chapter 5, be a pleasure that comes from condemnation (the punishment stands in for validation and gratification), it is always hard to have one's words twisted into distortions that, ironically, are symptomatic of the panic and anxiety that one's book is about. Levine's text is about the dangers of child protectionism in the arena of sex, and regrettably, although not surprisingly, it became an example of that from which social conservatives wish to protect their kids. In other words, the book became the problem that it was meant to document and interrogate. I can relate. The same thing happened to my writing but in the form of an article that later became a chapter in this book.

What follows is a series of methodological memoirs, journal entries that I wrote while researching and writing this book. By way of conclusion, I wish to share three entries to illuminate academic disciplinary practices but, more important, to hear the reverberations of what Kincaid calls the "belch" of sex research. In other words, I am interested in the noise and interference (Britzman 1998) that perverse sex research causes in heteronormative education and its imaginations. By "perverse," I mean to refer to all that is nonreproductive or anti-future – the practices, ideas, and desires that do not lend themselves to domestication in nuclear, monogamous, and white familial institutions, ensembles, and their imaginations. The perverse does not concern itself with professionalism or reproductive futurity and is unapologetically about what Foucault (1997) explained to be the pursuit of pleasure in new and previously unimagined ways of being with oneself and others.

Deborah Britzman (1998, 66) tells us that there is a form of sex education (or research) that is not yet tolerated: "the polymorphously perverse." This sex education "conceptualizes sexuality as movement and as otherness and, as such, as a part of the imaginary domain that means to refuse to stabilize sexuality through the consolation of place," time, and normalizing regimes. It is not about familial geographies, heterosexual and developmental time, stable and intelligible identities, eugenics, or even social hygiene for national betterment. It is queer and doesn't care much about the future as heterosexuality, eugenics, and professional education envision it. The polymorphously perverse incites a pedagogy based on difficult knowledge, interference, and a politics and poetics of transgression that interfere with education's future and approach to sex as negation. I am intrigued by the possibility of a queer pedagogy that troubles what Britzman (1998) conceives of as passions for ignorance and with an education that incites, as opposed to foreclosing upon, curiosity. In the realm of sexuality, passionate ignorances cannot tolerate or know about perverse or nonprocreative desires without upset. I continue to be curious about why adults cannot cope with Eros in the pedagogical encounter and about how this inability to cope may be used in my sex research as a moment to run interference, to stop heterosexual time, so that we can do something other than moralize and condemn in the time and place of school sex scandals. Queer pedagogies and sex researchers must interrogate the certainty that we have about "innocence and guilt, normality and deviance" (Britzman 1998, 74). I use the scandal of sex research to make such trouble.

It is the job of what Britzman (1998, 77) calls the "little sex researcher" to study pleasures, including one's own, and the otherness of "others" and to get curious about what education, moralities, and professionals claim to know, "for when one becomes a little sex researcher, one is interested in the study of pleasures and in the detours taken. When one can study the histories sex provokes, the love it might imagine and perform, then one is likely to engage as well the study of where knowledge breaks down, becomes anxious, is built again. The curriculum moves toward the polymorphously perverse and onto Bataille's notion of 'eroticism,' when the problem becomes the making of questions that can unsettle the docility of education." The polymorphous perversity of queer theory and pedagogy offers up new questions and opportunities. How are we to be curious about the differences of race, age, gender, sexuality, class, history, and culture without defaulting into anxious policies and teachings about social hygiene, professional practice, and health education, the legacies of which are to be found in modern-day eugenics and racisms? Instead, queer pedagogies offer up a means to think about social difference as calls for ethical engagements *as opposed to calls for moralities and for discipline and punishment.* In my capacity as a "little sex researcher" of sex panics in education, I have been curious about what upsets heteronormative high school cultures and about why the body of the child or teen is central to this upset. My intention in this chapter is to map, or locate, a conceptual trajectory whereby something new can be thought about Eros in the pedagogical encounter, in intergenerational desire, in child and teen sexualities, and in adult entanglements with, in, and about these realities. The time of learning is not always the time of education, as Britzman tells us, and queer pedagogies are similarly belated as they traverse diasporic, psychic, and temporal horizons. Queer timelines, as I discuss throughout this book, reverberate, and I ask the reader to listen to what is not said, to what cannot be said, and to what upsets the heteronormativity of academic and high school cultures. In the moment of scandal, something new about Eros in the pedagogical encounter may emerge and be subject to scholarly analysis; once the content is censored, it is sent back to the underground domain of the scholarly and professional unconscious. Promise lies in the echo, and it is here that I wish not to conclude but to begin again with my disturbing remembrances.

> *In June 2002 I received a letter from the Faculty Research Publications Committee of a university at which I am no longer employed, to which I had applied for funding to support my research project on the recent outbreak of school sex scandals involving female teachers and underage boy-students in the media. Although my proposal was funded, the project had the dubious honour of receiving the following, somewhat ominous warning in a formal letter authored by my dean: "In reviewing your application the committee identified a matter that I would like to share. It goes without saying that your research is in an area of public controversy and that academic freedom protects your right to pursue controversial topics. The cases you identify also raise questions about ethics, professional conduct and the law. While these issues are not the focus of your research, it is felt that some reference to these matters would be appropriate in your proposal and/or research." (Cavanagh, personal methodological memoir, 2002)*

> *In April 2003 I received an official notification from the Social Sciences and Humanities Research Council of Canada (SSHRC) stating that they weren't able to offer support for my program of research. The reviewer comments were enclosed, and one reviewer wrote: "The researcher makes a disturbing assumption that somehow these female teachers are not really at fault, even if they have crossed the line of what constitutes an ethical practice in their relationship with particular male students. Moreover, suggesting that discomfort with female teacher sexual deviance can somehow be equated with broader discomfort with female [sexual] deviance is baffling and disconcerting. Certainly feminist educators valuing teacher professionalism and promoting ethical teaching practices would also be baffled and disconcerted. The researcher would do well to rethink her study in light of ethical guidelines and codes of professional conduct developed by teachers' associations/federations across Canada." (Cavanagh, personal methodological memoir, 2002)*

> *I submitted a paper on the Annie Markson sex scandal to an academic journal in education. I was formally notified by the section editor in a letter that the paper had been accepted for publication and that the three reviews of my manuscript were overwhelmingly*

> *positive. I then received an e-mail message from the section editor, two months later, stating that "the editorial board has concerns about possible interpretations of your writing in reference to the specific case." (None of these concerns were expressed in the three reviews of the paper written by the external reviewers.) The editor would not commit these alleged concerns to paper, but through telephone conversations I was told that the chief editor believed that the paper could be read as condoning pedophilia. Even though allegations of sexual activity were found to be untrue in the scandal about which I was writing, the mere accusation of pedophilia in the case (not to mention the analysis of Eros in the pedagogical encounter) was enough to make people think that the teacher and I were both pedophiles!!*
>
> *I asked whether the editorial board had considered how censoring academic discussion about Eros in the pedagogical encounter contributed to a dangerous school climate for children. I also pointed out that by presuming childhood sexual innocence and refusing to talk openly about the pedophilic imagination (even though I was not doing so in my paper), we contribute to the construction of a societal taboo around childhood sexuality that produces the possibility of pederasty and makes it difficult for children to see themselves as having agency, decision, and choice in any sexual encounter. How can youth establish their physical and emotional boundaries when they are not supposed to know or speak openly about what they feel or about what adults do to them? In other words, I insisted that it is the silence surrounding the taboo (not my manuscript) that is productive – and hence dangerous. Besides, where else can conversations about Eros be had and seriously analyzed if not in scholarly journals?*
>
> *Instead of engaging in a discussion about the politics of censorship, child welfare, and the place of sexual moralism in school culture, the chief editor responded by stating that her decision was final; she did not want to discuss the matter further. Evidently, she did not want to take the time to discuss what she saw as serious enough to warrant censorship. (Cavanagh, personal methodological memoir, 2002)*

Curiously, people deal with their troubles by foreclosing on academic discussion, through ignorance and censorship, and as a last resort, by not reading about what is taken to be difficult or upsetting to white heteronormativity. The master narrative of child sexual abuse always wants the last word, and how better to get it than by branding the author a pedophile – a danger or threat to what professional education and its pedagogies care so very much about, the white sexually innocent child. So I am left with the question of what happens when one's book is read as a problem. How are the critically queer reflections that one offers up by way of analysis erased and effaced by the powers that be? Do queer engagements with normative ideas about the sexualities of youth necessarily upset, and what can be done or made of this upset? Might we analyze the deep-seated anxieties that ignite scandals as opposed to opting for a politic of academic censorship?

I suggest that authors do not have a transparent, linear, or obvious relation to that about which they write; interpretations can be made and narratives offered up for analysis, but an essential truth, as Michel Foucault (1978) theorizes it, does not exist. Feminist methodologists call for us to locate ourselves in relation to our research, and usually this is structured by an invitation to identify one's subject position and to articulate an academic and political interest befitting this identification. The equations between identity, academic agendas, and politics are too often seen as self-evident and knowable. I suggest that there is a danger in claiming to know too much about the author or the intentions that organize our research agendas. I wonder what the relationality between the two entails and how it gets used to override scholarly analysis and transfer reading difficulty on to authors themselves. The identity or politics of the author become a defence against difficult knowledge. Investments in research are never clear or transparent; it is foolhardy to assume that a truth or essence of the researcher can be gleaned from what he or she writes. This is not to say that researchers cannot be self-reflective, or that we need not be held responsible for what we write, but that we shouldn't be mistaken for what we write. I wonder how we might forge a pedagogy based on a politics of engagement as opposed to a practice of negation and identification. Why must we dismiss sex research because we claim to know a pedophilic truth about the "little sex researcher," as was the case with Kincaid and Heins – even when that "truth" is a fallacy? I see it as a problem when sex researchers become the focus of outrage as opposed to the trouble the reader has with the content of the research. How better to defend one's passion for ignorance than by making knowledge about the author a topic of concern? "Little sex researchers" study what most of us prefer to ignore or leave alone. Investments in not knowing are not benign or impotent; they structure relations to legitimate knowledge that aren't always apparent. Not knowing about child and teen sexualities, for example, supports heterosexualities and their investments in reproductive futures, as I argue throughout this book. I am deeply concerned about what people insist they don't know and its proximity to scandal. Ignorance is sometimes managed by demonizing authors (or teachers), which is a fundamental problem in learning and not learning about sexuality in contemporary

Western cultures committed to innocence, negation, morality, and white heteronormativities. The issue is one of conceptualizing education *as interference* (Britzman 1998); we cannot learn without upset, and education is nothing if not traumatic. Where there is education, there is resistance, and sometimes this resistance manifests itself in scandal.

I am troubled by scandals because they are structured by negations that inflict injury on others. But I am also excited by their promise. I contend that scandals serve important pedagogical and queer functions, as they are also injurious to those whom we cast as scapegoats in our morality plays. These injuries in the educational milieu are poignantly dramatized in the recent British films *Notes on a Scandal* and *The History Boys;* both underscore the queer and multifarious nature of the pedagogical exchange as they illustrate the harm that gets done in the name of child protectionism. I suggest that it is possible to harness the queer pedagogy and promise of sex scandals in education, as represented in these films and in the news reports of lascivious female teachers in the domain of the real, to do less harm. "Education must interfere with psychic and social development, with the pushes and pulls of superstitious and stereotypical thought, and with narcissism that so easily becomes attached to and defended by all sorts of prejudices" (Britzman 1998, 9), so the best that we can do is less harm. As I discuss in Chapter 5, I am critical of pedagogies of love and salvation because they are aggressive, as Anna Freud tells us, without appearing to be so and thus produce the very harm that they are set up to oppose. We must abandon our investments in unsullied maternal love, rescue, and salvation for a more modest but potentially important investment in lessening the harm that we inflict on others in the name of education, professionalism, and the child.

Kincaid (2004, 15) writes: "The only way, though, to rewrite the script is ... first to jar loose the present one, to drain its power by drawing it into the trap that scandal can set and then spring. Disgrace can do that, can revise the narrative, perhaps into one kinder to us and to children as well." There are two mutually reinforcing narratives here: one of the predatory pedophile and one of salvation. Kincaid suggests that we take the wind out of the pedophilic sail by exploiting and interrogating *it* as scandalous. I suggest that we do the same for the pedagogy of salvation, which perversely depends on the pederasty that it cannot tolerate. By exploiting teacher sex scandals as the upset occasioned by the interdiction against pedophilia and by the call for salvation, we come to see the panic itself as a symptom of a troubling equation in education: the mutual reliance and dependence on harm in the will to save. Education wants to see itself as saving children while depending on the pedophile and the pederastic imagination to discipline students and teachers in the name of salvation. Sex panics, as I show throughout this book, inflict injury and harm on those whom we constitute as predatory evil-doers along with those students whom we wish to save and protect. The great paradox is that education needs the pedophile even as it wants to expunge her, which is the crux of the matter – the difficult knowledge on which moral education is founded.

Queer readings of scandal demand that we let go of our passions for ignorance. Queer pedagogies of scandal trip the cultural censors and open the Pandora's box of scandal on which education relies to police teacher and student sexualities, gender and racially specific identifications. I suggest that as queer pedagogues and researchers we question the criminalization of consensual sexual activities between teachers and students. The invocation of pedophilia is used to police and set parameters on thought as it is, also, used to persecute those who transgress laws prohibiting sex with the underaged. It is important to challenge discursive structures that render sex demons in education thinkable as it is also important to be thoughtful about how to implement child-protection policies. We must not foreclose upon common sense in our rush to persecute those in breach of professional codes of conduct governing sexual infractions.

I wonder if we might be able to refuse an ethic of censorship and policing in order to study the differences between a more obvious abuse of professional power and a consensual sexual relationship between a teacher and a developmentally mature older teen. This is not to negate pedagogically important questions about professional boundary violations but to ensure that they are not overdetermined by master narratives of child sexual abuse. It is important to disentangle coercion from consent, criminal activity from what might better be called a professional boundary violation. We know little about the impact of teacher professional boundary violations precisely because they are subsumed into overarching abuse narratives. By refusing to censor discussions about sex in schools we would be less afraid to intervene and to offer students useful information about sexuality. We would also be less likely to default into protectionist and salvation-oriented pedagogies that call for negation, morality, and policing. As queer pedagogues we could more readily teach what students *really* need to know about birth control, safer-sex practices, nonprocreative sexualities, queer sex, and the possibilities of desire, love, and affection that accompany sexual engagements with ourselves and others. Might we incite what Britzman (1998) calls curiosities, as opposed to negations that foreclose on pleasure and the present as they exploit otherness in their dreams of healthy bodies, social hygiene, professional practice, and white heteronormative purity?

Is it possible to loosen the censorial and societal grip on the pedophilic jar by spilling the taboos that it is meant to contain? The school sex panics discussed in this book are noteworthy because they flourish without victims. But could they proliferate without scapegoats, demonic enemies, and diabolical threats to reproductive futurity, professionalism, heteronormativity, whiteness, and binary genders organized by heterosexual matrixes? I suggest that they could not and that abuse, like heterosexual futurity, can stop here. In other words, by refusing to criminalize teachers who have committed professional infractions (not against but *with* teenagers who have offered up social consent), we can exploit sex panics *and* make trouble for the conditions in which child sexual abuses are allowed to flourish. Fear, silence, and negations, not social consent, create a climate of social danger for children in the school.

Child sexual abuse is a problem, and I don't wish this book to be taken as evidence to the contrary. Adults do harm children, and childhood sexual abuse is devastating to ego development, but pedagogies of salvation also cause harm for which we have yet to account in professional education. Our ideas about sexual abuse and salvation are expansive and imperialist in content and focus. Conceptions of child sexual abuse tend to be more far-reaching than appeals to student welfare lead us to believe, and there *is* danger in the overspill. The discourse of child sexual abuse is expansive, colonizing, and ironically, as Kincaid tells us, responsible for the violence against younger people to which we claim to be opposed. It also leads to unhappiness and to fear of our bodies, our desires, and our sexualities, not to mention fear of social difference in the realm of education. Because we focus on abuse and sexual victimization, we do not offer up what Michelle Fine (1988) calls the missing discourse of desire in sex education. Young people must "elaborate themselves, learning the fragile work of loving others while they work through theories of sexuality that do run from the ridiculous to the sublime ... bodies experiment with their capacity for passionate relationality and experience however awkwardly or gracefully their potential to love and to be the beloved" (Britzman 1998, 77). Students are also "little sex researchers" (to borrow Britzman's terminology), and their queer curiosities, their explorations, and their entanglements with others are confronted by painful negations, censors, and prohibitions originating with adults who, ironically, talk about child protectionism without thinking much about what it means for young people.

As teachers and administrators, we censor discussion about safer sex in an era when AIDS has become an international health emergency. We refuse to give teens the information that they need to be safe and well informed about their sexual practices because we infantilize them and brand them innocent. High school teachers talk about being afraid to touch students or to even talk about genders, bodies, and sexualities in class without professional reprisal. The mandate of silence, censorship, and innocence allows for the possibility of abuse and sexual danger even as it claims to protect and sanctify the allegedly innocent child or teen. We are captivated and intrigued by the idea of sex between teachers and students *because* it is taboo, and there is nothing like silence, negation, and innocence to excite and romanticize sexual and professional prohibitions. The ironies on which teacher professionalism and child protectionism are based are perverse, although not in good conscience or in any ethical way.

I conclude this book by contending that the sex scandals involving white female teachers that have made headline news in the past decade or so are not really about child protectionism but about a will to protect an investment in reproductive futurity with its narcissistic hold on the white nuclear family, heterosexuality, and binary genders. Queer ways of being must be rooted out, and even heterosexualities that are inhospitable to the future (because they are primarily sexual as opposed to reproductive, intergenerational, and/or dependent on gender-role reversals) are shunned and subject to professional discipline or criminal investigations. Heterosexual imaginations are invested in ideas about childhood sexual innocence, and the courts are unable to recognize sex, desire, and flirtations between teacher and student as anything but evidence of gross indecency and child sexual abuse (regardless of age, social consent, gender, sexual maturity of the student, context, and so forth). Student accounts of a sexual encounter that has or has not transpired are often denied by the courts, school administrators, psychologists, parents, and the like, and the master narrative of child sexual abuse reigns supreme. To topple the abuse narrative or even to question its accuracy in the contemporary teacher sex scandals is to threaten the reproductive future, the sanctity of the white child, heteronormativity, gender binaries, and the heterosexual matrix.

Queer pedagogy demands that we refuse to override student testimonies and experiences of sexuality with adult protection and salvation-oriented policies. To take teenage voices seriously and to grapple with the polemics and professional problematics of Eros in the educational encounter is to interrogate the presumptions of innocence and the sexual negations that now permeate the official curriculum of the North American and British high school. Intergenerational sex and/or flirtations are worrisome, and people are right to consider the possibility of exploitation and abuse in schools. The presumption of and insistence on abuse, however, in the absence of a victim statement or student complaint is a problem and one that necessitates a queer interruption, analysis, and interrogation by a "little sex researcher."

By denying teenagers' sexual agency and choice in sexual partners, we negate their capacities to offer social consent and to have their own legitimate interpretations of the very events about which we, as adults, get upset. The problem, again, is with the adult, not with youth. Teenagers upset heterosexual and generational time because they are neither children nor adults; they are caught in between. Their sexualities are rarely reproductive or innocent. Many have sex for fun and in ways that adults don't understand or remember. By entering into the terrain of queer time, teenagers seem to upset adult holds on heteronormativity, reproductive futurism, and binary genders. If teenagers are not innocent children, who are they and, by extension, who are we? How can the future be assured when younger people are not innocent or budding heterosexuals? How may we establish heteronormative, binary gender, and generational matrixes when the pseudo-child (teen) is uninterested in the domesticated future-oriented sexualities on which adults depend?

I suggest that the problem is one of knowledge. The teacher sex scandals force educators, parents, administrators, psychologists, child protectionists, and the rest of us to grapple with difficult knowledge about those designated underage and their relation to adult sexualities. Queer pedagogies of scandal incite controversy and, in doing so, allow for a moment of reflection that can upset, unnerve, and undermine heteronormative claims to child sexual innocence. To be provocative is to be queer, and to insist that intergenerational sex between teacher and student is not criminal (but, perhaps, unprofessional) when based on social consent is to be perverse. The distance that gay and lesbian liberation movements in North America and Britain took from age-of-consent law reformers, gay youth, and those wrongly branded as pedophilic comes back to haunt us. As James T. Sears (1998, 76) so convincingly argues in his discussion of male homosexuality, queer pedagogy, and activism, "given the equation, male homosexual = child molester, homophile movement leaders and their organizations were reluctant to assist gay men under the age of 21, and ignored or joined in the chorus of condemnation against homosexual adults victimized because of intimate consensual relationships with teens." Gay and lesbian liberation (like professional education) was founded on a denial and a refusal of intergenerational desire, pederasty, and all that good, clean-living, white, heterosexual families oppose.

Similarly, gay and lesbian teachers found refuge in normativity as opposed to perversity by insisting that they were normal and that a homosexual orientation was not antithetical to futuristic agendas, child welfare, professional morality, responsible citizenship, and nuclear and reproduction-oriented families. Writes Sears (1998, 99), "Distancing ourselves from discussing the perversity of pederasty perhaps evidences our lack of comfort with the homoerotic liaisons – imagined, desired, actual – within schools." As outlined in Chapter 3, there is a long history of Eros in the pedagogical encounter, and sex was once instrumental (as opposed to detrimental) to knowledge acquisition. Queer pedagogies of today must account for our failures – as critical pedagogues – to grapple with the sexual, the perverse, and the pedophilic, which structure even the most mundane and blasé interactions between teacher and student in the educational milieu. The erotic and the pedophilic are not so much unusual, traumatic, and nullifying as foundational and commonplace. By this, I do not mean to say that teachers are pedophiles and that students are willing or unwilling participants in sex with adults. I mean to say that what gets read as perverse and pedophilic is deeply embedded in our social fabric. The sex that many female teachers are now alleged to be having with teenaged students is not new but old: "The legacy of pedagogical Eros extends from premodern to postmodern times, from the Greek gymnasium to the German *Wandervogelbewegung* (Sears 1998, 99). In discussing the everydayness of pedophilia, Kincaid (1992, 1998) reflects that he cannot imagine a culture in which adults were not, at some level, attracted to children. What else could sufficiently incline us to be with, care for, play with, parent, teach, feed, and tend to them? The processes through which these erotic parental engagements came to be seen as harmful to children is, of course, the central and important question.

If we are going to rescue the student (and teacher) from an ascetic pedagogy, we must understand the threat that *heteronormativity* and *futurity* pose to youth. I contend that it is the job of the queer pedagogue to release the student (coded as innocent child) from the clutches of heteronormative adults and protectionists who use his or her body for futuristic agendas that are more sinister and intricate than those of the pedophile could ever be. In short, a long legacy of compulsory heterosexuality has used and abused young people by making them into something that they are not: heterosexual and reproductive citizens for the good of the nation, its white citizenry, and its postcolonial strivings. Through the invocation of innocence, salvation, and protectionism, the young person has been denied a legitimate right to gender and sexual self-determination. More important, young people have been denied the right to have legitimate and consensual sex in whatever form it may take. The lascivious female teacher stands in as a central threat to youth but the actual threat is to be found in professional, legal, and protectionist discourses that negate legitimate claims to student sexual citizenship. By evoking the female teacher as pedophile, the profession and the public assure a student's entry into heterosexuality. But the time and pedagogy of school sex scandals is queer. The aim of queer theory is to embrace, interrogate, and grapple with the erotic, the pedophilic, and the present so that heteronormative futures, as Lee Edelman (2004) conceives of them, may stop here.

Notes

Chapter 1: Introduction

1 See Stanley Cohen (2002) for a discussion of moral panics.

2 Debra LaFave, a twenty-three-year-old married teacher in Florida, was accused of giving a fourteen-year-old boy-student oral sex in 2005. Because she was a former model and beauty-pageant winner, she has been featured in men's magazines and tabloids, and subject to extensive press coverage throughout the USA. See the article titled "Hot for Teacher" by Bart Blasengame (2005) in *Details* magazine for an example of the gendered and sensational coverage.

3 It would be wrong to remember the spinster-teacher as a subject without desire. As Geoffrey Galt Harpham (1987, 45) explains in his provocative discussion of the Christian ascetic imperative – a self-forming regiment akin to the orthodox disciplining of the white female teacher – asceticism is "essentially a mediation on, even an enactment of, desire." In short, the act of repudiating desire depends on an intimate relationship with the forbidden, so asceticism is a sexual orientation of sorts. In short, the spinster-teacher had desires and sexualities intimately related to the very taboos against extramarital sex she is thought to oppose (Cavanagh 2006a, 2006b).

The pedagogical function of asceticism is to produce an ethical self-formation that is seen to be innocent. "Childhood sexuality is exploited so that it can be dismissed, sacrificed on the altar of secular gender [and heterosexual] normativity" (Bruhm and Hurley 2004, xvii). But innocence as a literary trope – as Structuralism and French postmodern theory both remind us – depends on its opposite. The innocent child and innocent white female teacher need the diabolic, the forbidden, the threat of danger or evil incarnate in order to exist. It is not simply that one is good (asexual) or bad (dangerously sexual) but that both depend on an orientation to the law: the good abide by it, while the bad transgress it. Neither escapes the law. So it must be remembered that the production of the child and the teacher as innocent is a linguistic accomplishment, a cultural mandate, as I explain in subsequent chapters, and a psychic defence against a vision of the child and teacher as sexually uninhibited or queer. Childhood sexuality is unique because it is curious, unbounded, and not yet colonized by the institution of normative heterosexuality. Thus it must be contained or refused if the dominant order is to reproduce itself. I wonder whether the same can be said about the white female teacher – that her sexuality is somehow queer and/or off the grid of normative heterosexuality.

Chapter 2: Teacher's Pet

1 Christina Dress (2004), an inmate and friend of Letourneau's, wrote that because the infamous teacher was seen to be a child sex offender, she was subject to harassment by other inmates and unusually harsh and inhuman treatment from prison guards.

2 The media coverage of the Letourneau school sex scandal was unprecedented. During the Letourneau trial, reporters from *The Oprah Winfrey Show, CNN,* and *48 Hours* had cables set up to follow the court proceedings and then release the verdict to a concerned public.

Upon her imprisonment, Letourneau received "upward of thirty letters ... each day" (Olsen 1999, 311). Christina Dress, an inmate and friend of Mary Kay Letourneau's, wrote a book called *Mass with Mary: The Prison Years,* based on notes and letters smuggled out of prison. Several months after Audrey was born (the clandestine couple's first child), movie producers hounded Letourneau, her family, neighbours, former teachers, and parents of children formerly enrolled in her class for pictures, interviews, and any information that they could squeeze out of the otherwise overtold story.

Letourneau and Vili Fualaau wrote a book with a ghost writer entitled *Un seul crime, l'amour* (Only one crime, love, 1999) to raise awareness about the unjust criminalization of their love. (Letourneau has since said that the book was packed with lies and that the ghost writer, publishers, and lawyers in charge of the book didn't respect the story as she and Fualaau lived it.) The book was published and well received in France, as opposed to the United States, in part because American readers were, allegedly, uninterested in a sympathetic counterstory about a convicted "pedophile." *The Mary Kay Letourneau Affair* (2000) by James Robinson was also written about the teacher sex scandal. A made-for-television movie entitled *The Mary Kay Letourneau Story: All-American Girl* premiered in January 2000. The *Globe,* the *Insider,* and the *National Enquirer* published sensational stories and tabloid photos. In 2004, Letourneau and Fualaau were interviewed on *CNN: Larry King Live*. The now-famous teacher was also interviewed, via telephone, on *The Oprah Winfrey Show,* while Fualaau appeared on the show in person. The publicity and attention given to this case in popular American culture seemed endless: "Inmate no. 769014 was instantly the superstar of the Washington prison system, if not the most celebrated or notorious female face behind bars in the entire country" (Olsen 1999, 11).

People worried that the books and particularly the film glamorized pedophilia and, as Steve Olsen – who wrote his own book about Mary Kay Letourneau, *If Loving You Is Wrong: The Shocking True Story of Mary Kay Letourneau* (1999) – said, "there's a worldwide cult of pedophiles who use Mary as an example, and hold her up as an icon. Now, I don't think Mary is a pedophile, but she's inspired these people to use her for their cause" (Olsen, quoted in "Mary Kay movie" 2000). Although some had sympathy for Letourneau and did not see her as a pedophile, most were concerned about the implications of her case for child protection. For example, in a letter published in the *Seattle Times,* the contributor insisted that "predatory sexuality towards minors seriously affects their lives regardless of gender" ("Mary Letourneau" 1997). The *Austin American-Statesman* wrote that "child advocates are angered by the initial six-month jail sentence given to a teacher [Letourneau] who had sex with a 13-year-old boy, and say a man convicted of the same crime wouldn't get such a slap on the wrist." This newspaper also quoted Rebecca Roe, a prosecutor of sex offenders in King County, who said that "Letourneau might be getting a break because she doesn't look like most people's idea of a sex offender" ("Sentence" 1997). As Susann Betts, the teacher who replaced Letourneau at the now-infamous school in Seattle, said: "She's not the all-American girl – more like an American nightmare" ("Mary Kay movie" 2000). One writer for the *Indianapolis Recorder* wrote that she had a "14-year-old son and I can't imagine nor would I allow him in a relationship with a woman my age. I would prosecute her to the fullest extent of the law (if I didn't take the law into my own hands first)" (Hayes 1997).

3 Jenkins and others argue that pedophilia is not a sexual orientation completely separate from normative heterosexuality involving consenting adults. Erotic feelings toward children are common in adults, and these same feelings are also common between children of similar ages. Just because one "grows up" does not mean that he or she does not continue to have the same feelings for children that he or she had as a child. "Theories of pedophilia customarily assume that an individual fails to grow out of a quite normal early interest in fellow children, so that one's sexuality does not mature into the appropriate relationship with adults" (Jenkins 2001, 28-29). It is also, according to Jenkins, not uncommon for the adult pedophile to want the "kinds of interaction that characterize infantile fantasy and play – fondling, voyeurism, exhibitionism rather than penetrative sex" (29). In essence, pedophilic desire can be seen as a stage in heterosexual development, albeit a stage frozen in time and subject to anxious projections and pathological narration.

Chapter 3: Upsetting Desires in the Classroom

1 This list is compiled from news reports; from the Ontario College of Teachers' magazine, *Professionally Speaking,* which publishes the names of teachers facing disciplinary investigation and reprimand in Ontario; and from the British Columbia College of Teachers, which also publishes names of such teachers in their "Discipline Decisions" publication. The list is incomplete and biased toward Ontario and British Columbia teachers because all other provinces and territories do not publish such lists.

2 I suggest that the public preoccupation with the Markson case diverts attention away from the more legitimate cases of child sexual abuse in need of public attention. The media coverage surrounding this case makes it look as though the issue of childhood sexual abuse is being taken seriously when, in actual fact, the press provides an opportunity for readers to bask in the horror of the female teacher who refuses to renounce her desire in the pedagogical encounter.

3 For a discussion of male-adolescent fantasies of possessing the mother in incestuous relations, see Gabbard and Twemlow 1994.

4 The horror of the maternal body is also evident in underground pornographic materials of the sexy female teacher as sadistic disciplinarian.

5 Markson's clandestine flirtation offers insight into the "experience of women in assuming positions of authority over men in a culture that renders problematic the coexistence of sexuality and power in women" (Gornick 1986, 282). More so than in any other occupation, the profession of education requires women to renounce their sexuality. The marriage bans imposed on North American female teachers well into the 1950s are good examples of the intemperate sexual prohibitions imposed on female workers. In many occupational contexts, for women to be both sexual and powerful is an oxymoron. Therefore, it is not surprising that the white female teacher of elementary school children incites anxiety, formerly reserved for the legendary femme fatale, when she acts as a sexually dominant subject in the pedagogical encounter. "The dark woman of film noir had something her innocent sister lacked: access to her own sexuality (and thus to men's) and the power that this access unlocked" (Place 1998, 49).

Chapter 4: Sexing the Teacher

1 There is an important distinction to be made between a sex crime, which may include sexual assault or sexual harassment, and an unprofessional act or boundary violation, which may include fraternizing with students inside and outside the school. The former is a criminal offence, whereas the latter is a professional offence, but the two are often conflated in the media and in professional education's discourses about teacher-student sex. Although Gehring wasn't convicted of a crime, she was found to have been unprofessional in her social interactions with students. It is far more common that teachers found to have been unprofessional receive a professional reprimand as opposed to being excommunicated from the profession, so the response to the incident by the Ontario College of Teachers was unusually harsh.

2 Gehring did admit to at least one (and possibly a second) professional transgression involving schoolboys. She said that she may have had sex with a fifteen-year-old boy-student at a New Year's Eve party, although she couldn't be sure because she was too drunk to remember for certain. After hearing rumours circulating throughout the school that she did have sex with this boy in a bathroom, Gehring took the morning-after pill. The schoolboy, himself, could also not remember having sex with the teacher, so both depended on rumour, innuendo, and speculation to disentangle their fragmented memories.

Referring to the sexualized flirtations with schoolboys at the New Year's party, Gehring is quoted as saying that she was "too drunk. I wasn't myself. I was isolated. I was a kid really. They wanted it [sexual attention but not sex]. They initiated it. No one got hurt. It's all a bit embarrassing and that's all" ("Sex, lies" 2002). The maligned teacher did, however, admit to having had sex with a sixteen-year-old boy registered as a student in her previous place of employment, which at the time was legal in England because the boy was designated old enough to consent. This "confession" functioned to further ignite the media-induced panic.

3 The interesting thing about the definition of pornography is that it must be subject to the

threat of censor to be, strictly speaking, pornographic. As Angela Carter writes in *The Sadeian Woman and the Ideology of Pornography* (1978, 18): "When pornography serves – as with very rare exceptions it always does – to reinforce the prevailing system of values and ideas in a given society, it is tolerated; and when it does not, it is banned." Despite the sexually graphic representation of the Gehring story in the tabloids, it is not considered crudely pornographic by the mainstream public because it insists on the condemnation of the sexually promiscuous, wanton, and voracious single female characterized by the former teacher.

4 Not coincidentally, the sadomasochistic scenes inscribed by a professional dominatrix often involve the feminization (cross-dressing) of male clients (Highleyman 1997, 145). In her discussion of male fantasies, Nancy Friday (1993, 268) explains that "one of the major themes in male fantasy is the abdication of activity in favour of passivity. Role reversal." The femme dominant uses leather and chain accoutrements and sets an erotic scene through stage-like scripts, costume, and theatrical performance that enable gender transformations. Not unlike the mythology suggesting that the hermaphrodite had transcendent powers, the dominatrix seems to wield a power that can effect a change in one's gender identity.

As Gilles Deleuze (1991, 68) contends, in "sadism it becomes possible for the boy to play the role of a girl in relation to a projection of the father. We might say that the masochist is hermaphrodite and the sadist androgynous." The boy-student/adult male consents to a masochistic enactment in which the "feminine impulse is projected in the role of the mother; but in point of fact the two impulses constitute one single figure; femininity is posited as lacking in nothing and placed alongside a virility suspended in disavowal (just as the absence of a penis need not indicate lack of the phallus)." In the sadomasochistic scene, heterosexual bifurcations of gender – masculinity and femininity, organized along binary poles – cease to exist as fixed poles, and fantasy becomes more exciting or psychically meaningful than the real. The penis doesn't matter, and the female possesses the phallus as she adopts an allegiance to female dominance.

5 I wish to emphasize that it is possible for female teachers to sexually abuse and harm teenaged boy-students. It is also possible to understand the giggles as nervous reactions and the bravado as requirements of masculine social scripts. However, I do contend that a distinction needs to be made between a consensual amorous flirtation based on social consent – however unprofessional – and indecent sexual assault involving minors, which is not based on social consent.

6 Mary Calderone (1984, 134) writes that "to deny the sensual nature of children places them in a precarious position of intensely experiencing something that their own loved adults deny or, even worse, punish. It has been pointed out that to deny something that an intelligent child knows full well exists can have schizoid effects." I contend that by denying childhood sexuality and the erotic desires of adult, parental figures in teaching roles – no matter how taboo – we negate childhood sexualities and produce anxious feelings about sexuality in our children.

7 Focusing on the harm-to-minors thesis, Heins (2001, 134) demonstrates that "judges and school officials generally embraced the philosophy that students, even of high school age, must be shielded from the presumed shock or moral corruption of sexual subjects, or at least socialized to regard them as taboo." The compulsion to protect children by censoring sexual material in the school and the associated commitment to talk about sexually dangerous subjects (such as the pedophile) functioned not to protect children but to insert them into discourses about sexual danger by insisting on their vulnerability. In *Child-Loving* (1992, 4-5), Kincaid summarizes: "By insisting so loudly on the innocence, purity, and asexuality of the child, we have created a subversive echo: experience, corruption, eroticism. More than that, by attributing to the child the central features of desirability in our culture – purity, innocence, emptiness, Otherness – we have made absolutely essential figures who would enact this desire." The insistence on childhood sexual innocence produces the pedophile and does not protect the child from intergenerational sex: "Defining the child as an object of desire, we create the pedophile as the one who desires, as a complex image of projection and denial: the pedophile acts out the range of attitudes and behaviors made compulsory by the role we have given the child" (5). Ironically, moral

sensibilities call for a stern disciplining (and censoring) of the pedophilic imagination even though this same moral sensibility is predicated on the existence of pedophiles and cannot survive without them.

Chapter 5: Erotic Discipline

1 The situation was strikingly similar to an earlier British Columbia case involving a female volleyball coach at Prince George High School who allegedly had sex with up to fifteen of her male students. In the Prince George case, none of the alleged victims would file a complaint with the Royal Canadian Mounted Police, despite being asked to do so by authorities. They did not see themselves as victims. As a result, there was no evidence to support the allegations as reported by Adrian Humphreys (2000a).

2 There has been a host of studies on corporal punishment in North America that identify a sexual component to school-based discipline throughout the twentieth century. See, for example, Bakan 1971; Maurer 1974; Monroe 1913; Morris 1969; Newell 1972; Pinar 2005.

Arnold H. Modell (1997, 71) writes that in the early twentieth century, in "Western Europe and probably in North America as well, public beatings in classrooms were part of everyday life in school. Today children no longer suffer such humiliating corporal punishment, and there is some suggestion that beating phantasies in children are today somewhat uncommon." This observation lends credence to the speculation that the clandestine desire between female teacher and boy-student rebel is now channelled into a more overtly sexual pedagogical exchange. The punishment once administered by a female teacher is now channelled into sacrificial love, but the power and sexual dynamic remains intact. The analytic of beating has assumed a modern guise that needs to be subject to scholarly inquiry.

3 It goes without saying that actual beatings and familial incest are damaging to ego development and that it is incumbent on psychoanalysts, like teachers, to ascertain whether a violation has actually taken place. But this does not negate that the Oedipal complex involves not only fantasies of sex, but also incestuous and murderous impulses.

4 The great irony in the case, according to Ingram (2003), is that her court-ordered sentence to house arrest (real-life punishment) brought her closer to her teenage student lover because she became dependent on him to bring her groceries and to do other tasks that she could not leave her home to do, so their lives were more profoundly entwined, and he eventually moved in. The punishment brought with it not only a regressive substitute, but also the very thing against which it was supposedly designed to guard.

Chapter 6: Sex in the Lesbian Teacher's Closet

1 Each report about the lesbian-teacher sex scandal was written by journalist Neal Hall for the *Vancouver Sun*. Unlike the female-teacher sex scandals involving boy-students, this case did not receive nationwide publicity or international coverage.

2 This list of lesbian teachers' improprieties is in no way complete but depends on select media reports and on case reports involving teachers' disciplinary proceedings in Ontario and British Columbia. These two provinces make information about teacher unprofessional conduct available to the public, unlike other provinces and territories in Canada. Because the sexual offences of lesbian teachers are less likely to be reported in the media, it is exceedingly difficult to determine their frequency. There is a culture of professional secrecy surrounding lesbianism in Canadian schools. This is especially evident in Manitoba, where a twenty-five-year-old lesbian teacher of English, Gale M'Lot, was forbidden to discuss her sexual orientation in school by the Supreme Court of Canada. She caused a stir not for having sex with a student but for refusing to abide by a court injunction prohibiting her to speak about her lesbianism. The teacher insisted that she will "answer honestly that she's a lesbian the next time a student asks" ("Manitoba lesbian" 2001).

Cases that have been reported in the Canadian media include one involving a teacher by the name of Darlene Smart in 1992. She was convicted of having lesbian affairs with students in British Columbia. In this instance, Smart was twenty-four years old at the time and convicted of "two counts of sexual exploitation for fondling and kissing two girls, ages 15 and 16, who were students at her school" (Robins 2000, 121). In 2003, another lesbian teacher in British Columbia was designated unprofessional (not criminal) by a provincial

College Hearing Sub-Committee for having a three-year relationship with a former student. Although the relationship was based on social consent and the two cohabited for three years following the student's graduation, the teacher was found to be unprofessional for having "engaged in a romantic relationship with a female student she had once taught and counseled" (College Hearing Sub-Committee report 2003). To the best of my knowledge, the former student was in no way harmed by the relationship and received financial support from the teacher following the break-up; still, the teacher had both her teaching certificate and her membership with the college cancelled.

Other notable lesbian-teacher sex scandals in Canada include the one involving Ontario teacher Susanne Gagné, bisexual, who was charged with sexually assaulting nine students in Trenton, a city just east of Toronto. In this case, the news reports were again sparse and the particular allegations were not released to the media, but a parent of one pupil, alleged to have been assaulted, said: "For such a small town with simple values this seems so strange. I've never heard of anything like this before" (Priest 1992). Also in Ontario, a female teacher was acquitted in 2000 of sexual offences involving a female student. "While the trial judge found that the teacher's relationship with her student was 'suspicious,' he was not satisfied beyond a reasonable doubt that the offences had been committed" (Robins 2000, 122).

Most recently, an Ontario teacher by the name of Leanne Carla Robinson (formerly known as Leanne Carla Hanselman) was found guilty by the Ontario College of Teachers for befriending a female twelfth-grade student, inviting her to dinner and to her apartment, kissing her, showing her pornographic videotapes, and engaging in sexual activity with the student and Robinson's boyfriend. Although the actions were not criminal or in any way coercive, the conduct of this teacher was found to be unprofessional, so her teaching certificate was revoked. By all accounts, the seventeen-year-old student was a willing participant. In comparison to the media coverage of the aforementioned sexual transgressions in Canada involving lesbian teachers, this one received unusually titillating and sensational press coverage.

3 It is important to note that in the Hollywood film adaptation of *The Children's Hour,* the student was not South Asian. Robert Martin (2001, 402) speculates that in the 1960s, the filmmaker could not "effectively record the sense of racial and class difference that comes from the Indian orphan." Even though the original trial was about lesbianism *and* colonialism, the film does not do justice to the interlocking panic about deviant sexuality and racialization in the postcolonial context.

4 The persecuted teacher also claimed that Harris pursued her mercilessly, initiated sex, and insisted that she was in love. Ava Dean, sister of the accused, recalled that the student admitted to having initiated the affair. According to the sister, the teen believed that the affair "had done [Beltain] good ... [because she was] not an uptight old maid any more" (McDowell 1995).

5 Because of the policies forbidding lesbian representation in Hollywood film, like the Motion Picture Production Code, which regulated and often prohibited representations of homosexuality right up to 1968, stories of lesbianism had to be relegated to the domain of the unspoken. For example, in his discussion of *Diabolique* – the Hollywood remake of the 1955 French film *Les Diaboliques* – featuring two female schoolteachers who plot to kill the male headmaster and take over the school, Chris Pizzello (1996, 37) writes that so "much of the relationship between the two women was not and could not be dealt with culturally at that time." Director Jeremiah Chechik said that in the remake, the "enigmatic and ever-fluctuating relationship between Mia and Nicole [the schoolteachers] is the heart of the film" (44), but he chose to cloak the film with mystery and evocative, sexual innuendo. The difference seems to lie, however, in the pedagogical intent of the film. The plot calls on the viewer to question the manifest content of the film, to rely less on what is seen and heard than on what is going on beneath the surface. The motivations behind the killing are more important than the attempted murder.

6 This is not to say that lesbians cannot abuse teenaged girls. I do not want to condone or criminalize sex between teachers and students. It is my position that more critical and sex-positive research needs to be done on the impact of Eros in the pedagogical encounter and on the impact of intergenerational relationships based on social consent. I maintain that

the courts have yet to recognize and affirm an important distinction between indecent assault and an intergenerational sexual relationship based on social consent (when the younger party has reached puberty). We may agree that sex between teachers and students is unprofessional and can upset the learning environment, but until student narratives and experiences of these relationships are taken seriously, it is difficult to ascertain the magnitude and significance of the professional offences. It could very well be that the professional and moral panic, along with the sensational media coverage, the criminal investigations, and the like, do more harm to students than an intergenerational relationship based on social consent could ever do.

7 For a critical psychoanalytic discussion of the equation of lesbianism with psychosis, see Buccino 2001.

8 It should be noted that, according to Kincaid, the insistence on childhood asexuality is what sustains the pedophilic imagination and leaves children vulnerable to abuse because it is, in this knowledge regime, difficult to speak about the unspeakable, let alone to act in self-defence against predatory adults. When children are seen as asexual and unable to speak about sexuality, it is difficult for them to tell adults about violations that have occurred and about boundaries that they wish to set. The thesis of child sexual innocence endangers children in this way, which is the hypocrisy that the female teacher sex scandals render visible.

9 In film noir, a genre based on the threat of death, uncertainty, and corruption in modern civilization, there is an extreme visual sensation of black and white. For instance, in the film *Diabolique,* a contemporary film noir featuring two female teachers who plot a murder of the headmaster in an attempt to take over the school, the contrasts between night and day, black and white, evil and good are instrumental to the construction of lesbian-teacher sexuality as mysterious, enigmatic, and deeply corrupt.

In *Desert Hearts* (1985), the professor named Vivian (i.e., the female teacher and lesbian) is "uptight, intellectual, traditionally moral ... and pale and fair, while raunchy, physical, artistic, promiscuous ... Cay is dark" (Dyer 1997, 60). *Maedchen in Uniform* (1931), a German film produced in the era immediately preceding Hitler's Nazi regime, portrayed a boarding school girl, Manuela, who expresses her love and passion for a female teacher, thus falling victim to the school's authoritarian regime based on austerity, repression, and self-denial. The pupil, who in the original version kills herself in a passionate declaration of love for her teacher, is filmed in an angelic, innocent light of whiteness and purity. Her angelic innocence stands in stark contrast to any real threat of lesbianism in the underworld of the girl's boarding school.

10 Not only were white female schoolteachers described as barren, but schoolgirls were believed to be vulnerable to perversions that ran rampant through women's educational institutes. Girls' boarding schools, in particular, were rumoured to be injurious to the normal development of girls (Faderman 1991) because they were populated by the female of the species. Young white girls were thought to be at risk of infectious disease (including homosexuality), rendering them ineligible or unfit for reproduction. Sexologists speculated that the all-female staff and student body in such schools would draw out unnatural urges, thereby producing instances of homosexuality that would not, under more normal circumstances, develop or manifest themselves.

References

Abrams, Dan, and Pete Williams. 2004. *MSNBC: Abrams Report,* 6 August.

"Acquitted teacher ..." 2002. *Toronto Star,* 12 February.

"Agent for Gehring ..." 2002. *Times* (London), 5 February.

Alcoff, Linda. 1996. "Dangerous Pleasures: Foucault and the Politics of Pedophilia." In Susan J. Hekman, ed., *Feminist Interpretations of Michel Foucault,* 99-136. University Park, PA: Pennsylvania State University Press.

"All-American teacher ..." 2002. *Daily Mail* (London), 18 February.

Alston, Kal. 1991. "Teaching, Philosophy, and *Eros:* Love as a Relation to Truth." *Educational Theory* 41, 4: 385-95.

–. 1998. "So Give Me Love, Love, Love, Love, Crazy Love: Teachers, Sex and Transference?" In Steven Tozer, ed., *Philosophy of Education,* 366-69. Urbana, IL: Philosophy of Education Society.

"Amy Gehring ..." 2002. *Sunday Mirror* (London), 10 February.

Au Set, Tanith. 2001. "Tanith Au Set." In Roy Turner, ed., *You Beat People Up for a Living, Don't You Mummy?* 197-208. Brighton, East Sussex: Absolute Elsewhere.

Bakan, David. 1971. "The Effects of Corporal Punishment in School." *Journal of the Ontario Association of Children's Aid Societies* (November): 1-13.

Baker, Bernadette M. 2001. *In Perpetual Motion: Theories of Power, Educational History, and the Child.* New York: Peter Lang.

Basset, Clara. 1931. *The School and Mental Health.* New York: The Commonwealth Fund.

Bataille, Georges. 1957. *Eroticism: Death and Sensuality.* San Francisco: City Lights Books.

Bauer, Dale M. 1998. "Indecent Proposals: Teachers in the Movies." *College English* 60, 3: 301-17.

Baumlin, James S. 2000. "Teaching, Classroom Authority, and the Psychology of Transference." *Journal of General Education* 49, 2: 75-87.

Bell, Kim. 2003. "Sex crimes by women ..." *St. Louis Post-Dispatch,* 24 March.

Bell, Mark, and Corinne Iverson. 1998. "Reality, Transference and the Classroom: *Ces Enfants de Ma Vie* by Gabrielle Roy." *Romantic Review* 89, 4: 621-35.

Bell, Vikki. 1993. *Interrogating Incest: Feminism, Foucault and the Law.* London and New York: Routledge.

Bellett, Gerry. 1995a. "Pupil started lesbian affair ..." *Vancouver Sun,* 13 January.

–. 1995b. "Counsellor feared being found out." *Vancouver Sun,* 16 January.

Benjamin, Jessica. 1995. *Like Subjects, Love Objects: Essays on Recognition and Sexual Difference.* New Haven and London: Yale University Press.

Berenstein, Isidoro. 1997. "'A Child Is Being Beaten' and the Battered Child." In Ethel Spector Person, ed., *On Freud's "A Child Is Being Beaten,"* 133-56. New Haven and London: Yale University Press.

Bersani, Leo. 2001. "Genital Chastity." In Tim Dean and Christopher Lane, eds., *Homosexuality and Psychoanalysis,* 351-66. Chicago and London: The University of Chicago Press.

Beuka, Robert. 2000. "Retrospectives: Just One Word ... Plastics: Suburban Malaise, Masculinity, and Oedipal Drive in *The Graduate*." *Journal of Popular Film and Television* 28, 1: 12-21.

Beveridge, John. 1998. "Sins of the mother." *Daily Telegraph* (London), 21 March.

Birch, Helen. 1993. *Moving Targets: Women, Murder and Representation*. London: Virago Press.

Bird, Heather. 2001. Column. *Toronto Sun*, 2 March.

Blasengame, Bart. 2005. "Hot for Teacher." *Details*, April, 96.

Bloom, Allan D. 1993. *Love and Friendship*. New York: Simon and Schuster.

Blount, J. 1996. "Manly Men and Womanly Women: Deviance, Gender Role Polarization, and the Shift in Women's School Employment." *Harvard Educational Review* 66, 2: 318-38.

–. 2000. "Spinsters, Bachelors, and Other Gender Transgressions in School Employment, 1850-1900." *Review of Educational Research* 70, 1: 83-101.

Bollas, Christopher. 2000. *Hysteria*. London and New York: Routledge.

Boozer, Jack. 1999-2000. "The Lethal *Femme Fatale* in the Noir Tradition." *Journal of Film and Video* 5, 1: 20-35.

Britzman, Deborah. 1995. "Is There a Queer Pedagogy? Or Stop Reading Straight?" *Educational Theory* 45, 2: 151-66.

–. 1998. *Lost Subjects, Contested Objects: Toward a Psychoanalytic Inquiry of Learning*. New York: State University of New York Press.

–. 2003. *After-Education*. New York: State University of New York.

–. 2006. *Novel Education: Psychoanalytic Studies of Learning and Not Learning*. New York: Peter Lang.

Britzman, Deborah P., and Alice J. Pitt. 1996. "Pedagogy and Transference: Casting the Past of Learning Into the Presence of Teaching." *Theory Into Practice* 35, 2: 117-23.

Brown, Wendy. 1995. *States of Injury: Power and Freedom in Late Modernity*. New Jersey: Princeton University Press.

–. 2001. *Politics out of History*. Princeton and Oxford: Princeton University Press.

Bruhm, Steven, and Natasha Hurley, eds. 2004. *Curiouser: On the Queerness of Children*. Minneapolis: University of Minnesota Press.

Buccino, Daniel L. 2001. "Homosexuality and Psychosis in the Clinic: Symptom or Structure?" In Tim Dean and Christopher Lane, eds., *Homosexuality and Psychoanalysis*, 265-87. Chicago and London: University of Chicago Press.

Burch, Kerry T. 1999. "Eros as the Educational Principle of Democracy." *Studies in Philosophy and Education* 18: 123-42.

–. 2000. *Eros as the Educational Principle of Democracy*. New York: Peter Lang.

Butler, Judith. 1990a. "The Force of Fantasy: Feminism, Mapplethorpe, and Discursive Excess." *Differences: A Feminist Journal of Cultural Studies* 2, 2: 105-25.

–. 1990b. *Gender Trouble: Feminism and the Subversion of Identity*. New York: Routledge.

–. 1995. "Melancholy Gender/Refused Identification." In Maurice Berger, Brian Wallis, and Simon Watson, eds., *Constructing Masculinity*, 21-36. New York and London: Routledge.

Calderone, Mary S. 1984. "Above and Beyond Politics: The Sexual Socialization of Children." In Carole S. Vance, ed., *Pleasure and Danger: Exploring Female Sexuality*, 131-37. London: Routledge and Kegan Paul.

Campbell, Kirsten. 2004. *Jacques Lacan and Feminist Epistemology*. New York: Routledge.

"Canadian teacher cleared of sex charges." 2002. *Toronto Star*, 15 February.

Cantin, Paul. 1998. "Teacher's aide ..." *Toronto Sun*, 13 June.

Caputi, Jane. 2004. *Goddesses and Monsters: Women, Myth, Power, and Popular Culture*. Madison, WI: University of Wisconsin Press/Popular Press.

Carroll, Sue. 2002. "Amy's pervy as any man." *Mirror* (London), 6 February.

Carter, Angela. 1978. *The Sadeian Woman and the Ideology of Pornography*. New York: Pantheon Books.

Cavanagh, Sheila L. 2003a. "The Gender of Professionalism and Occupational Closure: The Management of Tenure-Related Disputes by the 'Federation of Women Teachers' Associations of Ontario,' 1918-1949." *Gender and Education* 15, 1: 39-57.

–. 2003b. "Teacher Transsexuality: The Illusion of Sexual Difference and the Idea of Adolescent Trauma." *Sexualities: Studies in Culture and Society* 6, 3-4: 365-88.

–. 2004. "Upsetting Desires in the Classroom: School Sex Scandals and the Pedagogy of the Femme Fatale." *Psychoanalysis, Culture and Society* 9, 3: 315-32.

–. 2005a. "Female Teacher Gender and Sexuality in Twentieth-Century Ontario, Canada." *History of Education Quarterly* 45, 2: 247-73.

–. 2005b. "Sexing the Teacher: Voyeuristic Pleasure in the Amy Gehring Sex Panic." *Social Text* 23, 1 82: 111-34.

–. 2006a. "The Heterosexualization of the Ontario Woman Teacher in the Postwar Period." In Mona Gleason and Adele Perry, eds., *Rethinking Canada: The Promise of Women's History,* 5th ed., 278-86. Don Mills, ON: Oxford University Press.

–. 2006b. "Spinsters, Schoolmarms and Queers: Images of the Unmarried Teacher in Medicine and Psychoanalytic Theory." *Discourse: The Cultural Politics of Education* 27, 4: 421-40.

Chabram-Dernersesian, Angie. 1999. "On the Social Construction of Whiteness within Selected Chicana-o Discourses." In Ruth Frankenberg, ed., *Displacing Whiteness: Essays in Social and Cultural Criticism,* 107-23. Durham and London: Duke University Press.

Chancer, Lynn Sharon. 1993. "Prostitution, Feminist Theory, and Ambivalence: Notes from the Sociological Underground." *Social Text* 37: 143-71.

Churcher, Sharon. 2002. "Amy lied about her lust ..." *Mail on Sunday* (Tillsonburg), 17 February.

CKNW editorial. 2000. 19 April. Vancouver.

Cohen, Stanley. 2002. *Folk Devils and Moral Panics: The Creation of the Mods and Rockers.* London and New York: Routledge.

Cohen, Stanley J. 2000. "The Wish to Regress in Patient and Analyst." *Journal of the American Psycholoanalytic Association* 48, 3: 785-810.

Collins, Claire. 2002. "Amy loved sex ..." *The People* (Wortley), 10 February.

"Courtroom drama queens." 2002. *Evening Standard* (London), 13 February.

Crowther, Bosley. 1967. "'Up the Down Staircase' Opens: Crises in a City School Make Poignant Film." *New York Times,* 18 August. http://movies2.nytimes.com/mem/movies/review.html.

Danylewycz, Marta. 1987. *Taking the Veil: An Alternative to Marriage, Motherhood, and Spinsterhood in Quebec, 1840-1920.* Toronto: McClelland and Stewart.

de Lauretis, Teresa. 1984. *Alice Doesn't: Feminism, Semiotics, Cinema.* Bloomington: Indiana University Press.

–. 1999. "Letter to an Unknown Woman." In Ronnie C. Lesser and Erica Schoenberg, eds., *That Obscure Subject of Desire: Freud's Female Homosexual Revisited,* 37-53. New York and London: Routledge.

Deleuze, Gilles. 1991. *Masochism.* New York: Zone Books.

–. 1998. *Coldness and Cruelty.* New York: Zone Books.

DiPiero, Tomas. 1994. "White Men Aren't." *Camera Obscura* 30: 113-37.

Doctor, E. 1999. "Someone else's nightmare: Sexual misconduct in schools." Paper presented at the annual conference of the Canadian Association for the Practical Study of Law in Education, Toronto, 25-27 April.

Dolmage, Rod. 1995. "Accusations of Teacher Sexual Abuse of Students in Ontario Schools: Some Preliminary Findings." *Alberta Journal of Educational Research* 41, 2: 127-44.Dress, Christina, with Tama-Lisa Johnson and Mary Kay Letourneau. 2004. *Mass with Mary: The Prison Years.* Victoria, BC: Trafford.

Driedger, Sharon Doyle. 2003. "The Teacher's Lesson." *Maclean's,* 19 May.

Dworkin, Andrea. 1981. *Pornography: Men Possessing Women.* New York: Perigee.

Dyer, Richard. 1997. *White.* London and New York: Routledge.

–. 2002. *The Culture of Queers.* London and New York: Routledge.

Edelman, Lee. 1998. "The Future Is Kid's Stuff: Queer Theory, Disidentification, and the Death Drive." *Narrative* 6, 1: 18-30.

–. 2004. *No Future: Queer Theory and the Death Drive.* Durham and London: Duke University Press.

Edwards, Steven. 2002. "A Canadian teacher's ..." *National Post,* 27 May.

Eng, David L. 2001. *Racial Castration: Managing Masculinity in Asian America.* Durham and London: Duke University Press.

"Ex-counsellor jailed over sex with student." 1995. *Vancouver Sun,* 18 March.

"Exonerated teacher ..." 2002. *National Post,* 6 February.

Fabian, Cosi. 1997. "The Holy Whore: A Woman's Gateway to Power." In Jill Nagle, ed., *Whores and Other Feminists,* 44-54. New York and London: Routledge.

Faderman, Lillian. 1983. *Scotch Verdict: Miss Pirie and Miss Woods v. Dame Cumming Gordon.* New York: W. Morrow.

–. 1991. *Odd Girls and Twilight Lovers: A History of Lesbian Life in Twentieth-Century America.* New York: Penguin.

Felman, Shoshana. 1987. *Jacques Lacan and the Adventure of Insight: Psychoanalysis in Contemporary Culture.* Cambridge, MA: Harvard University Press.

Felman, Shoshana, and Dori Laub. 1992. *Testimony: Crisis of Witnessing in Literature, Psychoanalysis, and History.* New York: Routledge.

Finateri, Linda M. 1999. "Paradox of Pregnancy in Prison: Resistance, Control, and the Body." *Canadian Women's Studies* 19, 1-2: 136-43.

Fine, Michelle. 1988. "Sexuality, Schooling, and Adolescent Females: The Missing Discourse of Desire." *Harvard Educational Review,* 3, 2: 29-53.

Fitten, Ronald, Nancy Bartley, and *Seattle Times* staff reporters. 1997. "Ex-teacher pleads guilty in rape of boy." *Seattle Times,* 7 August.

Fitten, Ronald, and *Seattle Times* staff reporters. 1997. "Teacher's dad had affair, too ..." *Seattle Times,* 11 August.

"Focus six years ..." 2002. *Sunday Express* (London), 24 February.

Foucault, Michel. 1977. *Discipline and Punish: The Birth of the Prison.* Trans. Alan Sheridan. New York: Vintage Books.

–. 1978. *History of Sexuality.* Vol. 1, *An Introduction.* Trans. Robert Hurley. New York: Vintage Books.

–. 1997. "Friendship as a Way of Life." In Paul Rabinow, ed., *Ethics: Subjectivity and Truth,* 135-40. New York: New Press.

Francke, Lizzie. 1996. "Dangerous Minds." *Sight and Sound* 6, 1: 37.

Frank, Steven. 2000. "Caging Birds of Prey: A Spate of Investigations of Female Teacher-Male Student Liaisons Raises the Question: Is This Abuse?" *Time,* 22 May.

Frankel, Bruce, Cathy Nolan, and Alex Hardy. 1998. "Family Man." *People,* 2 November.

Freel, Mike. 2003. "Child Sexual Abuse and the Male Monopoly: An Empirical Exploration of Gender and a Sexual Interest in Children." *The British Journal of Social Work* 33, 4: 481-98.

Freely, Maureen. 2002. "Real Lives: Sex Education." *Guardian* (London), 5 February.

Freeman, Elizabeth. 1998. "Honeymoon with a Stranger: Pedophiliac Picaresques from Poe to Nabokov." *American Literature* 70, 4: 863-97.

Freud, Anna. 1966. *The Ego and the Mechanisms of Defense.* Rev. ed. Madison, CT: International Universities Press.

Freud, Sigmund. 1900. *The Interpretation of Dreams.* Standard ed. London: Hogarth Press and Institute for Psychoanalysis.

–. 1953. *The Standard Edition of the Complete Psychological Works of Sigmund Freud.* Vol. 7, *The Sexual Enlightenment of Children.* Trans. and ed. James Strachey. London: Penguin.

–. 1960. *Totem and Taboo: Resemblances between the Psychic Lives of Savages and Neurotics.* Authorized translation with an introduction by A.A. Brill. New York: Random House.

–. 1961. *Civilization and Its Discontents.* Trans. and ed. by James Strachey, with a biographical introduction by Peter Gay. New York and London: W.W. Norton and Company.

–. 1962. *Three Essays on the Theory of Sexuality.* Trans. and rev. James Strachey. New York: Basic Books.

–. 1974. *The Standard Edition of the Complete Psychological Works of Sigmund Freud.* Vol. 19, *The Economic Problem in Masochism.* Trans. and ed. James Strachey. London: Hogarth Press.

–. 1997. "A Child Is Being Beaten." In Ethel Spector Person, ed., *On Freud's "A Child Is Being Beaten,"* 3-204. New Haven and London: Yale University Press.

Friday, Nancy. 1993. *Men in Love: Men's Sexual Fantasies, the Triumph of Love over Rage.* London: Hutchinson.

Fryer, Alex. 2000. "How a very unusual romance has ended in a court battle." *Sunday Telegraph* (London), 23 April.

Gabbard, Glen O. 1996. *Love and Hate in the Analytic Setting*. London: Jason Aronson.

Gabbard, Glen O., and Stuart W. Twemlow. 1994. "The Role of Mother-Son Incest in the Pathogenesis of Narcissistic Personality Disorder." *Journal of the American Psychoanalytic Association* 42, 1: 171-89.

Gallagher, B. 2000. "The Extent and Nature of Known Cases of Institutional Child Sexual Abuse." *British Journal of Social Work,* 30: 795-817.

Gallop, Jane. 1985. "Keys to Dora." In Charles Bernheimer and Claire Kahane, eds., *In Dora's Case: Freud – Hysteria – Feminism,* 200-20. New York: Columbia University Press.

–. 1992. "Not a Love Story." *Yale Journal of Criticism* 5: 209-18.

–. 1995. *Pedagogy: The Question of Impersonation*. Bloomington and Indianapolis: Indiana University Press.

–. 1997. *Feminist Accused of Sexual Harassment*. Durham and London: Duke University Press.

Galloway, Gloria. 2001. "Women make news with school affairs." *Toronto Star,* 3 March.

"Gehring tells tabloid ..." 2002. *Globe and Mail,* 11 February.

Gibson, Charles. 2004. "Mary Kay Letourneau Preview of 20/20 Interview." *Good Morning America,* 24 September.

Gibson, Valerie. 2001. *Cougar: A Guide for Older Women Dating Younger Men*. Toronto: Key Porter Books.

Gill, Christopher. 1999. Introd. to *Symposium,* by Plato. New York: Penguin Books.

Gilman, Sander L. 1985. *Difference and Pathology: Stereotypes of Sexuality, Race and Madness*. Ithaca: Cornell University Press.

–. 1986. "Black Bodies, White Bodies: Toward an Iconography of Female Sexuality in Late-Nineteenth-Century Art, Medicine, and Literature." In Henry Louis Gates, Jr., ed., *"Race," Writing, and Difference,* 223-61. Chicago: University of Chicago Press.

Giovannetti, Mario De F. 1997. "The Scene and Its Reverse: Considerations on a Chain of Associations in Freud." In Ethel Spector Person, ed., *On Freud's "A Child Is Being Beaten,"* 95-111. New Haven and London: Yale University Press.

Givens, Ron. 2000. "A teacher's obsessive teen love." *New York Daily News,* 16 January, sports final edition.

Gledhill, Christine. 2000. "Klute 1: A Contemporary Film Noir and Feminist Criticism." In E. Ann Kaplan, ed., *Feminism and Film,* 66-85. Oxford and New York: Oxford University Press.

Goodson, Teri. 1997. "A Prostitute Joins NOW." In Jill Nagle, ed., *Whores and Other Feminists,* 248-51. New York: Routledge.

Gornick, Lisa K. 1986. "Developing A New Narrative: The Woman Therapist and the Male Patient." In Judith L. Alpert, ed., *Psychoanalysis and Women: Contemporary Reappraisals,* 257-86. New Jersey: The Analytic Press.

Grace, Kevin Michael. 2001. "Price of Innocence ..." *Report News Magazine* (Edmonton) 28: 41.

Granatstein, Rob. 2002. "Lusty lessons: Ontario teacher's fate now lies in hands of U.K. jury." *Toronto Sun,* 4 February.

Grant, Larry. 1997. "MAPping Accountability." In Jill Nagle, ed., *Whores and Other Feminists,* 242-47. New York and London: Routledge.

Gray, Brian. 2000. "Female teacher in ..." *Toronto Sun,* 27 October.

Grimshaw, Jean. 1997. "Ethics, Fantasy and Self-Transformation." In Alan Soble, ed., *The Philosophy of Sex: Contemporary Readings,* 175-87. Lanham, Boulder, New York, and Oxford: Rowman and Littlefield.

Grumet, Madeleine. 1988. *Bitter Milk: Women in Teaching*. Amherst: University of Massachusetts Press.

Haig-Brown, Celia. 1991. *Resistance and Renewal: Surviving the Indian Residential School*. Vancouver: Arsenal Pulp Press.

–. 1995. *Taking Control: Power and Contradiction in First Nations Adult Education*. Vancouver: UBC Press.

Halberstam, Judith. 1998. *Female Masculinity*. Durham and London: Duke University Press.

–. 2001. "Imagined Violence/Queer Violence: Representations and Resistance." In Martha MacCaughey, ed., *Violent Women in the Movies,* 244-66. Austin: University of Texas Press.
–. 2003. "What's That Smell? Queer Temporalities and Subcultural Lives." *International Journal of Cultural Studies* 6, 3: 313-33.
–. 2005. *In a Queer Time and Place: Transgender Bodies, Subcultural Lives.* New York and London: New York University Press.
Hall, Neal. 1993a. "Tune brings abuse memories, witness says." *Vancouver Sun,* 23 February.
–. 1993b. "Former teacher denies sexual relationship." *Vancouver Sun,* 25 February.
–. 1993c. "Ex-student's sexual charges called 'delusional.'" *Vancouver Sun,* 5 March.
–. 1993d. "Vice-principal faces probe in suspected cover-up." *Vancouver Sun,* 17 March.
–. 1993e. "Woman teacher jailed four months." *Vancouver Sun,* 1 April.
–. 1993f. "Delta vice-principal spared board action in alleged cover-up of female colleague." *Vancouver Sun,* 2 April.
Hannsberry, Karen B. 1998. *Femme noir: Bad girls of film.* Jefferson, NC: McFarland.
Harpham, Geoffrey Galt. 1987. *The Ascetic Imperative in Culture and Criticism.* Chicago and London: University of Chicago Press.
Hart, Lynda. 2001. "Lust for Innocence." In Tim Dean and Christopher Lane, eds., *Homosexuality and Psychoanalysis,* 288-304. Chicago and London: University of Chicago Press.
Hartigan, John J. 1999. "Locating White Detroit." In Ruth Frankenberg, ed., *Displacing Whiteness: Essays in Social and Cultural Criticism,* 180-213. Durham and London: Duke University Press.
Hayes, Connie Gaines. 1997. "Opinions: Adults should know better." *Indianapolis Recorder,* 22 November.
Heins, Marjorie. 2001. *Not in Front of the Children: "Indecency," Censorship, and the Innocence of Youth.* New York: Hill and Wang.
Hellman, Lillian. 1934. *The Children's Hour.* New York: Dramatists Play Service, ca. 1981.
Hendrie, C., and S. Drummond. 1998. "A Trust Betrayed: Sexual Abuse by Teachers." *Education Week,* 2, 9, 16 December.
Hewitt, B. 1998. "Out of Control." *People,* 30 March.
Higgins, C. 1998. "Transference Love from the Couch to the Classroom: A Psychoanalytic Perspective on the Ethics of Teacher-Student Romance." In S. Tozer, ed., *Philosophy of Education,* 357-65. Urbana, IL: Philosophy of Education Society.
Highleyman, Liz. 1997. "Professional Dominance: Power, Money, and Identity." In Jill Nagle, ed., *Whores and Other Feminists,* 145-55. New York: Routledge.
Hockenberry, John, Lea Thompson, and Matt Lauer. 2002. "Leaving Las Vegas; Story and Trial of Tanya Hadden, who had affair with 15-year-old student in California." *NBC News* transcripts, 29 October.
Hocquenghem, Guy. 1972. *Homosexual Desire.* Trans. Daniella Dangoor. Reprint, Durham: Duke University Press, 1993.
Horsnell, Michael. 2002. "Science mistress admits ..." *Times* (London), 29 January.
Humphreys, Adrian. 2000a. "B.C. RCMP investigates ..." *National Post,* 22 April.
–. 2000b. "Female teacher alleged ..." *National Post,* 26 April.
Ingram, Heather. 2003. *Risking It All: My Student, My Lover, My Story.* Vancouver, Toronto, and New York: Greystone Books.
Ivens, Andy. 1998. "Teacher seduced me ..." *Vancouver Province,* 18 November.
Ivy, Marilyn. 1993. "Have You Seen Me? Recovering the Inner Child in Late Twentieth-Century America." *Social Text* 37: 227-52.
Jagodzinski, Jan. 2002. *Pedagogical Desire: Authority, Seduction, Transference, and the Question of Ethics.* Westport, CT, and London: Bergin and Garvey.
Janus. 2001. "Janus." In Roy Turner, ed., *You Beat People Up for a Living, Don't You Mummy?* 75-88. Brighton, East Sussex: Absolute Elsewhere.
Jenkins, Philip. 2001. *Beyond Tolerance: Child Pornography on the Internet.* New York and London: New York University Press.
Jennings, D., and R. Tharp. 2003. "Betrayal of trust." *Dallas Morning News,* 4, 5, 6 May.
"Journalists face prison ..." 2002. *Times* (London), 6 March.
"A jury in Guildford ..." 2002. *London Free Press,* 4 February.
Kaplan, E. Ann, ed. 1998. *Women in Film Noir.* London: British Film Institute Publishing.

–, ed. 2000a. *Feminism and Film.* New York: Oxford University Press.
–. 2000b. "Is the Gaze Male?" In E. Ann Kaplan, ed., *Feminism and Film,* 119-38. Oxford and New York: Oxford University Press.
–. 2000c. "The Case of the Missing Mother: Maternal Issues in Vidor's *Stella Dallas.*" In E. Ann Kaplan, ed., *Feminism and Film,* 466-78. New York: Oxford University Press.
Kessler, Kari. 2002. "The Plain-Clothes Whore: Agency, Marginalization, and the Unmarked Prostitute Body." In Merri Lisa Johnson, ed., *Jane Sexes It Up: True Confessions of Feminist Desire,* 231-40. New York and London: Four Walls Eight Windows.
Khayatt, Madiha Didi. 1992. *Lesbian Teachers: An Invisible Presence.* New York: State University of New York Press.
Kincaid, James R. 1992. *Child-Loving: The Erotic Child and Victorian Culture.* New York and London: Routledge.
–. 1998. *Erotic Innocence: The Culture of Child Molesting.* Durham and London: Duke University Press.
–. 2004. "Producing Erotic Children." In Steven Bruhm and Natasha Hurley, eds., *Curiouser: On the Queerness of Children,* 3-16. Minneapolis: University of Minnesota Press.
Klein, Theodore J. 1989. "Teaching and Mother Love." *Educational Theory* 39, 4: 373-83.
Ko, Michael. 2004. "Mary Kay Letourneau's lover wants no-contact order lifted ..." *Record* (Seattle), 5 August.
Kristeva, Julia. 1976-77. "Stabat Mater." In *Tales of Love,* trans. Leon Roudiez, 234-63. New York: Columbia University Press, 1987.
–. 1982. *Powers of Horror: An Essay on Abjection.* Trans. Leon S. Roudiez. New York: Columbia University Press.
–. 1995. *New Maladies of the Soul.* New York: Columbia University Press.
Lady Amber. 2001. In Roy Turner, ed., *You Beat People Up for a Living, Don't You Mummy?* 305-14. Brighton, East Sussex: Absolute Elsewhere.
Langmuir, Val. 1996. "Pansexual." In Cherie Matrix, ed., *Tales from the Clit: A Female Experience of Pornography,* 107-11. Edinburgh and San Francisco: AK Press.
Lauer, Matt. 1997. "Teacher Who Pled Guilty to Two Counts of Rape after Having Sex with Her Sixth-Grade Student Will Be Sentenced Today in Seattle." *SHOW: TODAY,* 14 November.
"The Law Must Protect Young Boys from These Women Sex Perverts." 1998. *Male View,* 30 June.
Lawrence, Bonita. 2004. *"Real" Indians and Others: Mixed-Blood Urban Native Peoples and Indigenous Nationhood.* Vancouver: UBC Press.
Leader, Darian. 2000. "Beating Fantasies and Sexuality." In Renata Salecl, ed., *Sexuation,* 106-30. Durham and London: Duke University Press.
Lee, Adrian. 2002. "Boy tells jury ..." *Daily Express* (London), 23 January.
Lee, Jeff. 1995. "Counsellor 'lured high-school student' ..." *Vancouver Sun,* 11 January.
"Lesbian teacher jailed after affairs with students." 1992. *Kitchener-Waterloo Record,* 1 February.
Letourneau, Mary Kay, and Vili Fualaau. 1999. *Un seul crime, l'amour.* Paris, France: Robert Laffont.
Levett, Ann. 2003. "Problems of Cultural Imperialism in the Study of Child Sexual Abuse." In Paula Reavey and Sam Warner, eds., *New Feminist Stories of Child Sexual Abuse: Sexual Scripts and Dangerous Dialogues,* 52-76. London and New York: Routledge.
Levine, Judith. 2002. *Harmful to Minors: The Perils of Protecting Children from Sex.* New York: Thunder's Mouth Press.
Litvak, Joseph. 1995. "Discipline, Spectacle and Melancholia in and around the Gay Studies Classroom." In Jane Gallop, ed., *Pedagogy: The Question of Impersonation,* 19-27. Bloomington and Indianapolis: Indiana University Press.
Lukes, H.N. 2001. "Unrequited Love: Lesbian Transference and Revenge in Psychoanalysis." In Tim Dean and Christopher Lane, eds., *Homosexuality and Psychoanalysis,* 250-64. Chicago and London: University of Chicago Press.
Lutzenberger, Jennifer. 2002. "Cutting, Craving, and the Self I Was Saving." In Merri Lisa Johnson, ed., *Jane Sexes It Up: True Confessions of Feminist Desire,* 107-25. New York and London: Four Walls Eight Windows.
Macdonald, Moira. 2001a. "Romance isn't ..." *Toronto Star,* 6 March.

–. 2001b. "Teachers who strip ..." *National Post,* 19 September.
–. 2001c. "Sex affair teacher ..." *National Post,* 20 September.
Mackenzie, Christobel. 1996. "XXX." In Cherie Matrix, ed., *Tales from the Clit: A Female Experience of Pornography,* 27-31. Edinburgh and San Francisco: AK Press.
Madame Tachibana. 2001. "Madame Tachibana." In Roy Turner, ed., *You Beat People Up for a Living, Don't You Mummy?* 209-16. Brighton, East Sussex: Absolute Elsewhere.
"Manitoba lesbian to keep answering students' questions on orientation." 2001. Canadian Press Newswire, 1 March.
Martin, Robert K. 2001. "*The Children's Hour:* A Postcolonial Turn of the Screw." *Canadian Review of American Studies* 31, 1: 401-7.
"Mary Kay movie called a crock." 2000. *New York Post,* 16 January.
"Mary Letourneau – Equally sexual beings." 1997. Letter to the editor. *Seattle Times,* 30 November.
Matthews, J.K., J. Raymaker, and K. Speltz. 1991. "Female Sexual Offenders: A Typology." In M.Q. Patton, ed., *Family Sexual Abuse: Frontline Research and Evaluation,* 147-61. Newbury Park, CA: Sage.
Maurer, Adah. 1974. "Corporal Punishment: A Review." *American Psychologist* (August): 614.
McClintock, Anne. 1995. *Imperial Leather: Race, Gender, and Sexuality in the Colonial Contest.* New York: Routledge.
McClintock, Anne, Aamir Mufti, and Ella Shohat. 1997. *Dangerous Liaisons: Gender, Nation, and Postcolonial Perspectives.* Minneapolis and London: University of Minnesota Press.
McCrae, S., Vander Voet, and L. Palmer Nye. 1994. *Violence Free Schools: Developing and Implementing Sexual Assault Prevention Policy.* Toronto: Metropolitan Action Committee on Public Violence Against Women and Children.
McDowell, Jim. 1995. "Counselled with Lesbian Sex: A Teacher Is Convicted." *BC Report,* 20 February.
McWilliam, Erica. 1996. "Seductress or Schoolmarm: On the Improbability of the Great Female Teacher." *Interchange* 27, 1: 1-11.
–. 1999. *Pedagogical Pleasures.* New York: Peter Lang.
Mickleburgh, Rod. 2003. "The rapper, the teacher, the scandal." *Globe and Mail,* 7 May.
Miller, Jacques-Alain. 1998. *On Feminine Sexuality, the Limits of Love and Knowledge: The Seminar of Jacques Lacan, Book XX, Encore.* Translated with notes by Bruce Fink. New York: W.W. Norton and Company.
Miller, Neil. 2002. *Sex-Crime Panic: A Journey to the Paranoid Heart of the 1950s.* Los Angeles and New York: Alyson Books.
"Miss Filth tried ..." 2002. *The People* (Wortley), 17 February.
Miss Prim. 2001. "Miss Prim." In Roy Turner, ed., *You Beat People Up for a Living, Don't You Mummy?* 241-46. Brighton, East Sussex: Absolute Elsewhere.
Miss Sara Dale. 2001. "Miss Sara Dale." In Roy Turner, ed., *You Beat People Up for a Living, Don't You Mummy?* 295-304. Brighton, East Sussex: Absolute Elsewhere.
Mistress Adelle. 2001. "Mistress Adelle." In Roy Turner, ed., *You Beat People Up for a Living, Don't You Mummy?* 337-46. Brighton, East Sussex: Absolute Elsewhere.
Mistress Antoinette. 2001. "Mistress Antoinette." In Roy Turner, ed., *You Beat People Up for a Living, Don't You Mummy?* 139-46. Brighton, East Sussex: Absolute Elsewhere.
Mistress Chrystalle. 2001. "Mistress Chrystalle." In Roy Turner, ed., *You Beat People Up for a Living, Don't You Mummy?* 117-32. Brighton, East Sussex: Absolute Elsewhere.
Mistress Eva. 2001. "Mistress Eva." In Roy Turner, ed., *You Beat People Up for a Living, Don't You Mummy?* 191-96. Brighton, East Sussex: Absolute Elsewhere.
Mistress R. 2001. "Mistress R." In Roy Turner, ed., *You Beat People Up For a Living, Don't You, Mummy?* 105-16. Brighton, East Sussex: Absolute Elsewhere.
Mistress Shane. 2001. "Mistress Shane." In Roy Turner, ed., *You Beat People Up for a Living, Don't You Mummy?* 217-22. Brighton, East Sussex: Absolute Elsewhere.
Mitchell, Stephen A. 2001. "Psychoanalysis and the Degradation of Romance." In Muriel Dimen and Adrienne Harris, ed., *Storms in Her Head: Freud and the Construction of Hysteria,* 201-22. New York: Other Press.
Modell, Arnold H. 1997. "Humiliating Fantasies and the Pursuit of Unpleasure." In Ethel

Spector Person, ed., *On Freud's "A Child Is Being Beaten,"* 67-75. New Haven and London: Yale University Press.

"Mom tells of ..." 2001. *Kitchener-Waterloo Record,* 28 February.

Monet, Veronica. 1997. "Sedition." In Jill Nagle, ed., *Whores and Other Feminists,* 217-22. New York and London: Routledge.

Monroe, Paul. 1913. *Cyclopaedia of Education.* Vol. 5. New York: Macmillan.

Moote, Nancy. 2000. "Teacher charged over affair with her student." *National Post,* 11 March.

Moreau, Vivian. 2003. "A minor infraction?" *Globe and Mail,* 25 July.

Morris, Desmond. 1969. *The Naked Ape.* New York: Dell.

Morrison, Richard. 2002. "Inappropriate behaviour – Reportage." *Times* (London), 5 February.

Muir, D.P.E. 2000. "Friendship in Education and the Desire for the Good: An Interpretation of Plato's *Phaedrus.*" *Educational Philosophy and Theory* 32, 2: 233-47.

Nagle, Jill, ed. 1997. *Whores and Other Feminists.* New York and London: Routledge.

Napolitano, Andrew. 2004. "Interview with Stacey Honowitz." *Fox News: The Big Story with John Gibson,* 4 August.

Nelson, Marissa. 2001. "Teacher was setting ..." *Globe and Mail,* 17 May.

Newell, Peter. 1972. *A Last Resort: Corporal Punishment in Schools.* London: Penguin.

Noddings, Nel. 1984. *Caring: A Feminist Approach to Ethics and Moral Education.* Berkeley: University of California Press.

O'Dell, Lindsay. 2003. "The 'Harm' Story in Childhood Sexual Abuse: Contested Understandings, Disputed Knowledges." In Paula Reavey and Sam Warner, eds., *New Feminist Stories of Child Sexual Abuse: Sexual Scripts and Dangerous Dialogues,* 131-47. London and New York: Routledge.

Ohi, Kevin. 2004. "Narrating the Child's Queerness in *What Maisie Knew.*" In Steven Bruhm and Natasha Hurley, eds., *Curiouser: On the Queerness of Children,* 81-106. Minneapolis: University of Minnesota Press.

Oliver, Kelly, and Benigno Trigo. 2003. *Noir Anxiety.* Minneapolis and London: University of Minnesota Press.

Olsen, Gregg. 1999. *If Loving You Is Wrong: The Shocking True Story of Mary Kay Letourneau.* New York: St. Martin's Press.

"Ontario teacher ..." 2002. *National Post,* 5 February.

Oprah Winfrey transcripts. 2004. "The Worst Mistake of My Life." Harpo Productions, 13 February.

Oram, Alison M. 1983. "The Introduction of a Marriage Bar in Teaching in the 1920s." In London Feminist History Group, eds., *The Sexual Dynamics of History: Men's Power, Women's Resistance,* 134-48. London: Pluto Press.

–. 1989. "Embittered, Sexless or Homosexual: Attacks On Spinster Teachers 1918-39." In Lesbian History Group, ed., *Not a Passing Phase: Reclaiming Lesbians in History 1840-1985,* 99-118. London: Women's Press.

Orbach, Susie. 2000. *The Impossibility of Sex: Stories of the Intimate Relationship between Therapist and Patient.* New York: Scribner.

O'Reilly, Bill. 2004. "Talking Points Memo; Top Story: Mary Kay Letourneau Is Released from Prison." *Fox News: The O'Reilly Factor,* 4 August.

Patton, Cindy, and Benigno Sanchez-Eppler, eds. 2000. *Queer Diasporas.* Durham and London: Duke University Press.

Pendleton, Eva. 1997. "Love for Sale: Queering Heterosexuality." In Jill Nagle, ed., *Whores and Other Feminists,* 73-82. New York and London: Routledge.

Perks, Marcelle. 1996. "DIY Pornography." In Cherie Matrix, ed., *Tales from the Clit: A Female Experience of Pornography,* 66-70. Edinburgh and San Francisco: AK Press.

Person, Ethel Spector, ed. 1997. *On Freud's "A Child Is Being Beaten."* New Haven and London: Yale University Press.

Phillips, Adam. 2002. *Promises, Promises: Essays on Literature and Psychoanalysis.* London: Faber and Faber.

Pidduck, Julianne. 1995. "The 1990s Hollywood Fatal Femme: (Dis)Figuring Feminism, Family, Irony, Violence." *cineaction: radical film criticism and theory* 28: 64-72.

Pinar, William, F. 2005. "A Visible/Invisible Binary: Visuality and Sexuality in the Discursive Figuration of the Child." *Journal of Gay and Lesbian Issues in Education: An International Quarterly Devoted to Research, Policy and Practice* 2, 4: 23-47.
–, ed. 1998. *Queer Theory in Education*. Mahwah, NJ: Lawrence Erlbaum.
Pizzello, Chris. 1996. "Bringing the Dark Side of Character to Light in *Diabolique*." *American Cinematographer* 26, 4: 36-42.
Place, Janey. 1998. "Women in Film Noir." In E. Ann Kaplan, ed., *Women in Film Noir*, 47-68. London: British Film Institute Publishing.
Power, Elizabeth. 1999. "The Cinematic Art of Nympholepsy: Movie Star Culture as Loser Culture in Nabokov's Lolita." *Criticism* 41, 1: 101-18.
Priest, Lisa. 1992. "43-year-old female teacher faces sexual assault charges." *Toronto Star*, 23 April.
Quinodoz, Jean-Michel. 1997. "'A Child Is Being Beaten': A Seminar with Candidates from the Perspective of Contemporary Psychoanalysis." In Ethel Spector Person, ed., *On Freud's "A Child Is Being Beaten,"* 112-32. New Haven and London: Yale University Press.
Ramirez, Eddy, and Dawn Reiss. 2005. "Praise halts for teacher ..." *St. Petersburg Times*, 3 November.
"Raped dad 'can't wait to see my baby.'" 1998. *Calgary Herald*, 19 October.
Reavey, Paula, and Sam Warner, eds. 2003. *New Feminist Stories of Child Sexual Abuse: Sexual Scripts and Dangerous Dialogues*. London and New York: Routledge.
"Remnants of a previous life ..." 1999. *Sunday Times* (London), 28 February.
Rendon, Ruth. 2002. "Teacher charged with sex assault ..." *Houston Chronicle*, 2 November.
Reynolds, Celia. 1983. "Ontario Schoolteachers 1911-1971: A Portrait of Demographic Change." PhD diss., University of Toronto.
Rich, Adrienne. 1980. *Compulsory Heterosexuality and Lesbian Existence*. Denver, CO: Antelope Publications.
Roberts, Duncan. 2002. "Gehring: I did have sex ..." *Edinburgh Evening News*, 11 February.
Robertson, Douglas L. 2000. "Unconscious Displacements in College Teacher and Student Relationships: Conceptualizing, Identifying, and Managing Transference." *Innovative Higher Education* 23, 3: 151-69.
Robertson, Judith, P. 1997. "Fantasy's Confines: Popular Culture and the Education of the Female Primary School Teacher." *Canadian Journal of Education* 22, 2: 123-43.
Robins, Sydney L. 2000. *Protecting Our Students: A Review to Identify and Prevent Sexual Misconduct in Ontario Schools*. Toronto: Ontario Ministry of the Attorney General.
Robinson, James. 2000. *The Mary Kay Letourneau Affair*. Leawood: Leathers Publishing.
Roof, Judith. 2001. "'The Community of Dolphins' v. 'The Safe Sea of Women': Lesbian Sexuality and Psychosis." In Tim Dean and Christopher Lane, eds., *Homosexuality and Psychoanalysis*, 235-49. Chicago and London: University of Chicago Press.
Rothstein, Eric. 2000. "Lolita: Nymphet at Normal School." *Contemporary Literature* 41, 1: 22-55.
Rubin, Gayle. 1984. "Thinking Sex: Notes for a Radical Theory of the Politics of Sexuality." In Carole S. Vance, ed., *Pleasure and Danger: Exploring Female Sexuality I*, 267-319. Boston: Routledge and Kegan Paul.
Salecl, Renata, ed. 2000. *Sexuation*. Durham and London: Duke University Press.
Samuels, Laurel. 1985. "Female Psychotherapists as Portrayed in Film, Fiction and Nonfiction." *American Academy of Psychoanalysis* 13: 367-78.
Sanderson, Terry. 1996. *A Stranger in the Family: How to Cope If Your Child Is Gay*. London: Otherway.
Sarler, Carol. 2002. "Amy's caresses were wrong but not harmful." *The Express* (London), 13 February.
Sauer, David Kennedy. 2000. "*Oleanna* and *The Children's Hour:* Misreading Sexuality on the Post/Modern Realistic Stage." *Modern Drama* 43: 421-41.
Sawyer, Diane. 2004. "Mary Kay Letourneau Scandalized Teacher to Be Released from Prison." *ABC News: Good Morning America*, 12 July.
Schmidt, Sara. 2000. "Sleeping with the Teacher." *Elm Street*, summer.
Sears, James. 1998. "A Generational and Theoretical Analysis of Culture and Male

(Homo)Sexuality." In William Pinar, ed., *Queer Theory in Education,* 73-105. New Jersey: Lawrence Erlbaum Associates.

Sedgwick, Eve Kosofsky. 1990. *Epistemology of the Closet.* Berkeley and Los Angeles: University of California Press.

Seidman, Steven. 2003. "From Identity to Queer Politics: Shifts in Normative Heterosexuality." In Steven Seidman and Jeffrey C. Alexander, eds., *The New Social Theory Reader,* 353-60. London and New York: Routledge.

"Sentence for teacher angers child advocates." 1997. *Austin American-Statesman,* 16 November.

"Sex-charges teacher labeled risk by police." 2002. *Yorkshire Post,* 5 February.

"Sex, lies and hopeless ..." 2002. *Hamilton Spectator,* 12 February.

"Sex tales were ..." 2002. *Hamilton Spectator,* 1 February.

"Sexual predators lurk in Ontario schools." 2000. *Ottawa Citizen,* 7 April.

Shakeshaft, C., and A. Cohen. 1994. *In Loco Parentis: Sexual Abuse of Students in Schools (What Administrators Should Know).* New York: Administration and Policy Studies, Hofstra University.

Shamburg, Robin. 2001. *Mistress Ruby Ties It Together.* New York: AtRandom.

Shengold, Leonard. 1997. "Comments on Freud's 'A Child Is Being Beaten': A Contribution to the Study of the Origin of Sexual Perversion." In Ethel Spector Person, ed., *On Freud's "A Child Is Being Beaten,"* 76-94. New Haven and London: Yale University Press.

Sigel, Lisa Z. 2002. "Autobiography of a Flea: Scrutiny and the Female Porn Scholar." In Merri Lisa Johnson, ed., *Jane Sexes It Up: True Confessions of Feminist Desire,* 241-58. New York and London: Four Walls Eight Windows.

Small, Peter. 2001. "Teacher didn't abuse." *Toronto Star,* 1 March.

Smith, Paul. 1988. "Vas." *Camera Obscura: A Journal of Feminism and Film Theory* 17: 89-111.

Stallybrass, Peter, and Allon White. 1986. *The Politics and Poetics of Transgression.* Ithaca, NY: Cornell University Press.

Steedman, Carolyn. 1985. "'The Mother Made Conscious': The Historical Development of a Primary School Pedagogy." *History Workshop: A Journal of Socialist and Feminist Historians,* 20: 149-63.

Steffenhagen, Janet. 2001. "Parents faced wall ..." *Vancouver Sun,* 15 December.

Stockton, Kathryn Bond. 2004. "Growing Sideways, or Versions of the Queer Child: The Ghost, the Homosexual, the Freudian, the Innocent, and the Interval of Animal." In Steven Bruhm and Natasha Hurley, eds., *Curiouser: On the Queerness of Children,* 277-315. Minneapolis: University of Minnesota Press.

Stoler, Ann Laura. 1997. "Making Empire Respectable: The Politics of Race and Sexual Morality in Twentieth-Century Colonial Cultures." In Anne McClintock, Aamir Mufti, and Ella Shohat, eds., *Dangerous Liaisons: Gender, Nation, and Postcolonial Perspectives,* 344-73. Minneapolis and London: University of Minnesota Press.

–. 2000. *Race and the Education of Desire: Foucault's History of Sexuality and the Colonial Order of Things.* Durham and London: Duke University Press.

Stoller, R. 1975. *Perversion.* New York: Pantheon.

Studlar, Gaylyn. 2000. "Masochism and the Perverse Pleasures of the Cinema." In E. Ann Kaplan, ed., *Feminism and Film,* 203-25. Oxford and New York: Oxford University Press.

Sykes, Heather. 2003. "The Angel's Playground: Same-Sex Desires of Physical Education Teachers." *Journal of Gay and Lesbian Issues in Education* 1, 1: 3-31.

–. 2004. "Pedagogical Censorship, Injury, and Masochism: Teacher Responses to Homophobic Speech in Physical Education." *Journal of Curriculum Studies* 36, 1: 75-99.

"Teacher guilty of sex-ploitation." 2000. *Toronto Sun,* 30 May.

"Teacher who pled guilty ..." 1997. *NBC News* transcripts, 14 November.

"Teacher 'worked on ...'" 2002. *Journal* (Newcastle), 5 February.

Theweleit, Klaus. 1987. *Male Fantasies.* Trans. Stephen Conway, in collaboration with Erica Carter and Chris Turner. Minneapolis: University of Minnesota Press.

Tierney, William G., and Patrick Dilley. 1998. "Constructing Knowledge: Educational Research and Gay and Lesbian Studies." In William F. Pinar, ed., *Queer Theory in Education,* 49-72. Mahwah, NJ: Lawrence Erlbaum Associates.

"Timeplan boss told ..." 2002. *Mirror* (London), 10 February.

Tisdale, Sallie. 1994. *Talk Dirty to Me: An Intimate Philosophy of Sex*. New York: Anchor.

Todd, S., ed. 1997. *Learning Desire: Perspectives on Pedagogy, Culture, and the Unsaid*. New York and London: Routledge.

Trocme, Nico, and Kate Schumaker. 1999. "Reported Child Sexual Abuse in Canadian Schools and Recreational Facilities: Implications for Developing Effective Prevention Strategies." *Children and Youth Services Review* 21, 8: 621-42.

"True Crime Book Watch." 2004. Message Board, 8 August, http://www.karisable.com/mkl.htm.

Tuhkanen, Mikko. 2002. "Breeding (and) Reading: Lesbian Knowledge, Eugenic Discipline, and *The Children's Hour*." *Modern Fiction Studies* 48, 4: 1001-40.

Turner, Roy, ed. 2001. *You Beat People Up for a Living, Don't You Mummy?: Inside the World of the Dominatrix*. Brighton, East Sussex: Absolute Elsewhere.

Tweedie, James. 2000. "*Lolita's* Loose Ends: Nabokov and the Boundless Novel." *Twentieth Century Literature* 46, 2: 150-70.

Twitchell, James B. 1987. *Forbidden Partners: The Incest Taboo in Modern Culture*. New York: Columbia University Press.

Verhaeghe, Paul. 2000. "The Collapse of the Function of the Father and Its Effect on Gender Roles." In Renata Salecl, ed., *Sexuation*, 131-54. Durham and London: Duke University Press.

Vicinus, Martha. 1985. *Independent Women: Work and Community for Single Women, 1850-1920*. Chicago and London: University of Chicago Press.

Walkerdine, Valerie. 1990. *Schoolgirl Fictions*. London and New York: Verso.

Waller, Willard. 1932. *The Sociology of Teaching*. New York, London, and Sydney: John Wiley and Sons.

Ward, Marianne. 2000. "An Equal-Opportunity Vice: More Female Sexual Predators Are Being Exposed, though the Phenomenon Is Not New." Canadian Business and Current Affairs, *Report newsmagazine*, 27 March.

Webster, Paula. 1984. "The Forbidden: Eroticism and Taboo." In Carole S. Vance, ed., *Pleasure and Danger: Exploring Female Sexuality*, 385-98. London: Routledge and Kegan Paul.

Welles, Judith K., and Kimble Wrye. 1991. "The Maternal Erotic Countertransference." *International Journal of Psycho-Analysis* 72: 93-106.

Wente, Margaret. 2002. "What if the schoolmistress ..." *Globe and Mail*, 2 February.

Westhead, Robert. 2002a. "Sex case teacher 'in row after sex with brothers.'" Press Association, 24 January.

–. 2002b. "Teacher 'too drunk' to recall having sex with boy." Press Association, 28 January.

"Where do fallen ...?" 2002. *New Statesman* (London), 18 February.

Whiting, Frederick. 1998. "The Strange Particularity of the Lover's Preference: Pedophilia, Pornography, and the Anatomy of Monstrosity in Lolita." *American Literature* 70, 4: 833-62.

Williams, Alexandra, and Fiona Cummins. 2002. "Boozy teacher had alley sex with two underage boys and bedded a third." *Mirror* (London), 22 January.

Young, Cathy. 2002. "The bias against male victims." *Boston Globe*, 3 June.

Young, Robert. 1995. *Colonial Desire: Hybridity in Theory, Culture and Race*. London: Routledge.

"Young boys need ..." 2002. *Northern Echo*, 8 February.

Žižek, Slavoj. 1991. *The Ticklish Subject: The Absent Centre of Political Ontology*. New York: Verso Press.

Websites

http://www.karisable.com/mkl.htm. "True Crime Book Watch." Message Board, 8 August 2004.

http://www.local6.com/news/5241503/detail.html.

http://www.thesmokinggun.com/archive/1102051teach1.html.

http://www.worldnetdaily.com/news/article.asp?ARTICLE_ID=48421.

Index

Printed and bound in Canada by Friesens

Set in Stone by Robert Kroeger

Copy editor: Robert Lewis

Proofreader: Jillian Shoichet

Indexer: Patricia Buchanan